D0611197

Yale Publications in American Studies, 13

Published under the direction of the American Studies Program.

City of the West: Emerson, America, and Urban Metaphor

by Michael H. Cowan

New Haven and London, Yale University Press, 1967

Designed by Sheila de Bretteville,
set in Linotype Primer type,
and printed in the United States of America by
Connecticut Printers, Inc., Hartford, Conn.
Distributed in Canada by McGill University Press.

Library of Congress catalog card number: 67–24492

Published with assistance from the foundation
established in memory of Calvin Chapin of the
Class of 1788, Yale College.

To my parents
in love and gratitude

Preface

The title of this book represents my attempt to capture the spirit as much as the letter of Emerson's dialectical approach to life and thought. As I had continually to remind myself while writing and rewriting, I am by no means concerned solely with Emerson's artistic use of urban material. The city has been a means of focusing rather than of circumscribing my argument and carries the limits of that function. I find, in fact, that Emerson's dialectical strategy has influenced my own structure, and I trust I will not mislead the reader as I dart back and forth between West and East, City of God and City of Man, Europe and America, nature and the modern city, individual freedom and communal possibility. I also hope that my comparative use of Cooper, Hawthorne, Melville, Thoreau, and Whitman—and the heavy footnoting that made necessary—will reinforce rather than distract from the main points I have tried to make about Emerson and the literature of the American Renaissance.

Like Emerson's artistic efforts, my own literary excursion into the city has been a sometimes painful but often exhilarating pilgrimage. It would be impious of me to fail to acknowledge the wise guidance and encouragement of several Delectable Mountains. A young American scholar could not wish for more humane advisers than Norman Holmes Pearson, Donald Davie, and R. W. B. Lewis. David Hall and Ajodhia Kaul undertook sensitive readings of the manuscript and made possible useful revisions. My ideas have also profited from continuing dialogues with Charles Feidelson and Albert LaValley. Wayland Schmitt, Kathleen Roberts, and Edward White made my relationship with the Yale Press an education as well as a pleasure. The Houghton Memorial Library at Harvard was most accommodating during my research stay there, and I wish to thank the President and Fellows of Harvard College and the Ralph Waldo Emerson Memorial Association for permission to quote from unpublished Emerson lectures in that library's collection. Sandra Narot offered invaluable help in preparing the manuscript. And my wife Ann held my hand through it all.

Michael H. Cowan

New Haven
June 1967

Contents

List of Abbreviations

I have incorporated as many Emerson citations as possible into the text and refer to them by means of the abbreviations noted below:

Corr — *The Correspondence of Emerson and Carlyle*, ed. Joseph Slater, New York, Columbia University Press, 1964.

EL — *The Early Lectures of Ralph Waldo Emerson*, eds. Stephen E. Whicher and Robert E. Spiller, 2 vols. to date, Cambridge, Harvard University Press, 1961–64.

J — *The Journals of Ralph Waldo Emerson*, eds. Edward Waldo Emerson and Waldo Emerson Forbes, 10 vols. Boston, Houghton, Mifflin and Co., 1909–14.

JMN — *The Journals and Miscellaneous Notebooks of Ralph Waldo Emerson*, ed. William H. Gilman and others, 5 vols. to date, Cambridge, Harvard University Press, 1960–65.

L — *The Letters of Ralph Waldo Emerson*, ed. Ralph L. Rusk, 6 vols. New York, Columbia University Press, 1939.

U — *Uncollected Lectures by Ralph Waldo Emerson*, ed. Clarence Gohdes, New York, William Edwin Rudge, 1932.

W — *The Complete Works of Ralph Waldo Emerson*, ed. Edward Waldo Emerson, Centenary Edition, 12 vols. Boston, Houghton, Mifflin and Co., 1903–04.

City of the West

Y *Young Emerson Speaks. Uupublished Discourses on Many Subjects*, ed. Arthur Cushman McGiffert, Jr., Boston, Houghton, Mifflin and Co., 1938.

Emerson's unpublished manuscripts are identified by the manuscript numbers given them in the Houghton Memorial Library at Harvard University.

❦ Editions Used

I list here the editions of Cooper, Hawthorne, Melville, and Thoreau to which I have made extensive reference. Shortened titles of the editions are used in the footnotes.

Cooper

New York, ed. Dixon Ryan Fox, New York, William Farquhar Payson, 1930.

Notions of the Americans: Picked up by a Travelling Bachelor, 2 vols. London, Henry Colburn, 1828.

Gleanings in Europe: England, ed. Robert E. Spiller, New York, Oxford University Press, 1928.

Gleanings in Europe: France, ed. Robert E. Spiller, New York, Oxford University Press, 1930.

A Residence in France: with an Excursion up the Rhine, and a Second Visit to Switzerland, 2 vols. London, Richard Bentley, 1836.

Excursions in Switzerland, 2 vols. London, Richard Bentley, 1836.

Excursions in Italy, 2 vols. London, Richard Bentley, 1838.

Hawthorne

The Complete Works of Nathaniel Hawthorne, ed. George Parsons Lathrop, Riverside Edition, 12 vols. Boston, Houghton, Mifflin and Co., ca. 1882–99.

The American Notebooks, ed. Randall Stewart, New Haven, Yale University Press, 1932.

The English Notebooks, ed. Randall Stewart, New York, Modern Language Association, London, Oxford University Press, 1941.

Melville

The Works of Herman Melville, Standard Edition, 16 vols. London, Constable, 1922–24.

The Complete Stories of Herman Melville, ed. Jay Leyda, New York, Random House, 1949.

Thoreau

The Journals of Henry David Thoreau, eds. Bradford Torrey and Francis H. Allen, 14 vols. Boston, Houghton, Mifflin and Co., 1949.

The Correspondence of Henry David Thoreau, eds. Walter Harding and Carl Bode, New York, New York University Press, 1958.

Collected Poems of Henry Thoreau, ed. Carl Bode, Enlarged Edition, Baltimore, Johns Hopkins Press, 1964.

City of the West

❦ 1. Emerson and "The Age of Cities"

Let the river roll which way it will, cities will rise on its banks. (*J*, 8, 90)

If a man loves the city, so will his writings love the city. (*JMN*, 3, 196–97)

Men are all inventors sailing forth on a voyage of discovery. (*U*, 28)

In a study with as unlikely a subject as Emerson's artistic use of "urban" material, the reader deserves an initial explanation. I am not primarily interested in Emerson's role or accuracy as an urban sociologist, though inevitably I must discuss many of his observations concerning actual "cities" and actual "urban" life as we conventionally use these terms. More basically, this study examines the various ways in which Emerson treated urban material, whether derived from his personal observations or from his reading, as an occasion for artistic manipulation—in other words, as metaphors for larger or deeper concerns not specifically urban.

Emerson's use of urban metaphors was as varied as his own fertile mind. They served him in discussions of God, human history, the natural universe, morality, psychology, the artistic process itself, and particularly American civilization as a whole. Urban metaphors were not merely convenient literary vehicles for Emerson; they were among the essential tools of a writer deeply committed to a dialectical handling of experience.

Emerson was experimenting with one major element in

his dialectic when, in 1848, he called his era "the Age of Cities" (*J*, 7, 525).[1] Like other labels he applied strategically to his age—and the concept of strategy should be underlined—"the Age of Cities" is both historically relevant and artistically suggestive.[2] In its historical aspect it symbolizes his interest in the many roles urban civilization did and might play in America and the modern world. More than is generally realized, Emerson's evaluation of actual urban civilization was productively complex and shrewdly optimistic. Certainly he would be much less representative if he had not shared with many other Americans an interest in and even fascination with what it meant to live in "this towered and citied world" (*W*, 1, 311) that Europe already was and that America was rapidly becoming.

But Emerson was not primarily a historian. Like many major American writers, he was self-consciously anxious to deal poetically with "the matter of America"—to learn, as Robert Spiller has put it, "to reduce American experience to expression in aesthetic form."[3] To a man born in Boston this

1. "Let me remind the reader," Emerson said in one of his most striking defenses of imaginative process, "that I am only an experimenter. Do not set the least value on what I do, or the least discredit on what I do not, as if I pretended to settle any thing as true or false. I unsettle all things. No facts are to me sacred; none are profane. I simply experiment, an endless seeker with no Past at my back" (*W*, 2, 318). Representative of his frequent use of a dramatic analogy for this process is his statement in his late essay, "Natural History of Intellect": "Men go through the world each musing on a great fable dramatically pictured and rehearsed before him" (*W*, 12, 84).

2. That Emerson's application of labels to his age was experimental in spirit is indicated by their wide range: they included Trade and Idealism, Association and Individualism, Atheism and Subjectivity. For an early sample of such terms, see his 1827 listing of "Peculiarities of the present Age" (*JMN*, 3, 70–71).

3. Robert Spiller, "The American Literary Dilemma and Edgar

experience was increasingly urban in the modern sense of the term, and to a Romantically inclined poet this urban experience was an artistic challenge of the highest priority. As Emerson said in a sermon of 1829, presenting Jesus implicitly as a prototype of his own American Scholar:

> Our Lord in his discourses condescended to explain himself by allusions to every homely fact, to the boys in the market, to the persons dropping into the custom offices; to the food on the board, to the civilities shown him by the hospitality of his entertainers; and would he not, let me ask, if he addressed himself to the men of this age and of this country, appeal with equal frequency to those arts and objects by which we are surrounded, to the printing press and the loom, to the phenomena of steam and of gas, to the magnificence of towns, to free institutions, and a petulant and vain nation. (*Y*, 29)[4]

Emerson's own professional use of urban material, prefigured by this sermon, was to be fundamentally allusive or metaphorical. Cities were to prove important to him not as much in themselves as in their capacity to illuminate and even test both his most abstract concepts and his most personal goals. Because he believed that the "test or measure of poetic genius" was its ability to transform the circumstances "of the nineteenth century" into literary material, Emerson

---

Allan Poe," in Carl Bode, ed., *The Great Experiment in American Literature* (New York, 1961), p. 5.

4. Emerson's interest in Jesus as a type of his own ambition remained large even after he had separated from organized Christianity. In 1863 he said that when he had written *Representative Men* "I felt that Jesus was the 'Representative Man' whom I ought to sketch; but that the task required great gifts" (*J*, 9, 579).

wished intensely in his own writing "to convert the vivid energies acting at this hour in New York and Chicago and San Francisco into universal symbols" (*W*, 8, 34). In grappling dialectically with "the Age of Cities," as it played against other poles of his experience, he was attempting to remain true to his dictum that his nation and his era find "mythology, symbols, religion, of our own" (*W*, 8, 74).

Against this view must be set a more traditional claim that Emerson, as man, moralist, and writer, was basically hostile to urban civilization. Morton and Lucia White, for example, in their recent discussion, *The Intellectual Versus the City*, argue that Emerson "occupied a middle position among the Transcendental anti-urbanists" and that he "did nothing to encourage the American to love the American city." They stress that "Emerson seemed to think of his anti-urbanism as a theorem in a metaphysical system" and that his "opposition to the American city was elaborately linked with his world-view and epistemology."[5]

To dispute this traditional claim, we will need to go, in Melville's words, "a lower layer yet" into Emerson's life and thought. We must avoid the temptation to label his metaphysics, epistemology, or aesthetics as necessarily or even basically "anti-urban," in order to understand more fully his relationship to the facts and metaphors provided by urban civilization. Initially, however, we should not neglect the biographical and psychological case that can be made for Emerson as an urban man—urban in a way not uniquely but

5. Morton and Lucia White, *The Intellectual Versus the City from Thomas Jefferson to Frank Lloyd Wright* (Cambridge, Mass., 1962), pp. 24–35. The "versus" in the Whites' title is symptomatic of the ways in which they have limited and even prejudiced their approach.

characteristically American. Whatever larger world Emerson wished his writings to benefit, they also reflected intensely personal aims. Growing out of his own experiences as a young American, Emerson's literary efforts attempted not only to support his nation's aspirations but to aid his private quest for a richer and more perfect inner life.

We are sometimes inclined to forget that Emerson spent half his lifetime in cities. His primary urban allegiance, of course, was to Boston, where he was born in 1803 and where he spent most of his first thirty years. His life in Boston, during the maturing years at Harvard and in the pulpit of the Second Church, was by no means isolated from the modern city that was growing up around him. As minister he saw not only the comfortable beneficiaries but the victims of urbanization. In a sermon on charity in 1829 he reminded his congregation:

> We live in a fair city. It is full of commodious and spacious mansions. But the eye that sees the morning sun shine on long streets of decorated buildings is apt to forget how many obscure garrets, how many damp basements are here and there found amid this magnificence, that contain victims of great suffering, poor men and women reduced by consumptions or bedridden with rheumatisms, or worn with fruitless labors to meet demands the quarter day. (Y, 242)

Emerson's criticisms of various aspects of Boston's routines and values did not prevent his consistent loyalty to the city. Often he saw its peculiarities and foibles with affection: "Every city has its rival city, its ridiculous suburb, its old times, and its jokes. Boston has Hull ('All are but parts of one majestic Hull') and its banter with New York journalism" (*J*, 9, 564–65). Though he warned of the dangers attendant upon Boston's growth into a leading industrial city, he felt a vested interest in such development. Such an interest was perfectly natural in one who had been fathered, in Wordsworth's sense, by a child who used to drive the family cow down Beacon Street to the city common. Young Emerson had grown along with his city, and it was with pride in his Boston past that, on his sixty-ninth birthday, he explored the greatly altered neighborhood in which he had been born; it occurred to him "that few living persons ought to know so much of the families of this fast-growing city" (*J*, 10, 383).

After Emerson moved to Concord in 1834, partly (but only partly) in protest against the social and intellectual environment of his youth, he continued to spend a great deal of time in Boston. Even before the Civil War, in fact, Concord functioned for him as a suburb of Boston, to which he commuted at least once a week for business, lectures, club meetings, and visits with his many friends. His social neighborhood was not bound by Concord's borders, and he continued to be proud of the Americans his birthplace had produced: "I will tell you why I value Boston," he wrote in his journal for 1863; "because, when I go to enumerate its excellent names, I do not take down the Boston Directory, but the National History, to find them" (*J*, 9, 574).

For all his puttering at Concord with apple trees, cows, and gardens, Emerson never forgot that he was a "city-bred farmer" (*U*, 25).[6] When he delivered his lecture on Boston in

6. Though his lecture used the label unspecifically, a journal passage shows that Emerson was thinking of himself (*J*, 9, 421).

1861, neither he nor his audience sensed any inappropriateness when he referred to "*our* little city" (*W*, *12*, 211; my italics). Those who treat his move to Concord as mainly an escape from Boston and urban civilization neglect his continuing belief, expressed with fluctuating certainty, that he could fulfill his "vocation" or "calling" *within* the context of Boston. Even when he castigated Boston, he usually did so less out of hatred than out of love.[7]

If Emerson's personal ties allowed him to forgive many of Boston's faults, he was often less kind to cities in which he felt a less vested interest. His criticisms of such cities as New New York (one of his favorite domestic targets) sometimes smacked less of Transcendental morality than of New England provincialism,[8] and they did not always or even usually imply full or wholehearted condemnation of urban civilization as a whole. Rather, Emerson's strictures were often as much matters of temperament as of philosophy—his reactions while tired, lonely, or depressed to urban environments that physically were too far away from his family and friends in the Boston-Concord area. He knew that his criticisms of cities

7. See Frederick I. Carpenter, *American Literature and the Dream* (New York, 1955), pp. 19–20; and Darrell Abel, "Strangers in Nature—Arnold and Emerson," *University of Kansas City Review*, *15* (1949), 210–13.

8. John L. Stafford, in *The Literary Criticism of "Young America"* (Berkeley, 1952), pp. 10, 123–24, illustrates the provincial tendencies of Emerson's Bostonian peers in their literary rivalry with New York. But the New York writer could be equally condescending to the Bostonian. Cooper advised Horatio Greenough to send his statue group, the Cherubs, to New York rather than to Boston: "You will be covered with twaddling criticism in Boston, which is no better . . . than a gossiping town, though it has so many clever people" (*Letters and Journals*, ed. James Franklin Beard [Cambridge, Mass., 1960–], 2, 53).

often revealed as much about himself as about the cities. While lecturing in New York in 1842, he wrote Margaret Fuller:

> Pity me & comfort me, O my friend, in this city of magnificence & of steam. For a national, for an imperial prosperity, everything here seems irrevocably destined. What a Bay! what a River! what climate! what men! What ample interior domain, lake mountain & forest! What manners, what histories & poetry shall rapidly arise & for how long, and, it seems, endless date! Me my cabin fits better, yet very likely from a certain poorness of spirit; but in my next transmigration, I think I should choose New York. (*L*, 3, 20)[9]

Emerson might "shudder" when he approached New York, but approach it and other American cities he did—not a few times, but again and again. True, most of his entrances were not made primarily for pleasure (though he could reckon a city like Philadelphia "a good hospital" for a man weary of activity[10]). They were part of his lecture tours and, as such, represented in many ways vocational duties and business necessities. But if it was in America's cities that Emerson could most readily find audiences who would pay money to listen to him, the mere desire to earn a living does not adequately explain his choice of this particular vocation—one that put him on the road year after year during the uncomfortable lecture season of November through March, subjected him to weary-

9. See also *L*, 1, 369; *L*, 4, 189–90; *L*, 5, 134. In a letter to his brother William in 1842, Emerson spoke of New York as "the good city" (*L*, 3, 14).

10. *L*, 5, 217.

ing transportation, cold rooms, uncertain receipts, and uncomprehending audiences, and forced him to be away from his family for over a quarter of the most active part of his mature life.[11] William Charvat points to another and equally important reason for the lecture tours when he quotes Emerson as saying, "I hate the details, but the whole foray into a city teaches me much."[12] In fact, a comprehensive portrait of Emerson as lecturer must include a strong sense of his activity as explorer as well as preacher, regularly inspecting harbors, factories, schools, jails, and museums, feeling frustrated that he had not time or energy to see more, and expressing pleasure that "I see & learn much that I look not for."[13]

Certainly Emerson must have learned a great deal from the rapidly growing cities through which he traveled while lecturing. Between 1840 and 1860 alone he delivered at least forty lectures in and about New York City, appearing there at least every other year and frequently passing through on route to other engagements. Before 1860 he had appeared seven times and delivered twenty-five lectures in Philadelphia.[14] In

11. For a wry comment by Emerson on his problems as a lecturer, see *J*, 10, 91–92.

12. William Charvat, *Emerson's American Lecture Engagements: A Chronological List* (New York, 1961). p. 7. Most of the details of Emerson's lecturing have been gleaned from Charvat's useful listings.

13. See also *L*, 3, 149. What must have been Emerson's typical habits of exploring cities in which he lectured are documented in R. B. Nye, "Emerson in Michigan and the Northwest," *Michigan History*, 26 (1941), 159–72. See also Louise Hastings, "Emerson in Cincinnati," *New England Quarterly*, 11 (1938), 443–69, and Frederick E. Schortemeier, "Indianapolis Newspaper Accounts of Ralph Waldo Emerson," *Indiana Magazine of History*, 49 (1953), 307–12.

14. These figures do not include the sermons Emerson preached in Charleston, Washington, New York, and Philadelphia during 1826, 1827, and 1830.

the decade preceding the Civil War—a decade in which he averaged between forty-eight and sixty lectures a year—he journeyed west of the Appalachians five times, speaking in Cleveland, Cincinnati, Pittsburgh, St. Louis, Columbus, Chicago, and many other expanding towns. (In the decade of the 1860s he doubled this number of western trips.) Few other American writers or men of letters could have claimed to have made such early firsthand acquaintance with urbanization in the American West as could Emerson. As a mainstay of the lyceum, he was one of the West's first major literary pioneers.[15] By 1871, when he returned from a trip to California, he had lectured in at least twenty-two states. Though his public efforts were concentrated in New England (nearly 250 lectures in Boston alone), his lecturing experience was nevertheless national. He could not deny the increasingly urban character of America, even in the great agrarian West, for he himself had seen his nation's burgeoning cities. Emerson's major problem as he faced America's increasingly urban civilization was, like that of his contemporary literary giants, not to deny the fact of the city but to interpret and evaluate it.

Emerson's interest in the emerging metropolises of his time was, at its best, neither shallow nor provincial. It was based on an extensive acquaintance with the cities of history and with the literature such cities had produced. In this connection, his trips to Europe were important. Despite all of his nationalistic assertions (especially on his first voyage) that America need no longer be bound to a decaying European past, his European experience was a significant educational

15. The importance of Emerson's contribution to the American lyceum movement is stressed in Carl Bode, *The American Lyceum, Town Meeting of the Mind* (New York, 1956). See also C. E. Schorer, "Emerson and the Wisconsin Lyceum," *American Literature*, 24 (1953), 462–75.

factor in his development. His first two trips to Europe, in 1832–33 and 1847–48, even if they only slightly modified his basic beliefs, presented the challenge of new, fascinating, and occasionally overpowering empirical data. His cry in Naples in 1832, "Here's for the plain old Adam, the simple genuine Self against the whole world," was in part a defensive ploy—an attempt to keep his distance on this disturbing and stimulating new data until he could assimilate it to his own purposes. After proclaiming his independence of others' judgments of Naples ("I won't be imposed upon by a name"), he could feel secure enough to then admit that "Naples is a fine city" (*JMN*, *4*, 141).

Emerson's first European trip was made partly to recover health, and the second was officially to deliver lectures in England. Neither of these reasons, however, accounts adequately for the wearying pace he set for himself while he was abroad. One of the most striking aspects of his European journals is the purposeful and even self-conscious manner in which he explored the Old World, and to explore Europe meant to explore urban civilization. "He has not seen Europe," he wrote in 1849, "who has not seen its cities" (*J*, *8*, 45). It is important to note the rather systematic way in which Emerson, on his first trip, walked and rode through the streets of Rome, Syracuse, Naples, Paris, and other cities, and, on his second trip, made the exploration of London a major goal. Though he often dreaded the entrance into a city, with the unpleasant necessity of finding lodging and taking care of other mundane and tiring details of travel,[16] he did not for that reason forsake the entrance, any more than he avoided lecturing in American cities or in England's industrial centers. His doc-

16. See *L*, *1*, 364, 369–70.

trine of compensation held that out of such discomforting necessities would come a positive experience—at the least a moral lesson or an exercise in self-discipline, at the best an inspiration. His observations of the problems, patterns, and achievements of European cities provided a functional background against which he could study the rising cities of his own nation.[17]

Despite Emerson's almost provincial preference at moments for his quasi-rural Concord, his foreign travels helped make him relatively at home in many cities of America and Europe. Paris, in fact, seemed to offer to the aged traveler, on his last journey to Europe in 1873, a tempered version of the blithe stimulations that in his essay *Nature* he had described finding on the Concord Common:

> The enjoyment of travel is in the arrival at a new city, as Paris, or Florence, or Rome,—the feeling of free adventure, you have no duties,—nobody knows you, nobody has claims, you are like a boy on his first visit to the Common on Election Day. Old Civilization offers to you alone this huge city, all its wonders, architecture, gardens, ornaments, galleries, which had never cost you so much as a thought. For the first time for many years you wake master of the bright day, in a bright world without a claim on you;—only leave to enjoy. This dropping, for

17. The European journals, notebooks, and letters of Cooper, Melville, and Hawthorne—to name but a few writers of the period—provide equally interesting evidence of a similar use of the "European urban experience." Stanley T. Williams has remarked that "our facing toward Europe was less timid, less weak, than it was axiomatic, inevitable for a young and aspiring culture" ("Cosmopolitanism in American Literature," in Margaret Denny, ed., *The American Writer and the European Tradition* [Minneapolis, 1950], p. 48).

> the first time, the doleful bundle of Duty creates, day after day, a health of new youth. (*J*, 10, 413–14)

Such an observation marked the culmination of a cosmopolitan attitude that had been developing in Emerson for more than forty years.

To talk of an urbane or cosmopolitan man is not to deny the more common view of Emerson as a shy lover of wooded solitude and Walden Pond, but it does insist on the complexity of his "inner life." Just as moments of Transcendental inspiration were subject to fluxes of time and temperament,[18] so both Emerson's fear of and respect for urban civilization were as much an honest admission of his personal feelings as a prescription for others. As he noted in 1862, "Most of my values are very variable,—my estimate of America which sometimes runs very low, sometimes to ideal prophetic proportions" (*J*, 9, 361). Emerson generally tried to turn insights into his own nature into positive values, and his recognition of inner "fluxions" (to use his own term) was no exception. Seen optimistically, fluctuation was another name for imaginative experimentation. To find himself "always insincere, as always knowing there are other moods" (*W*, 3, 247), involved his recognition that the purposefully experimental force that seemed to run through external nature also ran through the individual soul. Therefore, that "one man's justice is another's injustice" (*W*, 2, 315) could be treated as a psychological fact indicat-

18. See Stephen E. Whicher, *Freedom and Fate: An Inner Life of Ralph Waldo Emerson* (Philadelphia, 1953), pp. 98–99; Sherman Paul, *Emerson's Angle of Vision: Man and Nature in American Experience* (Cambridge, Mass., 1952), pp. 144–48; Jonathan Bishop, *Emerson on the Soul* (Cambridge, Mass., 1964), pp. 165–93. "My days," Emerson admitted as early as 1827, "are made up of the irregular succession of very few different tones of feeling. These are my feasts & fasts" (*JMN*, 3, 99).

ing not an ultimate but a provisional relativism in man's search for ultimate values. "The ends of action are the same," he argued in a sermon which he preached four times between 1830 and 1837, "but the means and the manner are infinitely various. . . . The better is the state of the world, the more unlike will be men's characters, and the more similar their purposes" (Y, 106).

However Emerson's personal attitudes toward the city may have fluctuated, he was often cautious about imposing his temperamental judgments on others. Though he made a holy, creative life a moral imperative for all men, he prescribed no uniform or single means to this end. Even in his period of greatest Transcendental self-confidence, he could advise himself, "Pray heaven that you have a sympathy with all sorts of excellence even with those antipodal to your own" (*JMN*, 4, 354). Applying this advice in his well-known sermon "Find Your Calling," Emerson pointed to the many ways in which men might work under God's providence in an urban setting:

> Look at the great throng the city presents. Consider the variety of callings and pursuits. Here is one man toiling with a hod on his shoulder; and another with his saw and tools; a third with his books; a fourth driving bargains at the corners of the streets; another spreads his sail from the wharf toward the sea; another heals the sick; another draws a map; another is hasting to his entertainment and to dangerous pleasures; another is led to jail between officers; another takes his seat on a bench to judge him. They do not perceive, who make up this sad and cheerful scene, that they are placed in these circumstances to learn the laws of the universe. (Y, 163)

Those inspirations and insights that Emerson often gained in the woods might be found by other men, he admitted, more easily or congenially in the city. He wrote in 1830, "If a man loves the city so will his writings love the city, & if a man loves sweet fern & roams much in the pastures, his writings will smell of it" (*JMN*, 3, 196–97).[19]

Though Emerson the individual might attack the city, Emerson the Transcendental philosopher and poet found theoretical difficulties in doing so. Radical Transcendentalism offered no way to evaluate the city qua city. It reduced urban civilization, along with all other finite data, to "experience" and then treated all experience unitarily, either as surface illusion covering reality or as symbolic manifestation of reality.[20] From the Transcendentalist's ultimate "angle of vision," urban life and objects were equally as expressive of the Over-Soul as were rural life and nonhuman landscape. The light of the Universal Spirit was "no aristocrat, but shines as mellowly on gipsies as on emperors, on bride and corpse, on city and swamp" (*J*, 8, 62). Or, conversely, all experience, both urban and nonurban, was equally *ir*relevant to those who lived most fully in the mystical Spirit. "The moment I *am*," Emerson said

19. Paul, in *Emerson's Angle of Vision*, esp. pp. 73–84, discusses clearly Emerson's use of nature for inspiration, but he perhaps stresses unduly the handicaps to inspiration that Emerson found in the city. Vivian Hopkins, in *Spires of Form: A Study of Emerson's Aesthetic Theory* (Cambridge, Mass., 1951), p. 23, indicates that Emerson could also find inspiration in urban objects and processes.

20. These aspects of Emerson's idealism are treated most adequately in Charles Feidelson's *Symbolism and American Literature* (Chicago, 1953), esp. pp. 122–23, and in René Wellek, "Emerson's Literary Theory and Criticism," in Gustave Erdmann and Alfons Eichstaedt, eds., *Worte und Werte. Bruno Markwardt zum 60. Geburtstag* (Berlin, 1961), pp. 444–56.

in 1841, "I despise city and the seashore, yes, earth and the galaxy also" (*J*, 6, 6).[21]

Between Emerson's solely personal and the radically Transcendental approach to urban experience lay a third point of view—or, rather, a spectrum of all those viewpoints that attempted to mediate between the two extremes.[22] From various points on this spectrum Emerson attempted to transcend his personal prejudices against the city without denying the necessity or importance of evaluating the city at a supra-personal or "social" level. He could not always approach the city as spokesman of the Over-Soul, and his modesty and sense of personal inadequacies forbade him to present blandly his personal reactions as universally valid. But he had another alternative—to be spokesman for some real or imagined group of men who might evaluate the city from a common point of view. In attempting to discover the possibilities of both the American people and their environment, Emerson, like Whitman, could project himself into many such roles. "We write from aspiration and antagonism, as well as from experience," he argued. "We paint those qualities which we do not possess" (*W*, 2, 221).

21. Emerson's radical negations, of course, prompted men like Carlyle to warn him against the "danger of dividing [yourself] from the Fact of this present Universe" (*Corr*, 328). But Emerson's radical affirmations were really no more "empirical": "The subject—I must often say —" he wrote in 1863, "is indifferent; any word, every word in the language, every circumstance, becomes poetic, when in the hands of a higher thought" (*J*, 9, 540–41).

22. This third point of view, in fact, seemed actually to emerge from the tension engendered by the extremes of temperament and philosophy. Emerson wrote Carlyle in 1841, "My whole philosophy—which is very real—teaches acquiescence and optimism. Only when I see how much work is to be done, what room for a poet—for any spiritualist—in this great, intelligent, sensual, and avaricious America, I lament my fumbling fingers and stammering tongue" (*Corr*, 304).

Important aspects of Emerson are overlooked if he is not seen as one of the major nineteenth-century practitioners of negative capability. "There is a great *parallax* in human nature," he noted in 1832, "ascertained by observing it from different states of mind" (*JMN*, *4*, 22).[23] Just as he characteristically sought for a hopefully unitary reality by means of a dialectical method, so he often launched a similar exploration by means of a "multilogue" or conversational drama between a group of experimentally projected human types.[24] Whether figures of history, such as Plato and Goethe, or creatures of his imagination, such as the American Scholar and the Poet, Emerson's "Representative Men" were, as Henry Nash Smith has argued, "a collection of embryos that might have developed eventually into characters of fiction, save for the fact that Emerson did not have a truly dramatic imagination."[25] Smith underemphasizes what Stephen Whicher has usefully stressed —that Emerson conceived at least his own inner life in highly dramatic terms. "It is doubtless a vice to turn one's eyes inward too much," he said in 1833, "but I am my own comedy & tragedy" (*JMN*, *4*, 132).

Through his powers of projection and tentative suspension of disbelief, Emerson could become by turns each of his representative men. "In dreams we are true poets," he argued; "we create the persons of the drama" (*W*, *8*, 44). Although he never became "a kosmos, of Manhatten the son," to as radical an extent as did the great American poseur Whit-

23. Such a belief motivated his advice of 1834: "Pray heaven that you have a sympathy with all sorts of excellence even with those antipodal to your own" (*JMN*, *4*, 354).

24. This desire may help explain his fascination with Landor's imaginary dialogues (*W*, *12*, 340–47).

25. Henry Nash Smith, "Emerson's Problem of Vocation—A Note on 'The American Scholar,' " *New England Quarterly*, 12 (1939), 52–67.

man, he nevertheless believed that, as poet, he had the right and responsibility to speak not only for himself and for universal man but, on the national level, for the many-faced American. If he was a self-proclaimed voice of the American farmer, the American backwoodsman, the New Englander, and the American scholar, he also presumed to speak for those Americans who were building and dwelling in cities. By a provisional relativism, an application of dialectical method, and a use of what Whicher calls the "fallacy of rotation,"[26] he attempted to assimilate meaningfully the idea of the city into his total poetic vision.

If Emerson did not in practice write solely for or to himself,[27] neither was his audience some nebulous Everyman. He spoke not only for urban Americans but largely *to* them. As he dealt with a variety of audiences, his estimation of the varying limitations, needs, and aims of his specific listeners and readers affected not only his rhetoric but even the substance and structure of his writing.[28] It is significant, therefore, that, in language very similar to that used by Hawthorne in the preface to *The Scarlet Letter,* he could argue that "every book is written with a constant secret reference to the few intelligent persons whom the writer believes to exist [among]

26. Whicher, *Freedom and Fate,* p. 130.

27. See Paul Lauter's highly perceptive monograph, "Emerson's Rhetoric" (Unpublished doctoral dissertation, Yale University, 1958), and an article based on this study, "Emerson's Revisions of *Essays* (First Series)," *American Literature,* 33 (1961), 143–58. Also relevant is Hopkins, *Spires of Form,* pp. 40–60. Even Emerson's journals might be said to have had an ultimately public aim, considering the use that he made of them.

28. A useful theoretical framework for an understanding of the artist's reaction to his conception of an audience might be erected by using Erving Goffman's provocative study, *The Presentation of Self in Everyday Life* (Garden City, 1959).

the million" (*W*, 8, 219). Although Emerson could urge his American Scholar to speak apocalyptically to the large mass of common Americans, he himself tended to speak to a more restricted and more influential group—a group very much at the heart of American urbanization.

We will probably not stretch Emerson's conception of his public role unduly if we treat a passage in his 1863 lecture on "Education" as indicative of the audience he was most interested in reaching: "Happy the natural college thus self-instituted around every natural teacher; the young men of Athens around Socrates; of Alexandria around Plotinus; of Paris around Abelard; of Germany around Fichte, or Niebuhr, or Goethe: in short the natural sphere of every leading mind" (*W*, 10, 149). Emerson liked to conceive of himself as a "natural teacher," and a major element of his audience was the "young Americans" who were reading his books and whose movement in and out of the growing cities in which Emerson lectured was setting the basic tone for modern American life.[29] Such Americans, writes Anselm Strauss, "entered a great period of city building during the nineteenth century protestingly, metaphorically walking backward."[30] Emerson, both personally and as a self-conceived spokesman for this

29. In 1850 Emerson wrote,

> I would have a man of large designs use our little Boston and noisy New York as suburbs and villages to try his pieces on. . . . Then let him take them to London or to Paris, to whatever Rome his age affords him, and read them tentatively there, too, not trusting his audience much . . . with a reference still to his ultimate tribunal, namely, the few scattered, sensible men, two or three in the world at a time, who, scattered thinly over the ages, are called by excellence *posterity*, because they determine its opinion. (*J*, 8, 94)

Compare with Hawthorne, *Works*, 5, 2.

30. Anselm L. Strauss, *Images of the American City* (New York, 1961), p. 123.

group, often expressed its protest in his writings. But within his protest was also a poet's challenge to this same group of American citizens, particularly to the artists in this group, to come creatively to terms with their urban civilization.

In attempting to make his own artistic efforts relevant to an increasingly urban world, Emerson assumed two strategic roles, those of historian and Romantic prophet. As many of his essays indicate, he believed that the raw materials for authentic American poetry should come from the actual American experience, both by itself and in the context of world history. To examine the development of civilization in America meant inevitably to include the city both in and as history. Man in his finite aspects "cannot live without a world" (*W*, 2, 36), Emerson argued in his essay "History." Urban civilization was a necessary part of this world, an inevitable expression of man's inner nature. "We are made of ideas," he wrote in 1850. "Let the river roll which way it will, cities will rise on its banks" (*J*, 8, 90). Though cities did not constitute the whole of human history, they became increasingly for Emerson the most central symbol of this history. After a lifetime of thought and observation he could argue that "the test of civilization is the power of drawing the most benefits out of cities" (*J*, 10, 54). In evaluating the developing power of city dwellers to create both bad and good out of their urban resources, Emerson was essentially testing human possibilities as a whole.

As a literary artist, one of Emerson's major evaluative devices was that of prophecy. Throughout his writings he posited the vague outlines of a utopia against which actual American civilization could be measured.[31] Emerson's American Scholar, his Poet, his New Adam were prophetic figures, and these fig-

31. See Benjamin T. Spencer, *The Quest for Nationality* (Syracuse, 1957), p. 126 and passim.

ures needed a brave new world. Part of his strategy was to develop, at least in embryo, a vision of such an ideal environment. This ideal realm was by no means exclusively "urban": made up of bits of home, garden, church, empire, and wilderness, as well as city, it was characteristically American in its attempt to amalgamate the best of all possible worlds. Nevertheless, idealized urban material assumed a central symbolic position in the larger utopia which, like Augustine's City of God, served as a metaphor for values and possibilities that Emerson conceived as essential tools for evaluating actual civilization.

Emerson's strategic use of the concept of an ideal city paralleled explorations by several of his contemporary American writers. As A. N. Kaul has stressed, the major nineteenth-century American novelists "shared a critical attitude toward the actual society of the time on the one hand and a constant preoccupation with ideal community life on the other,"[32] and this attitude is in striking contrast to European writing of the same period. Their ideal communities were by no means conceived always or totally in urban terms, but, on balance, the dreams of American Romantics showed greater fascination with urbanity than did the dreams of Europeans. The great urban utopian visions of European literature had ceased to inspire more than a relatively few Old World writers after the beginning of the nineteenth century and the advent of the industrial age.[33] While William Blake's highly individual apoc-

32. A. N. Kaul, *The American Vision: Actual and Ideal Society in Nineteenth-Century Fiction* (New Haven, 1963), p. 43. Kaul's study is a skilled exploration of many aspects of the vision of "community" in nineteenth-century American fiction and thought, but it does not deal with what I would call the American urban vision.

33. R. A. Foakes, *The Romantic Assertion* (London, 1958), pp. 146–47, and Frank Kermode, *Romantic Image* (London, 1957), p. 4.

alyptic vision of New Jerusalem was, in the Europe of his time, an unrepresentative belief in an ideal city as significant artistic material, a generation after Blake's death Emerson was still speaking hopefully, if metaphorically, of the vital relationship of a Romantically conceived City of God and the actual cities of nineteenth-century men.

This lingering American interest in a visionary city is an excellent example of the ways in which American literature attempted to fuse European literature with American history. Though nineteenth-century versions of an urban utopia are borrowed in part from traditional Old World sources—the Bible, various religious and utopian tracts, even, as in Emerson's case, such contemporaries and near-contemporaries as Swedenborg and Carlyle—they can also be understood in terms of their traditional native manifestations. The Ideal City had first appeared as the New England Puritans' City on a Hill and, before and during the Revolutionary Period, had become linked also to a vision of renewed classical grandeur. By the nineteenth century it was taking many forms—a refurbished New Jerusalem, a New Rome, a western Eldorado, or some other figurative version of what proved to be the implicit master metaphor, the City of the West. During much of the nineteenth century, at least, the ambiguous and elusive image of an ideal city tended to be explored more earnestly and more hopefully in American than in European literature. Both despite and because of their many criticisms of actual European and American cities, the major American Romantics in the decades spanned by Emerson's most productive years continued to be intrigued by the literary possibilities of an urban utopia.

For a writer like Emerson both the city of history and the visionary city shared an important common function—as the source for metaphors. Regardless of their literal referents, terms such as "Babylon," "Rome," "London," "Atlantis," and "New Jerusalem" were all literary vehicles by which he could relate the external and the internal, the actual and the ideal, the realms of experience and belief. In using metaphors, Emerson involved himself inescapably in the writers archetypal need to create new literature out of "old" language. To a nineteenth-century American writer the inherited meanings of this language were both gratifyingly and frustratingly abundant: he had as a rich and perplexing resource all that literature of Western civilization in which urban material and articulated attitudes toward urban civilization play so important a role.

It must be understood, of course, that mere uncritical use or imitation of these urban literary resources was inimical both to Emerson's temperament and to his aesthetic theories. The many and greatly varying traditional uses of urban material could not be melded without accepting complex tensions and ambiguities, and he could never use such literary traditions without being aware of the imperfect civilizations out of which they emerged. For both literary and moral reasons, he recognized that such traditions need to be handled with great caution. The ideal American poet, he once argued,

> releases himself from the traditions in which he grew,—no longer looks back to Hebrew or Greek or English use or tradition in religion, laws or life, but sees so truly the omnipresence of the eternal cause that he can convert the daily and hourly event of New York, of Boston, into universal symbols. (*W*, *12*, 42–43)

Nevertheless, along with other self-conscious American writers of the nineteenth century, Emerson usually saw his task less as avoiding than as redeeming those traditions. The American poet did not "release" himself from past literature by turning his back on it as much as by consciously confronting it and experimenting with it—by "trying out" its usefulness, as did *Moby Dick*, in the context of modern and American civilization.[34] In the middle of the nineteenth century traditional urban metaphors and themes were being transformed by the heat and pressure of major American imaginations, and Emerson was certainly a representative agent of this transformation. Specifically, the task he and his contemporaries undertook involved recasting urban literary traditions to make them suitable to a nation that saw itself in its dreams as peopled by a community of hopeful New Adams, housed in a gigantic and beneficent natural environment—a nation breathing heady democratic theories of society and imaginative effort and stimulated in influential quarters by a Romantic revolution that stressed an organic approach to both society and art. It would be far beyond the scope of this study to document fully the patterns of this metamorphosis as they emerged in novels, historical writing, urban newspapers, plans and names for new cities and towns, political rhetoric, movements for urban reform, utopian and communitarian efforts, education circles, and painting and architecture. But a detailed analysis of

34. R. W. B. Lewis, in *The American Adam* (Chicago, 1955), comments provocatively on American writers' "trying-out" of European literature; see esp. p. 140. Remarks by Earl R. Wasserman, *The Subtler Language: Critical Readings of Neoclassic and Romantic Poems* (Baltimore, 1959), pp. 169–88, should remind us that language was undergoing a comparable metamorphosis in English literature throughout the eighteenth and early nineteenth centuries. In America, however, this metamorphosis took on special significance because of its participation in the task of establishing a new nation as well as a revitalized language. The factor of self-conscious experimentation is obviously crucial to any central view of Emerson or his era.

Emerson and "The Age of Cities"

Emerson's literary relationship as Romantic prophet and historian both to actual urban civilization and to traditional urban imagery can suggest ways in which his writings may point to major aspects of American literature and thought.

❦ 2. City of the West

From Washington, proverbially "the city of magnificent distances," through all its cities, states, and territories, it is a country of beginnings, of projects, of designs, of expectations. (W, 1, 371)

The history of any settlement is an illustration of the whole—first, the emigrant's camp, then the group of log cabins, then the cluster of white wooden towns—to the eye of the European traveller as ephemeral as the tents of the first stage of the swift succession—and almost as soon followed by the brick and granite cities, which in another country would stand for centuries, but which here must soon give place to the enduring marble. (U, 20)

Europe would lack the regenerating impulse, & America lie waste, had it not been for El Dorado. (JMN, 2, 194)

City of the West is in two ways an appropriate metaphor for Emerson's attitude toward the "matter" and meaning of America. On one hand it points to the external substance of American history as Emerson saw it—"Californian quartz mountains dumped down in New York to be repiled architecturally along shore from Canada to Cuba, & thence west to California again" (*Corr*, 499). On the other hand it points to an Emersonian and characteristically American vision of "inner" or Romantic ideality—"a Columbia of thought and art, which is the last and endless end of Columbus's adventure" (W, *11*, 387). Like those more commonly cited metaphors for America, West and frontier, City of the West represents Emerson's attempt to find a metaphorical structure that would be true both to the "appearance" of American development and to the Transcendental reality by which such development should be measured. In experimenting with several versions of this strategic figure, Emerson was attempting to fulfill a role he ascribed once to Plato: "to reconcile his poetry with the appearances of the world, and build a bridge from the streets of cities to the Atlantis" (*W*, 4, 61).

Even when applied to American writers of Emerson's generation, however, City of the West cannot, at its most literary level, be termed a specifically or exclusively American metaphor. Under such versions as Atlantis and Eldorado, it had often appeared in European literature as a conventional symbol of the lush, the golden, the exotic, the mysterious, the visionary—and, especially, the elusive object of any passionate longing, of any yearning of the romantic heart. As early as 1822, while still in the first flush of determination to be a writer, Emerson himself pointed to these conventional connotations of the urban metaphor:

> When I lie dreaming on the possible contents of pages, as dark to me as the characters on the Seal of Solomon, I console myself with calling it learning's El Dorado. Every man has a Fairy land just beyond the compass of his horizon; the natural philosopher yearned after his Stone; the moral philosopher for his Utopia; the merchant for some South Sea speculation; the mechanic for perpetual motion; the poet for—all unearthly things; and it is very natural that literature at large, should look for some fanciful stores of mind which surpassed example and possibility. (*L*, 1, 117)

Thoreau was operating within the convention when he found in a cloud-streaked July sunset a "city, the eternal city of the west, the phantom city, in whose streets no traveller has trod, over whose pavements the horses of the sun have already hurried, some Salamanca of the imagination."[1] Melville's Taji was impelled by a similar evening vision: "The entire western horizon piled with gold and crimson clouds; airy arches, domes, and minarets; as if the yellow Moorish sun were setting behind some vast Alhambra. Vistas seemed leading to worlds beyond."[2] To mention Poe's poem "Eldorado" is only to indicate how often such a term served as a personal metaphor for Romantic longing.

For all their traditional and personal connotations, however, the metaphorical varieties of City of the West seemed particularly appropriate to the writers of Emerson's era, for they allowed the American writer not only to postulate his own "inner" vision of ideality, but to talk about the hopes of his nation. In its various metaphorical guises, City of the West pointed not only to that "Fairy land just beyond the compass" of the American poet's horizon but to the path by which America itself might venture toward the horizon—not only to a metaphysical vision but to a social utopia. Cooper placed the metaphorical concept specifically in the American context when, in *The Prairie,* he described the pioneering Bush family as "a band of emigrants seeking for the Eldorado of the

1. Thoreau, *Journals,* 2, 296. Compare his reference to "an Atlantis of the West" (*Journals,* 5, 216). In 1856 Thoreau wrote, "I prize this western reserve chiefly for its intellectual value. That is the road to new life and freedom" (*Correspondence,* p. 436). For discussions of Thoreau's use of a Romantic image of the West, see Edwin Fussell, *Frontier: American Literature and the American West* (Princeton, 1965), Chap. 4; Leo Stoller, *After Walden: Thoreau's Changing Views of Economic Man* (Stanford, 1957), pp. 28–33; and Sherman Paul, *The Shores of America: Thoreau's Inward Exploration* (Urbana, 1958).

2. Melville, *Works,* 3, 7–8.

West."[3] Hawthorne made similar use of the metaphor in a sketch entitled "The Hall of Fantasy," in which he discussed the utopian dreams of radical American reformers:

> Cities to be built, as if by magic, in the heart of pathless forests; and . . . streets to be laid out where now the sea was tossing; and . . . mighty rivers to be stayed in their courses in order to turn the machinery of a cotton mill. It was only by an effort, and scarcely then, that the mind convinced itself that such speculations were as much a matter of fantasy as the old dream of Eldorado, or as Mammon's Cave, or any other vision of gold ever conjured up by the imagination of needy poet or romantic adventurer.[4]

Emerson was accounting not only for European interest in America but for his fellow Americans' nationalistic aspirations when in 1828 he wrote in his journal, "Europe would lack the regenerating impulse, & America lie waste, had it not been for El Dorado" (*JMN*, 2, 194).[5]

3. Cooper did not view this search with total optimism. "It has long struck me," he said in 1837,

> that the term "happy country" is singularly misapplied, as regards America. . . . By placing incentives before us to make exertions, the El Dorado of our wishes is never obtained, and we pass our lives in vain struggles to reach a goal that recedes as we advance. . . . I know very well this is merely a consequence of a society in the course of establishing itself, but it shows how vulnerable is our happiness. (*Gleanings in England*, p. 358)

4. Hawthorne, *Works*, 2, 201

5. See Howard Mumford Jones, *O Strange New World. American Culture: the Formative Years* (New York, 1964), Chaps. 1, 2. As late as 1829 the *Edinburgh Review* was speaking Romantically of an Eldorado in the American West (Ralph L. Rusk, *The Literature of the Middle Western Frontier* [New York, 1925], 2, 1).

One striking aspect, however, of the American use of such metaphors as Eldorado is the stress not on the unattainable but on the possible. Though Hawthorne might describe as "fantasy" the vision of "cities to be built, as if by magic, in the heart of pathless forests," he recognized that American history actually embodied many aspects of the fantastic. Visiting the "instantaneous city" of Rochester, New York, in 1832—a town "sprung up like a mushroom"—he admitted that "it is impossible to look at its worn pavements and conceive how lately the forest leaves have been swept away."[6] As Whitman watched thousands of young Americans rush westward in 1858 toward the prospect of quick riches in California, he asserted that "the new territory will be populated as if by magic and what is now a wilderness will be thickly studded with cities and towns."[7] America's phenomenal history, as Carlyle once phrased it in a letter to Emerson, was itself a true romance (*Corr*, 472). It was, he said on another occasion, "as if the 'golden west,' seen by Poets, were no longer a mere optical phenomenon, but growing a reality, and coining itself into solid blessings!" (*Corr*, 128).

To talk of a master metaphor that derives its connotations from both urban and Western referents is to point to a profound tension at the heart of the American dream. This tension can be seen in Americans' idealization of their nation as both a New Jerusalem and a New Eden, in their hopes of founding both a New Rome and a new Golden Age, in their desire to build cities that would be both industrial and "or-

6. Hawthorne, *Works*, 12, 19.

7. Walt Whitman, *I Sit and Look Out: Editorials from the Brooklyn Daily Times*, eds. Emory Holloway and Vernolian Schwartz (New York, 1932), p. 99.

ganic." In the present study, City of the West will be used as the summary concept for this characteristic American desire for the best of all possible worlds. It will stand for the American's unwillingness to admit that the polarities of his experience—between nature and civilization, between economic abundance and moral integrity, between individualistic desires and society's demands—were inevitable or necessary. Like the ambiguous image of the frontier, City of the West can describe a metaphorical area within which these various poles might confront each other and, when viewed most optimistically, be reconciled or transcended.[8]

The distinction between frontier and City of the West should not be blurred, however. Though the polarities implied by both are similar, the priority given to the polarities differs. In the drama configured by the "frontier experience," nature and natural man loom larger than the civilization and civilized man with whom they come in contact. In the dramatic experience implied by City of the West, the reverse is true. The difference could be expressed another way: at the heart of the frontier drama is what R. W. B. Lewis has called the individual man in space; at the heart of the drama of City of the West is a "society" or "city" in space. In *The Scarlet Letter* not only Hester Prynne but an entire Puritan village must confront the New England wilderness. The protagonist of the Mississippi River world of *The Confidence Man* is not one individual but an entire floating city. Even in *Huckleberry Finn,* the major dramatic confrontations do not take place in

8. Fussell's *Frontier* places great stress on the literary possibilities of the West as "neutral territory" or "meeting ground," but he does not deal with the notion that an "urban" area might perform this dramatic function.

the lonely Western Territories but in the societies along the river bank. At the very least, City of the West can function as a highly concentrated focal point for the forces and values symbolized by the West as a whole. At its best, the metaphor can point to "civilized" possibilities beyond those of the frontier. For both historical and literary reasons, City of the West is a useful conceptual tool for illuminating Emerson's attitudes toward both America and his own "inner" quest.

Like many of his contemporaries, Emerson believed that the westward development of his nation was to provide an urban as well as an agrarian lesson.[9] In 1836, while near the height of his Romantic assertiveness, he looked hopefully at the growth of an "urban frontier" in America: "The founding of cities to which the course of rivers, the richness of soils, & the meridians of climate predict enormous growth, we see laid. We see the camp pitched, & the fire lighted which shall never be extinguished until great natural revolutions set a limit to human empire" (*JMN*, 5, 239).[10]

9. Whitman, among others, recognized "the tendency even of the emigration westward . . . to settle in towns and cities—to inhabit or found urban rather than to populate rural localities" (*I Sit and Look Out*, p. 164).

10. One of the era's most strikingly optimistic proclamations of American urban development occurs in Cooper's overly neglected book, *Notions of the Americans* (1828). Standing on a high hill overlooking the Mohawk Valley, the narrator of *Notions* sees what he describes as "completely an American scene, embracing all that admixture of civilization, and of the forest, of the works of man, and of the reign of nature, that one can so easily imagine to belong to this country." Feeling "the excitement of a rapid and constantly progressive condition," he is willing to believe that "he who comes a century hence, may hear the din of a city rising" from what is now a shadowy wilderness "or find his faculties confused by the number and complexity of its works of art" (*Notions*, 1, 229–37).

To Emerson, this nineteenth-century American urbanization smacked of a spirit characteristically Western, whether it occurred along the Atlantic seaboard or in the great interior watershed of the Mississippi River. Traveling between Cleveland and Cincinnati in 1850, he was reminded that "cities are everywhere much the same thing" (*L*, *4*, 203). What made American cities Western was not so much their geographical location as their economic and psychological orientation. When Emerson referred to St. Louis in 1850 as "the Metropolis of the West" (*L*, *4*, 214), he was referring to its outlook as well as to its position. Similarly, he could argue as late as 1863 for the Western status of Boston. "Our Boston merchants have already a sea-door," he noted in his journal, "but they are pinched by the Hoosac Mountain—on the landside—and they want a land-door; so they have made an extension of their gallery to New York, and build their land-door here, in New York, facing St. Louis and Chicago and the Pacific Railroad" (*J*, *9*, 577–78). When he spoke of New York's "immense natural advantages" and its "capabilities of boundless growth" (*Corr*, 260), he was pointing to that city's status, to use James Fenimore Cooper's phrase, as "the great Western emporium."[11]

The Western qualities of American cities were based on more than their interests in the material opportunities of a great continent. Emerson believed that any American city that was truly Western would give a perspective not only on the economic but on the qualitative possibilities of its national hinterland. Throughout his life he argued that "the point which decided the welfare of a people" was *"which way does it*

11. Cooper sometimes used the phrase satirically. More usually, however, he showed kind feelings toward this "western god-child" (*Notions*, *1*, 149).

look?" (*W*, 8, 103–04).[12] Time and again he stressed that a truly American city should apply much of its energy toward the realization of a symbolic Western vision of moral possibility. Significantly, he made this stricture the measure of his hope for the nation's capital city. After standing on the capitol steps in Washington one January evening in 1843, he wrote his brother that "at sunset I seemed to look westward far into the heart of the continent from this commanding position" (*L*, 3, 127).[13]

If emerging American cities seemed, at their most "American," to embody a characteristically Western outlook or allegiance, many aspects of the physically nonurban West seemed to embody an urban perspective. As Emerson used the term, "urban" was as psychologically relative as "Western." For this reason, he was willing to venture at times that all America, both within and outside its actual cities, might be seen under the aspect of a figuratively urban environment. "It becomes the young American," he wrote in 1836, "to learn the geography of his country in these days as much as it did our fathers

12. Emerson was aware that the answer to this question was not always easy. Actual American cities seemed to exemplify in their attitudes what Carl Bridenbaugh said of Colonial American cities: "Janus-like, they faced two ways" (*Cities in the Wilderness: Urban Life in America, 1625–1742* [New York, 1938], p. 138). Much of the drama implied by City of the West derived from the tensions of this double-facing toward European civilization and American nature, the given past and the unknown future. The very names of American cities and towns—New London as against Independence, Athens as against Indianapolis—reveal this tension within Americans' conceptions of their civilization.

13. Similarly, in his fragmentary history of New York, Cooper could argue that that city "is essentially national in interests, position, and pursuits. No one thinks of the place as belonging to a particular State, but to the United States" (*New York*, p. 19). New York's growth, he believed, "must be . . . always in proportion to the infant vigour of the whole country" (*Notions, 1*, 167).

to know the streets of their town; for steam & rails convert roads into streets & regions into neighborhoods" (*JMN*, 5, 120). In discussing America as a whole, Emerson came increasingly to the belief that his entire nation was a new sort of urban complex—a "city" whose thrust was ideally implied by the most positive connotations of "Western," and a "West" whose highest values were connoted by the most ideal meanings of "urban."

In postulating that America's ideal possibilities were those of a figurative City of the West—a fusing of the quintessential Western spirit and the most admirable form of cosmopolitanism—Emerson was by no means blind to the failure of most aspects of his nation's external environment to manifest these possibilities in more than a partial and unsatisfactory way. In fact, many aspects of American life seemed hostile to such an ideal vision. Emerson had begun to come to terms with some of these aspects as early as 1828, when he was forced to travel to Florida for his health. Finding himself "an exile" in St. Augustine, he took the opportunity to make comparisons between this "oldest town of Europeans in North America" and Tallahassee, the young capital of Florida "200 miles west of St. Augustine" (*JMN*, 3, 115). To a young man who had never been to Europe, St. Augustine embodied many "romantic things" of the Old World, but it also illustrated sadly that "the colonies observed the customs of the parent country however ill they may be adapted to the new territory" (*JMN*, 3, 113, 124). On the other hand, although Tallahassee had certainly shown skill in adapting to many of the demands of a Western frontier experience, Emerson disapproved of the results. It was "a grotesque place selected 3 years since as a suitable spot for the Capital of the territory, & since that day rapidly settled by public officers, land speculators & desperadoes." It had "much club law & little other" (*JMN*, 3, 115). As Emerson was beginning to realize, actual Western and urban experiences often seemed to be in conflict or to be allied on only the lowest common denominator of materialistic aims. It was difficult enough to find environments in America that would embody either admirable Western or admirable urban aspects, but it was infinitely more difficult to find one environment that would embody both.

In June 1850, while on one of his Western speaking tours, an older Emerson found an occasion for illustrating more concisely his sense of some of the problems inherent in a nation's attempting to become both Western and urban. After visiting Cairo, Illinois, a small town at the mouth of the Ohio River, he wrote his wife about his experiences there:

> Cairo, you know, is a tongue of low land . . . seized upon by speculators as a point that must necessarily be a depot of immense importance. The land for ten miles from the point was bought & lots were laid out & the biggest city of the world was to be here. The Rothschilds are or have been owners or mortgagees of the property. But the river during a large part of the year keeps the whole of it under water, and the houses that were built by the Companies are now wide open to every pedlar & boatman to enter & take possession, if he will. (*L*, 4, 209)

Here, in shorthand—with the telltale "but" signaling his duality of vision—is Emerson's recognition of a number of tensions in American civilization. Though projected as a new Western city, Cairo was to be built by Eastern or even European resources. Though promised to the future, it was mortgaged to the past. Though to be peopled by a basically Protestant population, it was owned by Old Testament interests (the

Jewish Rothschilds). Though claiming dreams of becoming "the biggest city of the world," its physical site was still the domain of a natural wilderness; its "water lots" symbolized not only the inflationary speculations from the East, but the power of rivers of the West to challenge this speculative faith. Though it was projected to be an intensely worldly city—"a depot of immense importance"—it was at the present merely a dream city—a product of the Eastern imagination. The realization of this projected city of the West rested on a precarious balancing of the partly cooperating, partly hostile forces of Eastern civilization and Western nature.

Emerson's response to his experience in Cairo, like his characteristic response to most experience, was twofold. On one hand, he believed it his duty to evaluate such "American" material from the standpoint of an ideal moral standard. On the other hand, he strongly wished to find in this material, however morally imperfect it was, its proper "literary" function. A few years after his trip to Cairo, in his essay "Art and Criticism," he had begun to convert his observations into the elements of both a moral lesson and a dramatic metaphor:

> I passed at one time through a place called New City, then supposed, like each of a hundred others, to be destined to greatness. I fell in with one of the founders who showed its advantages and its river and port and the capabilities: "Sixty houses, sir, were built in a night, like tents." After Chicago had secured the confluence of railroads to itself, I chanced to meet my founder again, but now removed to Chicago. He had transferred to that city the magnificent dreams which he had once communicated to me, and no longer remembered his first emporium. "Where is the town? Was there not," I asked, "a river

> and a harbor there?" "Oh yes, there was a guzzle out of a sand-bank." "And the town?" "There are still the sixty houses, but when I passed it, one owl was the only inhabitant." (*W*, *12*, 301)

In this new version, Cairo has been translated into a more metaphorical term, New City, and by adding a new dynamic term—Chicago—to his tale, Emerson demonstrates the relativity of the metaphor itself. Chicago too is a New City. Like many new American cities, it can exemplify "the magnificent dreams" and ironic tensions once symbolized by the hut-town of Cairo. The founder of New City is an older brother of Colonel Sellers in Mark Twain's *Gilded Age*, but he is also one of the primary actors in the epic drama of America that Emerson was creating in bits and snatches—a pioneer whose aim is not the establishment of freehold farms but the building of gigantic cities, not the husbandry of nature but the speculation in a powerful urban civilization. New City and its archetypal founder by no means represented the vision of transcendent reconciliation that Emerson posited as the most ideal meaning of "America," but the very tensions they embodied provided the conflicting elements that Emerson needed in trying to move dialectically from the imperfections of actual American development toward the better America implied by City of the West.[14] In the famous passage from his essay "The Poet," Emerson had urged the American mind to

14. A few years before the Civil War Emerson applied a revealing metaphor to such speculating pioneers:

> Tantalus, who in old times was seen vainly trying to quench his thirst with a flowing stream which ebbed whenever he approached it, has been seen again lately. He is in Paris, in New York, in Boston. He is now in great spirits; thinks he shall reach it yet; thinks he shall bottle the wave. It is however getting a little doubtful. Things have an ugly look still. No matter how many centuries of

find "in the barbarism and materialism of the times, another carnival of the same gods whose picture he so much admires in Homer; then in the Middle Age; then in Calvinism." Such materials, he argued, "rest on the same foundations of wonder as the town of Troy and the temple of Delphi" (*W*, 3, 37–38). By including the imperfect New Cities of the American West within an idealistic literary structure, Emerson was attempting to re-create the archetypal "sense of wonder" that would redeem these cities and the nation.

Emerson's own attempt to move, by literary means, from the actualities of an urbanizing West to a vision of an ideal America is usefully exemplified by his treatment of those characteristics that American cities seemed to share with and focus for their Western hinterland. Four of these characteristics appear as early as a journal entry of 1823, in which Emerson was beginning gingerly to touch on the possibilities and problems of his nation's extraordinary continent. Though the passage bears the marks of opinions current at the young Harvard graduate's alma mater, its final sentence is almost Melvillian in tone:

> Let the young American withdraw his eyes from all but his own country, and try if he can find employment there, considerable enough to task the vigorous intellect he brings. I am of opinion that the most extraordinary powers that ever were given to a human being would lose themselves in this vast sphere. Separated from the contamination which infects all other civilized lands this country has always boasted a great comparative purity.

> culture have preceded, the new man always finds himself standing on the brink of chaos, always in a crisis. (*W*, 7, 163–64)

It was out of the New Cities built by an American Tantalus, however, that Emerson hoped to find suggested features of a City of the West.

> At the same time, for obvious causes, it has leaped at once from infancy to manhood; has covered & is covering millions of square miles with a hardy & enterprizing population. . . . But the vast rapidity with which the desarts [sic] & forests of the interior of this country are peopled have led patriots to fear lest the nation grow *too fast* for its virtue & its peace. In the raw multitudes who lead the front of emigration men of respectability in mind & morals are rarely found. . . . The pioneers are commonly the offscouring of civilized society who have been led to embark in these enterprizes by the consciousness of ruined fortunes or perchance a desire for that greater license which belongs to a new & unsettled community. These men & their descendants compose the western frontier population of the United States and are rapidly expanding themselves. At this day, the axe is laid to the root of the forest; the Indian is driven from his hut & the bison from the plains;—in the bosom of mountains where white men never trod, already the voice of nations begins to be heard—haply heard in ominous & evil accents. Good men desire, & the great cause of human Nature demands that this abundant & overflowing richness wherewith God has blessed this country be not misapplied & made a curse of; that this new storehouse of nations shall never pour out upon the world an accursed tribe of barbarous robbers. (*JMN*, 2, 115–16)

Emerson's suspicion of the "raw multitudes" then settling the American West followed a typical Whig view of the frontier during the early decades of the nineteenth century.[15] But if

15. See Rush Welter, "The Frontier West as Image of American Society: Conservative Attitudes Before the Civil War," *Mississippi Valley Historical Review*, 46 (1960), 593–614.

we partly discount his suspicion in light of his later opinions, we are still left with a young man's critical awareness of at least four major variables that were being tested in the West —newness, overwhelming space ("the vast sphere"), rapid settlement and consequent compression of the American time-scale ("leaped at once from infancy to manhood"), and the heterogeneous people who were converting the new area into a "new storehouse of nations."

These four factors—newness, large scale, rapid motion, and heterogeneity—became for the mature Emerson crucial components describing not only the West but urbanizing America. None of these factors was in isolation uniquely Western. Each found its American orientation only in interaction with the other factors, and together they formed the major drama that Emerson and others saw in America's westward development: the attempt of a new and diverse people to confront and exploit rapidly the resources—psychological as well as material—of a large, newly discovered continent. These factors were not merely historical causes of American growth or socioeconomic reflections of contemporary American culture. For Emerson, in his capacities as poet and prophet, they were potentially dramatic metaphors by which one could explore symbolically the various possible meanings of America.

Underlying all other major components was that of newness. As Emerson applied the term to the most Western aspects of his nation, it pointed in part to how relatively recent had been the first confrontation of the white American and a natural wilderness. "In America everything looks new and recent," he stated in a lecture on "The Progress of Culture." "Our towns are still rude, the makeshifts of emigrants, and the whole architecture tent-like" (*W*, 8, 212). More important to Emerson, however, were the psychological implications of newness—the "youthful" reaction of Americans to the unexplored possibilities of the West. "America is another word for Opportunity," he said (*W*, *11*, 299). "That cosmical west wind . . . is alone broad enough to carry to every city and suburb . . . this new hope of mankind" (*W*, *8*, 211–12). Psychologically speaking, newness was a synonym for optimism. Thus Emerson reflected his own Americanness in his excitement about Western development, for in the West none of man's own works was a given. The West was at base a resource, a challenge, and a laboratory for free experimentation. " 'The Far West' is the right name for these verdant desarts [sic]," Emerson wrote Carlyle, after returning in 1851 from a lecture tour in the Mississippi River Valley. "On all the shores, interminable silent forest. If you land, there is prairie beyond prairie, forest beyond forest, sites of nations, [but] no nations. The raw bullion of nature; *what we call 'moral' value not yet stamped on it*" (*Corr*, 470; my italics). As historian, Emerson studied the West because he was fascinated by the civilizing process, by which a variety of possible values might be stamped onto what was, in one sense, a morally neutral region. Emerson's writings did not test the Western land itself so much as test the Americans who were newly and optimistically shaping that land. To the extent that he treated the natural West itself as a neutral tool he could emphasize the American population's own moral responsibility for what it wrought in its new cities of the West.

To Emerson, the American city-builder's confrontation of the opportunities and problems that Western newness presented was the historical or social counterpart of his own attempt to discover the literary or ideal implications of this newness. When he reacted most "youthfully" to the as-yet unexplored literary possibilities of Western material, Emerson was tempted to treat America almost ingenuously as a poem waiting only to be set to meter (*W*, 3, 38). "In the moments when my eyes are open," he wrote Carlyle in 1837, "I see that here are rich materials for the philosopher and poet." On the other hand, he admitted in the same letter, it was easier to affirm the richness of these materials in the abstract than to find them in the specific example. "America looks, to those who come hither," he said, "as unromantic & unexciting as the Dutch canals" (*Corr*, 162). At his most pessimistic, Emerson went so far as to argue in 1852 that such projects as the railroad-building efforts of St. Louis "cannot consist with much literature" (*L*, 4, 338–39). Between Emerson's most optimistic hope that urbanizing America would prove innately or at least ultimately poetic and his pessimistic reference to this America as "the unpoetic West" (*JMN*, 4, 297) lay his more characteristic attitude toward the literary implications of a newly emerging West. Just as the American city-builder could impress value on the morally neutral resources of a physical West, so Emerson as poet could treat Western urbanization as "neutral" in ideal implications until "settled" and "civilized" by the artist's imagination. To test the poetic and dramatic possibilities of this new America was thus really to test the "inner" possibilities of the poet himself.

Because of both their external and their metaphorical relation to newness, the Western components of large scale, speed, and diversity offered to both the city-builder and the civilizing poet similar "neutral" possibilities. Though each component had idealized connotations, it was capable of symbolizing the dark as well as the bright side of American actualities and dreams. Through the confrontation of those polarities, Emerson hoped to create a progressive drama in which the dark aspects would be redeemed or overcome by the bright. In his own practice, however, he found it all but impossible to embody this hope in convincing dramatic form. He was well aware that it was much easier to preach "the Gospel according to San Francisco" and "the Epistle to the Californians" (*J*, 9, 386) than it was to dramatize their implications. But even by listing the ambiguous connotations of newness, large space, rapid motion, and diversity as they converged in an urbanizing West, he attempted at least to outline the drama.

Certainly the ambiguities of large space, as applied to American cities, enhanced its dramatic and poetic possibilities. In physical terms, American cities were both products of large external space—that of the West itself—and manifestations of large interior scale. The power and "future greatness" of the American city, as Cooper argued in 1828 of New York, "is the immense and unprecedented range of interior which, by a bold and noble effort of policy, has recently been made tributary to its interests."[16] The resources of this spacious hinterland offered the city opportunities for expansion not only of its boundaries but of its internal components. To Emerson, St. Louis was typical of such cities, with its "spacious squares, & ample room to grow."[17] He praised the "magnificent" hotels of Cincinnati and Philadelphia and noted with pleasure the noble buildings and expansive vistas in Washington.[18]

He found vast urban scale most pleasing, however, for what it could symbolize ideally about America. It dramatized his belief that "the boundless America gives opportunities as

16. Cooper, *Notions*, 1, 168.

17. "Anglo-American" (Houghton manuscript 202.2). The lecture was delivered first in 1853.

18. *L*, 3, 121, 124; *L*, 4, 204; *J*, 6, 337.

wide as the morning" (*J*, *8*, 584). "These grand material dimensions," he argued, "cannot suggest dwarfish and stunted manners and policy. Everything on this side [of] the water inspires large and prospective action. America means opportunity, freedom, power" (*J*, *10*, 84). For this reason, he saw St. Louis' expanding size as a material reflection of "a certain largeness in the designs & enterprise of the people & a generosity." Such American cities represented "the American discovery that, it is as easy to occupy large space, & do much work, as, to occupy small space, & do little."[19]

The external manifestations of urban scale, however, were themselves neutral. The moral value of this scale rested in part on the values of the city-builders who had created it. Emerson judged urban size most harshly, therefore, when he thought it the product of low, selfish motives. When American attempts to exploit the possibilities of a large continent were not "supported by adequate mental and moral training," he believed, "they run into the grandiose, into exaggeration and vapouring" (*J*, *10*, 84). When he complained of "the miles of endless squares" of "the monstrous city of Philadelphia" (*L*, *3*, 132–33) or, while in New York, found himself intimidated by "the tyranny of Space I feel in this long long city" (*L*, *3*, 27), he was reflecting his belief that large urban space was not always used for "large" moral ends. He pointed to this misuse of Western space in a description of Washington in 1843:

> The two poles of an enormous political battery, galvanic coil on coil, self-increased by series on series of plates

19. "Anglo-American." In an editorial in 1857 on "Grand Buildings in New York City," Walt Whitman argued for urban buildings that would have "the grandeur of Americanism, originality, and appropriateness to their surroundings and intended use" (*I Sit and Look Out*, p. 129).

> from Mexico to Canada, & from the sea westward to the Rocky Mountains, meet & play, and make the air electric & violent. Yet one feels how little, more than how much, man is represented there. I think in the higher societies of the Universe, it will turn out that the angels are molecules, as the devils were always Titans, since the dulness [sic] of the world needs such mountainous demonstration, & the virtue is so modest & concentrating (*Corr,* 341–42).[20]

In suggesting a dramatic relationship between Titans and angels, however, or between electric political forces, Emerson was not merely condemning the darker implications of large space. He was indicating the way he, by literary means, could impress on this space a higher meaning than could the Washington politicians. Eloquence, he believed, needed a sense of extremes—"nothing less than the grandeur of absolute ideas, the splendors and shades of Heaven and Hell" (*W*, 7, 61). Arguing that the "tendency to combine antagonisms and evil . . . is the index of high civilization" (*W*, 7, 25), he hoped to find a literary framework in which America's hellish uses of the opportunities symbolized by large space would confront and give way to the angelic use of this space. He felt the large urban spaces of America at their most ideal implied grand "inner" possibilities for the poet's exploring imagination—"There is no country so extensive as a

20. Compare Melville's remarks in *Mardi* on the spacial basis of Vivenza's (America's) democracy: "It is because you overflow your redundancies within our own mighty borders; having a wild western waste, which many shepherds with their flocks could not overrun in a day. Yet overrun at last it will be; and then, the recoil must come" (*Works*, 4, 239–40). This passage has striking resemblances to Turner's frontier hypothesis.

thought," he said in 1832 (*JMN*, *4*, 14). Under the redemptive impulse of large, Romantic thoughts, America's urbanizing society could be, as Thoreau put it, "well spaced all at once, clean and handsome to the eye—a city of magnificent distances."[21]

The same ambiguities and symbolic possibilities applied to the rapid motion of the American city. "Everything in America is at a rapid rate," Emerson argued in 1853. "America means speedy in Europe as if the ingenuity of this country were directed on nothing so much."[22] As early as 1816, while visiting Boston's Long Wharf, an adolescent Emerson "was surprised to see how changed the Central or New Wharf appeared to be in so short a time—It was but a little time ago," he wrote his brother Edward, "when there was nothing but water to be seen there; and now, a long block of about 30 stores fill up the place" (*L*, *1*, 27). Visiting Bangor, Maine, in 1834, he noted that "a man goes out & puts up a frame of a house before breakfast as an ordinary morning's work" (*JMN*, *4*, 390). During the following two decades, he personally observed the same impetus toward rapid growth in even greater magnitude in New York, Philadelphia, Cincinnati, St. Louis, and Chicago.[23] His statement in the lecture "Social Aims" was a summary of this American growth:

> The history of any settlement is an illustration of the whole—first, the emigrant's camp, then the group of log cabins, then the cluster of white wooden towns—to the eye of the European traveller as ephemeral as the tents of the first stage of the swift succession—and almost as

21. Thoreau, *Journals*, 12, 417.
22. "Anglo-American."
23. For examples, see *J*, *9*, 76–77, and *L*, *4*, 204, 345, 414, 427, 434–35.

> soon followed by the brick and granite cities, which in another country would stand for centuries, but which here must soon give place to the enduring marble. (*U*, 20)

Great speed was "Western" only as it interacted with the other major components of American urbanization. It was, for one thing, a tool and consequence of the Americans' attempts to conquer large space—a product of their optimistic response to the possibilities of their abundant environment. This rapid movement, treated psychologically, also reinforced the Americans' sense of newness. As early as 1837 Emerson was quoting sympathetically Talleyrand's suggestion "that to go from the American coast one or two thousand miles into the wilderness was like going back one or two thousand years in time; you pass, in both, from the extreme of civilization to the extreme of barbarism" (*EL*, 2, 136). Such a suggestion, however, could be taken two ways. Carlyle, in a letter to Emerson, opted for one of these possibilities: "Only a hundred years ago," he wrote, "and the Mississippi has changed as never valley did: in 1751, older and stranger, looked at from *its* present date, than Balbec or Nineveh!" (*Corr*, 468). Emerson's response was perhaps more characteristically American. America's rapid motion, he felt, did not give Americans a feel for history as much as it gave them a reason for believing history irrelevant to their own tasks. Psychologically speaking, Americans had not had time to get used to their past, since it had changed so quickly. Moving rapidly, they inevitably gave less attention to their past than to the rapid succession of "new" presents and imminent futures.

The railroad was a central symbol of this rapid urbanization. "The chain of Western railroads from Chicago to the Pacific," Emerson noted shortly after the Civil War, "has planted cities and civilization in less time than it cost to bring an orchard into bearing" (*W*, 7, 160–61). By its speed, the railroad had "destroyed the old scale of distances" (*W*, *10*, 458–59) and, in doing so, had encouraged and aided the confrontation of the heterogeneous people, processes, and products that made up America's emerging civilization. "The railroad and telegraph are great unionists" (*J*, 8, 209), Emerson said. "I like it well," he could argue for the railroad at his most optimistic, "that in the heart of democracy I find such practical illustration of high theories" (*J*, 6, 337).[24]

Speed, however, was also a manifestation of the underside of American urbanization. "Everything is sacrificed for speed,—solidity and safety," Emerson complained in a lecture on his countrymen. "They would sail in a steamer built of Lucifer matches if it would go faster."[25] The reference to "Lucifer matches" was probably a pun, for the American stress on rapid development certainly had its devilish possibilities. Emerson noted in 1834 that a Concord farmer called the railroad "Hell in harness" (*JMN*, 4, 296). "Western" motion might imply rapid progress toward freedom, abundance, and national unity, but, as young Emerson had noted, the new nation might also "grow *too fast* for its virtue & its peace" (*JMN*, 2, 115). The American city-builder's value-giving mind might lag too far behind his material pace westward and be ruled for the moment by a narrow infatuation with the materials themselves. Impatient to reach the golden vision promised on the

24. See G. Ferris Cronkite, "The Transcendental Railroad," *New England Quarterly*, 24 (1951), 306–15.

25. "Anglo-American."

horizon of a spacious America's future, many of Emerson's hurrying contemporaries seemed to be blinding themselves to the necessary stepping-stones that must first be carefully laid before the vision could be reached. "Chicago grows so fast," Emerson argued after returning from a Western lecture tour in 1864, "that one ceases to respect civic growth: as if all these solid and stately squares which we are wont to see as the slow growth of a century had come to be done by machinery as cloth and hardware are made, and were therefore shoddy architecture without honor (*J*, *10*, 91). Several decades before this, he had phrased his complaint more generally:

> We are a puny and fickle folk . . . and the whole generation is discontented with the tardy rate of growth which contents every European community. America is . . . the country of small adventures, of short plans, of daring risks, not of patience, not of great combinations, not of long, persistent, close-woven schemes, demanding the utmost fortitude, temper, faith, and poverty. (*J*, 5, 529)

Americans should not neglect, he argued repeatedly, "the penalty that speed must pay"—products that were "hasty, incomplete, cheap, much of it counterfeit." Too often, the hurrying American, like a New Tantalus eager to grasp golden fruit beyond his reach, was carelessly flinging down on the westward path in front of him not solid stones but flimsy paper—watered stocks, inflated currency, grandiose blueprints for specious New Cities. Like the paper that filled the Slough of Despond in Hawthorne's short story, "The Celestial Railroad," the resulting road might not be at all adequate for its professed purposes. The American himself paid the largest price. In the rush to compete for economic abundance, Emerson argued, "every man is tasked beyond his strength, & grows early old."[26] In the American's rush to find a material Eldorado in the American interior, he ran the risk of not discovering the moral Eldorado within himself.[27]

Even the impatient materialism of Americans, however, considered in the proper dramatic context, might be considered as part of a grand epic tendency. In a thumbnail sketch of his fellow citizens in 1847, Emerson attempted to ally their speed with the fate of a natural universe: "Irresistibility of the American; no conscience; his motto, like Nature's, is 'Our Country, right or wrong.' . . . good race, but though an admirable fruit, you shall not find one good, sound, well-developed apple on the tree. Nature herself was in a hurry with these hasters and never finished one" (*J*, 7, 294). By taking an initially critical attitude toward the rush for California gold—the materialistic side of America's quest for Eldorado—as "a rush and scramble of needy adventurers," Emerson hoped to provide a dark beginning from which a dramatic affirmation could grow: "California gets peopled and subdued, civilized in this immoral way, and on this fiction a real prosperity is rooted and grown. . . . Out of Sabine rapes, and out of robber's forays, real Romes and their heroisms come in ful-

26. Ibid.

27. "Men rush to California and Australia as if the true gold were to be found in that direction," Thoreau wrote in 1855, "but that is to go to the very opposite extreme to where it lies. . . . Is not our native soil auriferous" (*Journals*, 7, 496). A similar attitude informed Melville's attack on the deluding lusts of "gold hunters" in the worlds of *Mardi* and *The Confidence Man* (*Works*, 4, 264–67; 12, 235, 237, 281). In *Moby Dick* he made the doubloon nailed by Ahab to the Pequod's mast a striking symbol of the ambiguously practical and Romantic motives that set men out in quest of golden dreams.

ness of time" (*W*, 6, 255–56).[28] Rapid motion, like great space, could work for Emerson's Romantic ends if properly structured by poetic vision; even the railroad, seen most poetically, was "a practical confirmation of the ideal philosophy that Matter is phenomenal whilst men & barns whiz by you as fast as the leaves of a dictionary" (*JMN*, 4, 296). The impatience of the materialist had its higher equivalent in the impatience of the idealist—in the hope for a rapid leap from an imperfect America to the City of the West. At the height of Emerson's Transcendental assertiveness, he could admit that "I never was on a coach which went fast enough for me" (*JMN*, 4, 316). In exploring the progressive possibilities of rapid speed in his nation's development, he was also exploring the powers of the inner American.

For this reason, Emerson placed great emphasis on a fourth major characteristic of American civilization at its most "Western"—the heterogeneous population that was forming a new urban culture. In his essay "Civilization," he underlined the essential human basis of the westering process:

> The true test of civilization is, not the census, nor the size of cities, nor the crops,—no, but the kind of man the

28. In a letter to Emerson in 1872, Carlyle offered a similar suggestion:

> There is something huge, painful, and almost appalling to me in that wild Western World of yours;—and especially I wonder at the gold-nuggeting there, while plainly every gold-nuggeter is no other than a criminal to Human Society . . . I conclude it is a bait used by All-Wise Providence to attract your people out thither, there to build towns, make roads, fell forests (or plant forests), and make ready a Dwelling-place for new Nations, who will find themselves called to quite other than nugget-hunting. (*Corr*, 588)

> country turns out. I see the vast advantages of this country, spanning the breadth of the temperate zone. I see the immense material prosperity,—towns on towns, states on states, and wealth piled in the massive architecture of cities: California quartz-mountains dumped down in New York to be repiled architecturally alongshore from Canada to Cuba, and thence westward to California again. But it is not New York streets, built by the confluence of workmen and wealth of all nations, though stretching out towards Philadelphia until they touch it, and northward until they touch New Haven, Hartford, Springfield, Worcester and Boston,—not these that make the real estimation. But when I look over this constellation of cities which animate and illustrate the land, and see how little the government has to do with their daily life, how self-helped and self-directed all families are . . . I see what cubic values America has, and in these a better certificate of civilization than great cities or enormous wealth. (*W*, 7, 31–32)

In giving close attention to "the confluence of workmen and wealth of all nations," Emerson was looking for human signs of America's "cubic values."

A major form and symbol of American heterogeneity was its mixture of ethnic groups. Emerson could treat such ethnic diversity most optimistically when it seemed to promise "the fusion of races and religion" into a new race that would take adequate advantages of the vast opportunities of the "wide continent" (*W*, 8, 207). In 1851 he stated,

> In the distinctions of the genius of the American race it is to be considered that it is not indiscriminate masses of

> Europe that are shipped hitherward, but the Atlantic is a sieve through which only or chiefly the liberal, adventurous, sensitive, *America-loving* part of each city, clan, family are brought. It is the light complexion, the blue eyes of Europe that come: the black eyes, the black drop, the Europe of Europe, is left. (*J*, *8*, 226)

The latent racism in this observation is much less important than the reflection of Emerson's search for an adequate vocabulary by which to describe American possibilities. It was perhaps natural that a Bostonian would see the Anglo-American "race" itself as a symbol of the best tendencies of fusion. In a lecture of 1853, Emerson portrayed America's ethnic majority as "a pushing, versatile, victorious race, with wonderful powers of absorption & appropriating. The Mississippi swallows the Illinois, the Missouri, the Ohio & Red Rivers and does not visibly widen; and this Anglo-American race absorbs into itself . . . millions of German, French, Irish, Norwegians, & Swedes, & remains unchanged."[29] Symbolically, the Anglo-American reflected America's ideal meaning—the "wonderful powers" of absorbing and appropriating lower materials for higher purposes. It was within the context of this symbol that

29. "Anglo-American." The merging of races on the American continent, sang Melville's Redburn, was producing a new people "whose blood is as the flood of the Amazon, made up of a thousand noble currents all pouring into one. We are not a nation," said Redburn, affirming the concept of a new cosmopolitanism, "so much as a world. . . . We are the heirs of all time, and with all nations we divide our inheritance. On this Western Hemisphere all tribes and people are forming into one federated whole" (*Works*, 5, 217). Compare this to the crew Melville assembles on the Pequod or to his more demonic description of the passengers of the *Fidèle* as "a cosmopolitan and confident tide" (*Works*, 7, 149–50, and 12, 9).

Emerson could "see with joy the Irish emigrants landing at Boston, at New York, and say to myself, There they go—to school" (*J*, 10, 153). The schooling was not basically in racial assimilation. Rather, it taught that all varieties of American diversity—"new divisions of labor or . . . new professions," as well as new ethnic groups—might "form . . . a new order" of ideal aims (*W*, 8, 210).

Like the other facets of Western urbanization, however, heterogeneity was primarily a tool of the civilizing process rather than a goal and was subject to the same abuses as large space and rapid motion. American commerce, for example, could provide at its best a diversity that would serve a new kind of social unity. Trade, Emerson argued in his lecture "The Present Age," in 1837,

> opens all doors. It perforates the world with roads. The old bonds of language, country, and king give way to the new connexions of trade. It destroys patriotism and substitutes cosmopolitanism. It makes peace and keeps peace. . . . It mingles all nations in its marts. What picturesque contrasts are crowded on us! . . . The South Sea Islander is on the wharf. The Indian squaw sells mats at our doors. And all those contrasts which commerce so fast abolishes are brought within a holiday excursion of more softness and refinement than was in Syria or Rome. (*EL*, 2, 160–61)

When Americans allowed such material diversity to become an end in itself, however, they cut themselves off from the possibilities of a higher form of cosmopolitanism. The only order that could come out of such a misplaced affection, Emerson believed, was a unification on the basis of the lowest materialistic denominators.[30] "The congregation of men into large masses and the universal facility of communication with metropolitan refinement and opinion," he argued at his most critical, "has had the effect of grinding off the asperities of individual character, introducing the dominion of fashion . . . and so substituting an universal regard to decorum for the sinews of virtue and intellect" (*EL*, 2, 161–62). Though the diverse material resources of America could impose on its heterogeneous population the metropolitan bonds of wealth and manners, it often seemed in a moral sense to leave them "strangers" not only to their past, but to their continent, to each other, and even to themselves. As Emerson interpreted his nation, this was its greatest dilemma. "My own quarrel with America, of course," he said in 1850, "was that the geography is sublime, but the men are not" (*J*, 8, 136).

In stating "the American dilemma" in human terms, however, Emerson was also attempting to indicate the key to its solution. Between the purely physical and "neutral" facts of newness, large space, rapid motion, and diversity and the "divine" meanings of these facts stood the American himself. As Emerson often argued, "A man should know himself for a

30. Cooper, like many other American writers, understood the dangers of assimilation that resulted from materialism. It was this aspect of New York that he attacked most harshly. "The great emporium of the West," he charged in 1838,

> is a congregation of adventurers, collected from the four quarters of the earth, that have shaken loose every tie of birthplace, every sentiment of nationality or of historical connexion; that know nothing of the hour, and care less for any greatness but that which is derived from the largeness of inventories. . . . [They] never rise far enough above the lowest of human propensities to come within the influence of any feeling above that which marks a life passed in the constant struggle for inordinate and grasping gain. (*Excursions in Italy*, 2, 203–04)

necessary actor. A link was wanting between two craving parts of nature, and he was hurled into being as the bridge over that yawning need, the mediator betwixt two else unmarriageable facts" (*W*, *1*, 207). In searching among the traits of imperfect American city-builders for the foreshadowings of the better American, Emerson was piecing together the lineaments of a New or American Cosmopolitan, the fit symbolic inhabitant of a metaphorical City of the West.[31] As a synecdoche of the City of the West, the American Cosmopolitan provided a "human" standard against which Americans could measure their own civilizing efforts. As a literary figure, he was grand enough to play a central role in an epic that dramatized America's discovery of its "Western" possibilities. Like City of the West, the American Cosmopolitan implied not only a Romantic ideal but the literary process by which Emerson might point toward this ideal.

It is therefore appropriate that one of Emerson's most sustained attempts to move from an actual toward a visionary America is in an essay significantly entitled "The Young American." Emerson first delivered the essay as a lecture to the Mercantile Library Association of Boston in 1844, the same year that James K. Polk was elected President on an

31. Most major writers of the American Renaissance posited various forms of the ideal American, whom Thoreau once called "the Man of the West" (*Journals*, *4*, 295). Each of these mythic American giants had his appropriate ideal environment. The American Adam, for example, found a fit home in an Edenic garden. The American Pioneer was a personification of the tensions of the frontier on which he lived. The American Immigrant retained the best of Europe as part of his landscape. In the figure of the American Cosmopolitan, all these figures and environments were merged harmoniously. Emerson's American Scholar was, of course, a preeminent version of the Cosmopolitan. But notice the insidious possibilities of the Cosmopolitan—as in Melville's *Confidence Man*—for a critical view of American civilization.

expansionist platform.[32] It is crucial to an understanding of Emerson's aims that he should lecture on a "Western" subject to a Bostonian audience, for the lessons drawn were to be applied to America as a whole. The essay is an exploration of the unifying tendencies of American civilization, which are found in each of the five major sections into which the essay is divided: a two-paragraph introduction; a seven-page discussion of the part that "land," "soil," or "natural wealth" plays in "creating an American sentiment"; a nine-page analysis of the similar functions of "anti-feudal" commerce or trade; an eleven-page discussion of the "appearance of new moral causes which are to modify the state"; and a four-page conclusion that reaffirms the "tendencies" implicit in the three central sections of the essay. In structure and imagery as well as theme, these sections form an arrow piercing the past and present, the West and its people, and pointing toward an ideal City of the West beyond the horizon of any actual present achievement.

The structure of "The Young American" reinforces the two central and interrelated tenets of the essay: first, that Europe is receding and the American continent beginning to assert itself in American thought (the psychological implications of this process are heavily underscored), and second, that the ameliorative tendency of history is proved by the movement in America from life dominated by brute nature to a society controlled by the moral and poetic mind of man—a society in which freedom is used to achieve order and unity. Around this central structural axis revolves what Vivian Hopkins has usefully referred to in another context as an ascend-

32. This essay is found in *W, I*, 363–95. A useful application of the essay can be found in Whicher, *Freedom and Fate*, pp. 139–40. See also Paul, *Emerson's Angle of Vision*, pp. 224–28.

ing spiral—a dialectic that, in continually circling back on itself as it moves forward toward a higher plane, alters and adds to the meaning of the terms of the dialectic. This circling not only presents the overall structure of "The Young American" but appears in miniature within each of the five sections and even in individual paragraphs and sentences. It is basically a movement from external referents to internal referents, from a description of the facts of history to a vision of the way in which such facts symbolize the inherent nature of man, his art, and the poetic process.

The opening paragraph of the essay establishes the movement toward the American West, toward improvement and unification of American civilization, and presents a symbol of this movement—the railroad. In the second paragraph Emerson discusses this "arrow in our quiver":

> This rage of road building is beneficent for America, where vast distance is so main a consideration in our domestic politics and trade, inasmuch as the great political promise of the invention is to hold the Union staunch. . . . Not only is distance annihilated, but when, as now, the locomotive and the steamboat, like enormous shuttles, shoot every day across the thousand various threads of national descent and employment and bind them fast in one web, an hourly assimilation goes forward, and there is no danger that local peculiarities and hostilities should be preserved. (*W*, *1*, 363–64)

Embedded in this passage are basic components of American urbanization—"vast distance," rapid movement ("it has given a new celerity to *time*," says Emerson in the following paragraph), and "hourly assimilation." As he presents these concepts, they form a structural pattern—the given (space), the process (movement) acting upon the given, and the result (assimilation) of the interaction. Vast land stimulates the American's assertion of an expanding freedom, and this assertion leads to a higher and more complex civilized unity based *on* this freedom.

The first major section of the essay deals with the concept of large space—"the boundless resources" of American land—although in its internal circling it also introduces the other two components of the pattern. Every paragraph of this section reminds us that Emerson is not as interested in the land itself as in what can be done with the land by Americans: "the task of surveying, planting, and building upon this immense tract" (p. 365). If America is to become a new and higher culture, it must cast off the "false" precedents of a Europe that is overcivilized because civilized in a wrong sense. At least in imagination the American nation must begin where all true civilization must begin—in the soil. In the essay, soil has both a literal and a figurative meaning. It refers both to real earth and to the "essential base" of any genuinely creative process. Land is the logical starting point for both a nation and a poet that wish to build anew—to build a new structure worthy of American space and abundant resources.

Emerson's desire to build both a society and an art probably explains why, in this section on land, he devotes so much space to the problem of education and art. Though he discusses farming and gardening extensively in this section, his major subject seems to be the artistic impulse that lies behind any creative effort. When he remarks that America's "natural wealth" has "given a strong direction to the wishes and aims of active young men, to withdraw from cities and cultivate the soil" (p. 366), he is using "cultivate" in an intellectual as well as agricultural sense. He is challenging his young Boston audience not so much to work the actual land as to cultivate the essential "idea" of the land. Like Thoreau's beanfield, the land has moral and aesthetic as well as physical value, and the Young American's first task should be to search for these symbolic values. Working the land is not an end but a means: "It is the fine art which is left for us, now that sculpture, painting, and religious and civil architecture have become effete, and have passed into second childhood" (p. 367). Emerson is not here rejecting the traditional fine arts per se, but their degradation. Land well used in both its physical and symbolic senses may be the essential initial element of the arts' purification and revitalization. The withdrawal—at least in imagination—from existing American cities is not an ultimate rejection of civilization but an initial strategic movement in preparation either for establishing new cities of the West or for reforming old ones.

Such a reading of Emerson's strategy gives greater complexity to what, on surface reading, might seem to be damnation of American cities:

> The cities drain the country of the best part of its population: the flower of the youth, of both sexes, goes into the towns, and the country is cultivated by a so much inferior class. The land,—travel a whole day together,—looks poverty-stricken, and the buildings plain and poor. In Europe, where society has an aristocratic structure, the land is full of men of the best stock and the best culture, whose interest and pride it is to remain half the year on their estates, and to fill them with every convenience and ornament. Of course, these make model farms, and model architecture, and are a constant education to the

> eye of the surrounding population. Whatever events in progress shall go to disgust men with cities and infuse into them the passion for country life and country pleasure, will render a service to the whole face of this continent, and will further the most poetic of all the occupations of real life, the bringing out by art the native but hidden graces of the landscape. (p. 368)

The criticism is not of cities per se but of the breakdown in a creative dialectical relationship between city and country—a relationship at the very heart of the metaphor of City of the West. When Emerson notes the advantages of having an aristocracy live in the country for half—but only half—of the year, he is not only stressing an ideal social policy but offering a dialectical proposition. As he reminds his urban audience, "the new modes of traveling . . . [make] it easy to cultivate very distant tracts and yet remain in strict intercourse with the centres of trade and population" (p. 367). The term "cultivate" is again used figuratively as well as literally. The imaginative Young American may cultivate "very distant tracts"—that is, see their value as symbols of moral and artistic truths—even while sitting in Boston. The basic advantage of urban America's patronage of rural America (and it cannot be denied that Emerson's attitude toward the real American farmer is, in this passage, patronizing) is intellectual—to introduce education and art into the thoughtless, artless drabness of rural life. Though farming is vital to national well-being and unity, it needs the proper "architecture" created by urban man to bring out "the native but hidden graces of the landscape." Western land is not an end; it is a "beginning" that all Americans must share.

Emerson's citation of the European aristocracy in the

above-quoted passage is also less praise of Europe than a strategic device, like the citation of the values of rural nature, for commenting on American civilization. By playing the polar concepts of European civilization and Western nature against each other, he can more adequately define the central concept of Western civilization. In the concluding paragraph of the section on land, he notes that "the vast majority of the people of this country live by the land, and carry its quality in their manners and opinions" (p. 369). (The reference to "quality" should again alert the reader to the metaphorical dimension of "land.") The problem is that the urban leaders of the American people—the nearest American equivalent of an aristocracy—do not always do so. Emerson's Bostonian audience was representative of the group he most wished his remarks to reach—not the "vast majority" of Americans, but the urban leaders whose education and abilities made them most capable of using (or misusing) the vast new power offered by Western land.

> We in the Atlantic states, by position, have been commercial, and have . . . imbibed easily an European culture. Luckily for us, now that steam has narrowed the Atlantic to a strait, the nervous, rocky West is intruding a new and continental element into the national mind, and we shall yet have an American genius. (pp. 369–70)

The ultimate concern is not the new land but "the national mind." (Note the metaphorical implications of "nervous" and "continental.") Emerson's goal is a new urban American leadership that can make this vast new land poetic in fact and in figure.

This use of vast power is developed further in the next

section of the essay, which deals with "the uprise and culmination of the new and anti-feudal power of Commerce" (p. 370). "We cannot look on the freedom of this country, in connexion with its youth," Emerson argues, "without a presentiment that here shall laws and institutions exist on some scale of proportion to the majesty of nature" (p. 370). From the figurative application of the majestic scale of American nature to commercial institutions, it is only a step to the figurative use of "commerce" and "trade" themselves. At the heart of both terms is the concept of reciprocal motion—in its most positive connotation, a creative dialectic. Though both terms can imply products, they basically refer to processes—the processes of communication and, at an even higher level, communion.

This process of creative interaction, it cannot be stressed too strongly, is central to Emerson's optimistic attitude toward Western urbanization. It is therefore significant that, in his section on commerce, he explicitly places cities of the West in the reciprocal context of the American continent and offers a central vision of a new American population that, by moving through vast space, is striving to mold its heterogeneity into a new cosmopolitanism:

> A heterogeneous population crowding on all ships from all corners of the world to the great gates of North America, namely Boston, New York, and New Orleans, and thence proceeding inward to the prairie and the mountains, and quickly contributing their private thought to the public opinion, their toll to the treasury, and their vote to the election, it cannot be doubted that the legislation of this country should become more catholic and cosmopolitan than that of any other. It seems so easy for

> America to inspire and express the most expansive and humane spirit; new-born, free, healthful, strong, the land of the laborer, of the democrat, of the philanthropist, of the believer, of the saint, she should speak for the human race. It is the country of the Future. From Washington, proverbially "the city of magnificent distances," through all its cities, states, and territories, it is a country of beginnings, of projects, of designs, of expectations. (pp. 370–71)

In both its factual and figurative meanings, commerce, like land, is an essential part and developer of these beginnings. It is most inadequate when still tied to older historical restrictions and immoralities ("We have feudal governments in a commercial age," complains Emerson) and most useful when tied to "the beneficent tendency" of historical development (p. 375)—when it is willing to lose present material gains in order to achieve better life for the following generation. Despite its most selfish self, therefore, trade, like land, is an educational and therefore liberating force. Even more than land, it gives man's imagination a primary place in the scheme of things. It allows him to make the land a tool: "It is a new agent in the world, and one of great function; it is a very intellectual force. This displaces physical strength, and instals [sic] computation, combination, information, science, in its room" (pp. 377–78). Trade in America—or the essential ideal of Trade—thus becomes a synecdoche for City of the West. Its movement (a movement both physical and intellectual) combines heterogeneous materials, forces, and ideas "in its room" in the interest of freeing man for higher ends. "The philosopher and lover of man," Emerson comments, "have much harm to say of trade; but the historian will see that trade was the principle of Liberty, that trade planted America and destroyed Feudalism; that it makes peace and keeps peace, and it will abolish slavery" (p. 378). Emerson is projecting himself into both sides of the evaluative dialectic: as humane philosopher and historian he can see both the evils of actual trade and the ideal meaning of trade. Linking a natural metaphor ("planted") to trade, he points both to its organic base and civil potential. If nature has "planted" trade, trade has in turn "planted America"—that is, has interacted creatively with the American continent to produce the beginnings of a higher civilized society than the world has yet known.

Commerce's most important function, concludes Emerson, is its impact on American man himself. Trade has erected "a new aristocracy on the ruins of the aristocracy it destroyed" (p. 378). Although very imperfect, the new leadership is at least based "on merit of some kind" and is thus an improvement over an effete feudal leadership. Not complacently, but optimistically, Emerson incorporates America's commercial metropolises in a larger vision of a more comprehensive and adequate American community of the future. "Our part," he states, borrowing a significant metaphor from the railroad, "is plainly not to throw ourselves across the track, to block improvement and sit till we are stone, but to watch the uprise of successive mornings and to conspire with the new works of new days" (p. 379). Trade too, in its present form, will inevitably be replaced, but it has been an essential part of the growth of human civilization in general and American society in particular. "Government has been a fossil," says Emerson; "it should be a plant." To the extent that a Commerce rooted in the soil has shown organic growth, it has worked with the divine purpose and not against it. It has been the stem of the plant of American civilization growing in the vast garden of the continent.

Emerson describes the emerging flower of that plant in the following section on new moral causes. One sign of these causes is the movement of national government (so Emerson hopes) from the service of commerce to the service of man—from merely economic to moral and aesthetic functions. Commerce has taught man how to use nature; in the next stage of development man must learn consciously to use nature *correctly*. The leaders of America must begin to use their trained minds to benefit not only themselves but society as a whole; they must cease to be exploiters and must become educators. Theory must join practice on a national scale. "Here," says Emerson,

> are Etzlers and mechanical projectors, who, with the Fourierists, undoubtedly affirm that the smallest union would make every man rich;—and, on the other side, a multitude of poor men and women seeking work, and who cannot find enough to pay their board. The science is confident, and surely the poverty is real. If any means could be found to bring these two together! (p. 382)

Emerson is not here talking about a gap between European or American, Easterner or Westerner, or even city dweller and farmer. He is talking about members of an increasingly urban world—the home of labor unions (and, of course, "the smallest union" has larger dimensions when pressed metaphorically) and of the members of the laboring force who must work to "pay their board." The movement of this section attempts, at least rhetorically, to bring the aristocrat and the common man, the theoretician and the practitioner, together in the cities of the West, for a new and better American society can be created only through such union.

In the movement toward a higher and more complex unity both urban and Western, the term "community" becomes central. Emerson initially uses the term to discuss several specific reformist groups, such as the Fourierists, that have sprung up in New England. Whatever initial success they have had, he notes, results from their basing their work on the same organic principles that have made farming and commerce successful. Such principles cannot be neglected by any group desiring to save its virtuous aims from impotence. But these communities have moved toward a higher and broader stratum of human development because their aims ultimately are to educate rather than to exploit: "the Communities aimed at a higher success in securing to all their members an equal and thorough education" (p. 384). Such communities are microcosmic hints as to what Emerson would like America to become, and he turns from the problem of specific communities to the problem of the very meaning of Community.

All America, Emerson argues, should be a single organic community, in which the government would be not so much an economic servant as a moral and aesthetic educator: "Yes, Government must educate the poor man. Look across the country from any hill-side around us, and the landscape seems to crave Government" (p. 384). In making this striking statement, Emerson is not calling for a society where all are farmers nor a society where all are equal in every sense. He is not asking that his urban audience become gentlemen farmers, working with "the poor man" in a democratic version of benevolent feudalism for physical control of the rural landscape. Rather, he is urging the urban leadership to learn to "govern" the image of the West in order to discover and respond to its inner meaning. The "landscape" Emerson is referring to is really a metaphor for a human community that, like neutral nature, is only potentially humane (in the sense of being a creative adjunct to human development) until governed by man's best tendencies. Repeatedly, Emerson stresses that he is using "land" as a metaphor for human nature. A "*land* lord" is one who can unify such nature into a genuinely creative community.

> The actual differences of men must be acknowledged, and met with love and wisdom. These rising grounds which command the champaign below, seem to ask for lords, true lords, *land* lords, who understand the land and its uses and the applicabilities of men, and whose government would be what it should, namely *mediation* [my italics] between want and supply. (p. 384)
>
> We must have kings, and we must have nobles. Nature provides such in every society,—and let us have the real instead of the titular. Let us have our leading and our inspiration from the best. (p. 386)

The American "land lord" must be a poet in action and in thought; he must recognize the inner meaning of an external world and hence find the West in himself. "That were his duty and stint,—to keep himself pure and purifying, the leaven of his nation . . . by making his life secretly beautiful" (p. 387).

The Young American aristocrat thus becomes both the ultimate subject and the ultimate audience of Emerson's essay. He must be a cosmopolitan—a worthy resident of the City of the West—in the highest sense—that of seeing his vital spiritual relationship to every resource and every other human being in his society. The Young American is blood brother of the American Scholar, whose eternally youthful energy and vision is challenged again to public service:

> I call upon you, young men, to obey your heart and be the nobility of this land. In every age of the world there has been a leading nation, one of a more generous sentiment, whose eminent citizens were willing to stand for the interests of general justice and humanity, at the risk of being called, by the men of the moment, chimerical and fantastic. Which should be that nation but these States? Which should lead that movement, if not New England? Who should lead the leaders, but the Young American? (pp. 387–88)

Emerson began the essay by stating that a continental America—home for a cosmopolitan outlook—was beginning to assert itself to the American imagination. Now he asks the Young New Englander to lead that continent, for all men who realize the value and beauty of the land and its reciprocal relationship to an ideally civilized future are Western in spirit—perhaps more Western than those who actually lead thoughtless, drab lives on the Western farm or frontier. Such "common" men must be led by those trained not only by land but by cities and commerce—by Young Americans equally at home (at least in spirit) on the Western farm and in the cities of the West.

Emerson's concluding section once again circles through his major themes—themes that have spiraled upward in the course of the essay to new significance: "One thing is plain for all men of common sense and common conscience, that here, here in America, is the home of man" (p. 391). Land and commerce are important only so far as they contribute to a new and better "home" for men and hence to the development of a new and better form of man. In America land and commerce are on a scale never seen before in human history. American society must therefore assume, under the guidance of the Young American, a similar "spaciousness" of aim. In America there are possibilities for "organic simplicity and liberty" and for the greatest possibility of all, "opportunity to the human mind not known in any other region" (p. 392). The natural resources of America are a given, but the key to the future lies in the development of a new national leadership and a new poetic insight that will use the freedom created by such resources for the betterment and unification of American civilization:

> Here stars, here woods, here hills, here animals, here men abound, and the vast tendencies concur of a new order. If only the men are employed in conspiring with the designs of the Spirit who led us hither and is leading us still, we shall quickly enough advance out of all hearing of others' censures, out of all regrets of our own, into a new and more excellent social state than history has yet recorded. (p. 395)

This conclusion to "The Young American," like the conclusion of a prolonged meditation, is not analytic in tone; rather, it is an emotional response to the most optimistic connotations of the West—a West in which urban civilization can play its fullest part. Emerson's concluding vision, like many of his concluding visions, tends toward the apocalyptic and the abstract. The conclusion of the essay does not describe in any detail the "new and more excellent social state" to be achieved. What it does is to imply the necessity that such a civilization be both urban and Western in the best figurative sense of both concepts. Nature alone could not create a new

America, any more than it could write a poem. Both the nation and the poem depend on nature's interaction with the affirmative visions of a cosmopolitan American leadership that, like Whitman's Adamic Cosmopolitan, was "Crossing the prairies—dwelling again in Chicago—dwelling in many towns." Though Emerson, even at his most optimistic, recognized that America "has not fulfilled what seemed the reasonable expectation of mankind," he continued to assert hopefully that his nation would produce "a brood of Titans, who should laugh and leap in the continent, and run up the mountains of the West with the errand of genius and of love" (*W*, 1, 156). Out of the efforts of those Americans of epic stature—epic both in themselves and because of the poet's vision of their possibilities—might come a nation whose urban leaders would ally themselves organically with the resources of nature not only to benefit all American citizens materially but to free their souls for willing service of the divine forces that presided over their enterprise. In the complex unity of a civilization that was organic, grand, free, and holy lay the basis for a metaphorical City of the West.

❦ 3. The City of God

Art lives and thrills in new use and combining of contrasts, and mining into the dark evermore for blacker pits of night. What would painter do, or what would poet or saint, but for crucifixions and hells? (W, 6, 255)

Must I call the heaven and the earth a maypole and country fair with booths, or an anthill, or an old coat, in order to give you the shock of pleasure which the imagination loves and the sense of spiritual greatness? (J, 6, 18)

Obey the Genius when he seems to lead to uninhabitable deserts . . . and presently when men are whispered by the gods to go and hunt in that direction they shall find that they cannot get to the point which they would reach without passing over that highway which you have built. Your hermit's lodge shall [be] the Holy City and the Fair of the whole world. (J, 5, 530–31)

In searching for a literary structure to contrast strategically actual American civilization and its ideal possibilities, Emerson often turned to religious rhetoric. He argued that America's quest for the ideal civilization implied by City of the West should be essentially an attempt to found a holy community—a community that traditionally had been described by an urban metaphor, the New Jerusalem. One version of this metaphor had been given an American setting as early as John Winthrop's justly famous dictum to the settlers of Massachusetts Bay: "wee must Consider that wee shall be as a Citty upon a Hill, the eies of all people are vppon vs."[1] To a Protestant nation whose rhetoric was saturated with a sense of the imagery and stories of the Bible, the American enterprise naturally called for comparison with the Jewish peoples' escape from Egypt (Europe, in the American version), their period of testing and moral strengthening in the wilderness, and their founding of a Jerusalem in a land abounding with milk and honey. The American errand into the wilderness, however, differed in one crucial respect from its Old Testament "type": it was made possible by the sacrifices and principles symbolized by Christ and his New Testament. Melville's linking of both biblical and Western metaphors in *White Jacket* is a striking expression of feelings often heard in Emerson's era:

> We Americans are the peculiar, chosen people—the Israel of our time; we bear the ark of the liberties of the world. . . . We are the pioneers of the world; the advance-guard, sent on through the wilderness of untried things, to break a new path in the New World that is ours. . . . The political Messiah . . . has come in *us*, if we would but give utterance to his promptings.[2]

1. John Winthrop, "A Model of Christian Charity," in Perry Miller and Thomas H. Johnson, eds., *The Puritans* (New York, 1938), p. 199. The Puritans' City on a Hill was intended to be not only a community to which "the eyes of all people" would turn; it would be a community from which the saints could look down upon all people. Its founders hoped to erect not only an example to the world but a perspective on that world. Emerson was suggesting a similar strategy for his own work when he argued in 1840 that "the use of literature is to afford us a platform whence we may command a view of our present life" (*J*, 5, 408).

2. Melville, *White Jacket* (*Works*, 6, 189).

Emerson too, as early as an 1826 journal passage, was bringing together the Christian drama and the American enterprise. "It is the order of Providence that great objects must be purchased by great sacrifices," he argued. "The best thing in the world[,] the New Testament[,] rests its genuineness . . . on the flood of the purest human blood which was shed to seal its authenticity. The next best thing in human possession is the American Constitution which hundreds & thousands of valiant patriots perished to obtain" (*JMN*, 3, 14).

In pointing to the religious implications of the American enterprise, however, Emerson was not only using the Judeo-Christian drama of a community journey. He was also applying Christian literature's more fundamental drama—the search of the individual soul for the City of God. As a Protestant and Romantic individualist, Emerson stressed that America's communal attempt to found in history itself a holy City on a Hill could succeed only if each American's soul searched for a Celestial City that transcended history. In order for the eternal City of God to manifest itself on earth in the form of a New Jerusalem, Americans as individuals needed first to discover citizenship in this eternal City. It is quite significant that Emerson applied this Christian urban metaphor to his conception of inner ideality most frequently during the five- or six-year period that saw his withdrawal from the Unitarian ministry and his most fervent Transcendental self-assertion—the period in which he apocalyptically argued, "It would give scope for many truths in experimental religion to preach from the text of 'There shall be new heavens & a new earth' " (*JMN*, 4, 347). Emerson was not merely looking for a moral metaphor to describe his personal forays into "experimental religion." He was searching for a dramatic structure that would adequately ally his imperfect self to his higher possibilities and to universal reality. The metaphor of pilgrimage that structured Christianity's traditional drama of the soul seemed particularly appropriate to a young man who had grown up on strong doses of the Bible, Bunyan, and Milton and who, by 1830, was well versed in Augustine and Dante.[3]

In some ways, in fact, the dramatic aspects of the Christian drama appealed more than its moral affirmations to a son of the Puritans who was setting out self-consciously on a literary career. "Art," he argued later in his career, "lives and thrills in new use and combining of contrasts, and mining into the dark evermore for blacker pits of night. What would painter do, or what would poet or saint, but for crucifixions and hells?" (*W*, 6, 255).[4] In the Christian drama's melodra-

3. "The Bible is an engine of education of the first power," Emerson argued in 1827, shortly after entering the Unitarian ministry. "It does more than all other books. It is an index every where of light" (*JMN*, 3, 71). But even as a youth he also admired it for its melodramatic and epic power, and with increasing age he placed increasing stress on its literary importance. "The Bible," he argued, "has been the literature as well as the religion of large portions of Europe" (*W*, 7, 194). The King James version was a supreme reflection, as he put it in a significantly "urban" reference, of "the great metropolitan English speech" (*W*, 7, 204). Similarly, *Paradise Lost* offered Emerson not only moral lessons but "lofty images" (*JMN*, 2, 317). "It is said of Milton's 'Paradise Lost,'" he noted in 1835, "that the theological dogmas there taught are continually confronted with the teachings of Scripture" (*EL*, 1, 307). In fact the literary and moral power of such works were closely related. Emerson argued in 1824 that Milton and Bunyan could "bewitch young hearts by eloquent verses to the love of goodness" (*JMN*, 2, 220–21). Profiting from his own experiences, he strongly recommended *Pilgrim's Progress* as useful reading for a child (*W*, 7, 106).

4. In 1827 Emerson made a striking attempt to explore Christ's crucifixion for its melodramatic possibilities (*JMN*, 3, 63). A provoca-

matic struggle between the City of God and the Dis-drawn City of Man Emerson found such thrilling contrasts. Since the dramatic arena for these metaphorical cities was the soul of the individual pilgrim—one's powers, Emerson argued characteristically in a Miltonic paraphrase, "are your heaven, or they are your hell" (*JMN*, 4, 42)—Emerson's application of the pilgrimage to his own inner life was an attempt to give structure to a quest for both moral perfection and literary excellence. In portraying himself as the chief actor in his own Pilgrim's Progress, he was attempting in a characteristically Romantic way to find an adequate religious rhetoric by which he could evaluate his fellow Americans and to develop a prophetic literary guide to stimulate their own individual pilgrimages. Only out of such individual efforts to find and become worthy of a Transcendental City of God could a community of pilgrims emerge that might erect a lasting holy City in the American environment.

As a nineteenth-century American and a self-conscious Romantic poet, however, Emerson did not use the Christian urban drama uncritically. "Every man," he argued in 1830, "makes his own religion, his own God, his own charity; takes none of these from the Bible or his neighbour, entire" (*JMN*, 3, 179). In borrowing from a literary structure that he considered metaphorical rather than literally true, Emerson modified the drama so as to make its implicit meanings more apparent, more relevant, and hence more persuasive to himself and his era.[5] To an extent, in fact, he allowed his City of

---

tive, if debatable, modern study of the literary implications of dichotomy can be found in Northrop Frye, *Anatomy of Criticism* (Princeton, 1957), in his section on "Archetypal Criticism: Theory of Myths," esp. pp. 131–58.

5. "The subject of the Times is not an abstract question," Emer-

God to take on some architectural characteristics of an ideal City of the West, and his pilgrim began partly to resemble an American Cosmopolitan. However, his use of inward pilgrimage took him beyond merely nationalistic aims. If on one hand he wished to make the archetypal Christian drama relevant to nineteenth-century American civilization, on the other he did not wish to degrade the drama into a mere justification of that civilization. By treating the individual pilgrimage as much more than merely American and yet at the same time stressing those elements of American experience that might usefully symbolize the pilgrim's proper path, Emerson was attempting to be faithful both to his dream of an ideal America and to his inner quest for self-perfection.

In devoting this chapter primarily to Emerson's use of the metaphor of an inward pilgrimage, therefore, we are by no means leaving our discussion of urban metaphor or our interest in its specific application to American civilization. The traditional Christian pilgrimage could not have existed independently of its urban metaphors; its structure was necessarily based on a movement between the Christian drama's two major urban centers, the City of Destruction and the City of God. Even when Emerson did not name these cities explicitly, they stood as a pervading context around his portrayal of the pilgrimage itself. Similarly, his attempt to define his own infinite quest was made against the implicit background of his nation's finite quest. In a modified version of that metaphorical drama whose resolution was the City of God, Emerson found both a means for defining his personal

son said in 1841. "If you speak of the age, you mean your own platoon of people, as Dante and Milton painted in colossal their platoons, and called them Heaven and Hell" (*W*, I, 161).

goal and a strategic perspective from which to evaluate America's performance and possibilities.

Emerson's abiding interest in the metaphor of a personal pilgrimage emerged from his childhood experiences with a Puritanism upon which he often looked back with nostalgic affection. "What a debt is ours," he argued in 1841, "to that old religion which, in the childhood of most of us, still dwelt like a sabbath morning in the country of New England, teaching privation, self-denial and sorrow! (*W*, *1*, 220). Raised on Puritan rhetoric, if not theology, young Emerson treated his early life as a painful pilgrimage of self-purification. To Mary Moody Emerson, his provocative Calvinist aunt, he wrote in 1826 that "the light of nature countenances the notion of a proper Purgatory, of an island between evil and good where the poor tempest-driven sufferers must perform quarantine to purge out the sores of human nature that might infect or offend the society of heaven" (*J*, 2, 91).

By the time of his Unitarian ministry, however, Emerson was making a strong attempt to liberate himself from some of the darker tendencies in the Puritan version of this Christian drama. This is indicated best by his increasing emphasis on the place of Christ in the drama. For Emerson, Christ was not only the archetypal Christian pilgrim—the supreme citizen of the City of God who suffered through and transcended the trials of the City of Man—but the very basis of the pilgrimage for others. Because of his personal sacrifice and resurrection, finite men might experience not only the necessary pains but the highest possibilities of the pilgrimage. Even after Emerson had ceased to believe in the unique divinity of the historical Jesus, he continued to treat him as a metaphor for the joyful conclusion of the Christian drama. As he argued in his striking 1838 address at the Harvard Divinity School, "Jesus Christ belonged to the true race of prophets. He saw with open eye the mystery of the soul. . . . Alone in all history he estimated the greatness of man" (*W*, *1*, 128).[6]

Puritanism, in contrast to Christ's own example, was still too much a part of an Old Testament or "Jewish" vision of the world. Bunyan, Emerson once argued, had shown that in the Puritans "the whole Jewish history became flesh and blood" (*W*, *10*, 244). "These men," he said of his New England ancestors in 1861, "are a bridge to us between the unparalleled piety of the Hebrew epoch, & our own." His highest praise of the Puritans was that they "were a high tragic school, & found much of their own belief in the grander traits of the Greek mythology,—Nemesis, the Fates, & the Eumenides" (*L*, 5, 145). Puritanism, however, embodied not only the strengths but the limitations of a tragic interpretation of the Christian drama. In attempting to deal courageously with "the sorrows and sins of this transitory life" (*Y*, 137), the Puritans had tended to treat the sorrows as ends in themselves and to neglect the optimistic implications of the pilgrimage. By stressing the power of God's overwhelming Providence, wrathful justice, and severe moral demands, they often neglected the joy of the "New Testament" Celestial City—a divine vision of freedom, love, and beauty for which Christ himself was a

6. For ways in which modern American literature has humanized the figure of Christ, see Ursala Brumm, "The Figure of Christ in American Literature," *Partisan Review*, 24 (1957), 403–13. Emerson argued in 1827 that modern ethics needed to progress beyond "the ritual, the offering, & the altar of Moses," to "cast off the superstitions that were the swaddling clothes of Christianity" (*JMN*, 3, 61). But he also recognized that the literary strength of the Old Testament made such ethical modernization difficult: "The oldest vision of the prophet communing with God only," he admitted in 1835, "is confined & coloured & expressed according to the resistless example of the Jewish" (*JMN*, 5, 5–6).

metaphor. When, in attempting to combat the degrading materialism of their era, they stressed the overwhelming moral duties that attended human existence, the beauty of this existence

> straightway vanished; . . . an obligation, a sadness, as of piled mountains, fell on them, and life became ghastly, joyless, a pilgrim's progress, a probation, beleaguered round with doleful histories of Adam's fall and curse behind us; with doomsdays and purgatorial and penal fires before us; and the heart of the seer and of the listener sank in them. (*W*, *4*, 219)

Nevertheless, Emerson greatly preferred the truncated Christian pilgrimage of the Puritans to those "modern" beliefs of his own era that preached no need for a painful journey of self-discipline and self-sacrifice. Emerson, of course, shared many of these modern hopes. During his period of greatest Transcendental assertion he attempted to sketch the pilgrimage in as joyous colors as possible—and, at his most optimistic, to argue that the soul might attain the Celestial City more easily than the Puritans had believed. But the Puritan in him continued to argue that the liberal could never "construct that heavenly society you prate of out of foolish, sick, selfish men and women, such as we know them to be" (*W*, *1*, 250). Modern liberalism, he believed, had taken the metaphor of salvation too complacently, without examining closely enough the higher truth for which it stood. It had treated Christ's message too little as a hopeful call for a life of reform and too much as a justification of imperfect vested interests. To Emerson, this complacent rationalization was dangerously close to a doctrine that ruled the Old Testament's Cities of the Plains. "It was a refined, a well born, a rich, a selfish heaven that filled the imagination of the ancient pagans," he argued in 1828. "The other world recognized the distinctions of this" (*JMN*, 3, 147). The lesson was clear: the imperfections of nineteenth-century man were "argument as significant as a visible finger out of the sky that we should not fabricate a heaven in our heads & then square life to that fiction" (*JMN*, 4, 42).

Emerson believed that the complacent materialism and selfish optimism of his time was reason enough for arguing that the Christian urban drama was still relevant to his era and that the pilgrimage was still necessary for any man in search of inner perfection. "Satan who plays so prominent a part in the theology of the last age," he argued in 1834, "is a hollow word now but the evil principles which the word designated are no whit abated in virulence" (*JMN*, 4, 330). Like the writers of the Puritan jeremiads, he believed it his task to remind his nation that, for all its pretensions to being a New Jerusalem, it was still far from being a godly City on a Hill. This belief formed the basis for the "Fast Sermon" in 1828:

> When our fathers shook off the dust of the old world from their feet did they shake off all its pollutions? Was theirs an emigration from the passions & from the sins as well as from prelacy & corrupt institutions? When they came out of the roar of crowded cities into the desolate sea, did they leave behind them also that whisper of Temptation that is always heard in human ears? Like the Pilgrim in the simple story of Bunyan as they went up the steep mountain of Difficulty did the burden of vice fall forever from their shoulders? Then why this solemn rite? Why did they leave us this dismal tradition appointing us with each returning spring equinox a day of Fast-

> ing, Humiliation, & Prayer? No, my brethren, human nature doth not change with change of place, with change of Condition. . . . Man is the same & if the events have been different which have attended that colony of the race, which have grown up here it is owing to the mercy of God. (*JMN*, 3, 121–22)

By retaining the pilgrimage—even in modified form—Emerson was reminding Americans of the difficult private journey they must take before they could join to build a human community that would be metaphorically a City on a Hill. He was also reminding himself of the difficulties that faced a poet who felt called to be a prophet of that higher community to his own imperfect nation.

The American prophet's pilgrimage, like the archetypal Christian pilgrimage, was a drama that opened in the City of Man, the pilgrim's temporary home in a fallen world. Following a strong American predisposition to contrast his nation's symbolically ideal possibilities to the corruptions of European civilization, Emerson was often willing to see European civilization under the metaphorical aspect of a City of Cain.[7] After reading Thackeray's *Vanity Fair*, he had argued that the book was both "pathetic in its name" and in Thackeray's "use of the name; an admission it is from a man of fashion in the London of 1850 that poor old Puritan Bunyan was right in his

7. This sort of comparison was quite common among writers of Emerson's era. At fair time, London reminded Hawthorne "of Bunyan's description of Vanity Fair" (*Works*, 12, 281–82). Cooper treated that city as "the modern Babylon" (*Afloat and Ashore*, Chap. 10). Melville's darker vision saw London in *Israel Potter* as an image of Dis (*Works*, 11, 212); in various short stories he treated London as "the Pit of the Lost," Babylon, and Tartarus (*Complete Stories*, pp. 155–59, 179). These same terms might also be given an American context. Hawthorne's short story, "The Celestial Railroad," presents a well-known

perception of the London of 1650" (*J*, *8*, 113–14). But he also criticized his nation's failings in similar terms. "We say Paradise was; Adam fell; the Golden Age; & the like," he noted in 1837. "We mean man is not as he ought to be; but our way of painting this is on Time, and we say *Was*" (*JMN*, 5, 371). To the extent that American civilization symbolized and reinforced the American's temptations to be less than he ought to be, it too, like European civilization, was metaphorically comparable to the Old Testament's Cities of the Plains. As a Bostonian, Emerson was quick to call New York "our Babylonian city" (*Corr*, 268) and, using a Bunyanesque metaphor, to argue in 1834 that "Broadway is Trade & Vanity made flesh" (*JMN*, *4*, 331). But he was equally prepared to treat Boston's failings in the same manner. In his 1841 lecture "Man the Reformer," he argued that

> Americans have many virtues, but they have not Faith and Hope. I know no two words whose meaning is more lost sight of. We use these words as if they were as obsolete as Selah and Amen. And yet they have the broadest meaning, and the most cogent application to Boston in this year. (*W*, *1*, 249)

In stating that "I always seem to suffer some loss of faith on entering cities" (*Corr*, 260), Emerson was pointing to the primary reason for treating his civilization as a fallen City of Man. Referring in an 1838 lecture, "Holiness," to the archetypal builder of this City, he argued that the "soul which is without God in the world" was a "chill, houseless, fatherless,

---

version of a nineteenth-century Vanity Fair. When the Cosmopolitan, in *The Confidence Man,* refers to the *Fidèle* as "our Fair," he is probably suggesting its relationship to Bunyan's destructive city.

aimless Cain" (*EL*, 2, 342).[8] To an extent the American city was a new Vanity Fair—"the paradise of trifles" as he once called it (*J*, 7, 316)—because it contained so few genuine pilgrims, so few citizens who saw the ideal possibilities that could redeem their own City of Man. "In our large cities," he stressed in his essay "Worship," "the population is godless, materialized,—no bond, no fellow-feeling, no enthusiasm. These are not men, but hungers, thirsts, fevers and appetites walking. How is it people manage to live on,—so aimless as they are?" (*W*, 6, 208). Emerson was not referring to lack of economic ambition but to lack of spiritual or imaginative direction, and it was this lack of direction—the disbelief in the possibilities of a pilgrimage—that made the City of Man into a City of Destruction. He felt he could justly borrow a metaphor from Dante's Inferno in order to argue that the "meanness and sterility" of Boston conveyed a message of "leave-all-hope-behind" to the man of sensibility (*J*, 8, 363–64). By searching for ways to adequately protest against this psychological destructiveness, the prophetic Emerson, like Bunyan's Christian, began his pilgrimage.

The American prophet became a pilgrim reluctantly, however. Despite its failures the City of Man offered many seductive possibilities, even to the prophet. Early in 1826,

8. This description of Cain seems to allude less to the Bible than to Augustine's *City of God* or perhaps to such a work as Byron's "Cain." Augustine remarks that "Of [the] first two parents of the human race . . . Cain was the first-born, and he belonged to the city of man; after him was born Abel, who belonged to the city of God. . . . Accordingly, it is recorded of Cain that he built a city, but Abel, being a sojourner, built none." This passage also offers an archetypal definition of "pilgrim": "the citizen of the city of God . . . by grace a stranger below and by grace a citizen above" (*The City of God*, trans. Marcus Dods [New York, Modern Library, 1950] Bk. 15, Pt. 2).

shortly after recovering full use of his eyes ("when I came back to books," he wrote his aunt Mary, "I felt like Columbus on the new shore"),[9] the young minister indicated the nature of these seductions:

> I rejoice that I live when the world is so old. There is the same difference between living with Adam & living with me as in going into a new house unfinished damp & empty, & going into a long occupied house where the time & taste of its inhabitants has accumulated a thousand useful contrivances[,] has furnished the chambers[,] stocked the cellars and filled the library. In the new house every comer must do all for himself. In the old mansion there are butlers, cooks, grooms, & valets. In the new house all must work & work with the hands. In the old one there are poets who sing, actors who play & ladies who dress & smile. O ye lovers of the past, judge between my houses. I would not be elsewhere than I am. (*JMN*, 2, 340)

To a prophet like Emerson, who appreciated the immense pleasures offered by the "old mansion" of civilized society, the path of the pilgrim was in human terms often solitary and lonely (*W*, 2, 296). "Solitude," he argued in a dark moment in 1838, "is fearsome & heavy hearted" (*JMN*, 5, 454). Even one of his most hopefully conceived pilgrims, the American Scholar, had to pay this price for his redemptive quest: "He must accept—how often!—poverty and solitude. For the ease and pleasure of treading the old road, accepting the fashions, the education, the religion of society, he takes the cross of making his own" (*W*, 1, 101).

9. *J*, 2, 99–100. The metaphor is significantly "Western" in orientation.

Mere personal suffering, however, was no valid reason in itself to cause the prophet to forswear his solitary pilgrimage. Suffering was justifiable only as a means to the heavenly goal of the pilgrim. "If man is immortal," Emerson had argued in 1826, "the world is his place of discipline & the value of pain is then disclosed" (*JMN*, 3, 48). While still in the Unitarian ministry, therefore, he argued that martyrdom was "the height of human virtue" and that "Martyrs are finished men wise beyond their former measure having attained in the last days of life the full enjoyment of every moral & intellectual power" (*JMN*, 3, 95). He later used the martyr analogy to justify the sufferings of his Transcendental saint, the scholar: "A self-denial no less austere than the saint's is demanded of the scholar. He must worship truth, and forego all things for that, and choose defeat and pain, so that his treasure in thought is thereby augmented" (*W*, 2, 341). Without a compelling affirmation of possibilities beyond the suffering, solitude was a dangerous tool in the hands of the prophet. "I praise no absurd sacrifices," he wrote in 1825.

> I praise no wolfish misanthropy that retreats to thickets from cheerful towns, and scrapes the ground for roots and acorns, either out of a grovelling soul or a hunger for glory that has mistaken grimace for philosophy. It is not the solitude of place but the solitude of soul which is so inestimable to us. . . . It is not that you should avoid men, but that you should not be hurt by them. Not to break the brotherhood of the race but to enable you to contribute to it a greater good. (*JMN*, 2, 326)[10]

10. Though Emerson sometimes felt that he had "no skill to live with men, that is, with such men as the world is made of, & such as I delight in," he continued—even in his more individualistic moments—to ask himself the question that he asked of every prophetic pilgrim: "But

Emerson's emphasis on the pilgrim's potential contribution to the "brotherhood of the race" is highly revealing. In attempting to justify the "solitude" of the pilgrim's soul as a necessary means to the higher prophetic task of redeeming the City of Man, he continually referred to the individual pilgrimage as a metaphorically "social" experience. In the sermon "The Choice of Theisms," which he delivered at least eleven times between 1831 and 1837, Emerson advised his listeners, as he advised others during the rest of his active career, to go "within the doors of his own soul" to find the "source of all truth, of all generous humane affections, a source of power to produce great and beneficent changes in the world. There, in the soul, in the eternal Temple of God," he argued, "he who watches his thoughts will find that he can at once make a calm solitude in the midst of the thickest multitude, yes, and the sweetest society in total solitude" (*Y*, 158–59). Solitude's goal, he stated in his essay "Culture," was "more catholic and humane relations. . . . The saint and poet seek privacy to ends the most public and universal" (*W*, 6, 157). Linking such rhetoric to his concept of pilgrimage in 1841, he advised the prophet to

> obey the Genius when he seems to lead to uninhabitable deserts, penetrate to the bottom of the fact which draws you, although no newspaper, no poet, no man has ever yet found life and beauty in that region, and presently when men are whispered by the gods to go and hunt in that direction they shall find that they cannot get to the

would it not be cowardly to flee out of society & live in the woods?" (*JMN*, 4 74). In *JMN*, 2, 97–98, he attaches this attitude to a specifically religious context.

point which they would reach without passing over that highway which you have built. Your hermit's lodge shall [be] the Holy City and the Fair of the whole world. (*J*, 5, 530–31)

In defending the solitary pilgrimage in the name of society, Emerson was thus making use of a rhetorical strategy central to his literary practice and theory—a manipulation of the ambiguities of metaphor in the interest of affirmative drama. This strategy was part of his description of the Transcendentalists: "They say to themselves, It is better to be alone than in bad company. And it is really a wish to be met,—the wish to find society for their hope and religion,—which prompts them to shun what is called society" (*W*, *1*, 347). The solitary pilgrimage represented an escape from a lower or external meaning of "society" in order to search for a higher or inner meaning of the term—a metaphorical journey from the City of Man to the City of God. In using this strategy, Emerson was actually borrowing Augustine's classic definition of the two Cities. The author of *The City of God* had argued that the human race is "distributed into two parts, the one consisting of those who live according to man, the other such who live according to God. And these we also mystically call the two cities, or the two communities of men, of which the one is predestined to reign eternally with God, and the other to suffer eternal punishment with the devil."[11] One of the important lessons that Emerson found in Augustine's presentation was that the human community of saints—the "symbol and foreshadowing" of the City of God—need not find architectural embodiment or geographical cohesiveness on earth. The com-

11. Augustine, *City of God*, Bk. 15, Pt. 1.

munity of saints was not definable by its "visibility," but by its members' communion in the status of "salvation"—their sharing of the love and mercy of God. Such a community, Emerson argued while a Unitarian minister, "peoples every solitude" of the living individual who has faith (*Y*, 142). If asked to write a sample of his own verse in an admirer's autograph album, he often wrote the following lines:

> O what is Heaven but the fellowship
> Of minds that each can stand against the world
> By its own meek but incorruptible will. (*JMN*, 4, 341)

On the basis of this Transcendental doctrine of community, Emerson could defend the pilgrim's strategy of self-reliance. By 1838 he was arguing that in the individual soul itself "is the city which hath foundations whose builder and maker is God" (*J*, 5, 150). In 1840, after reading in the Bible, he was moved to praise the soul of "rich, leopard-skinned man! who art a palace of sweet sounds and sights, and carriest in thy brain the City of God" (*J*, 5, 375).[12] Though he warned against the dangers of confusing selfish subjectivity for individual salvation, he continued to argue that the best form of self-reliance was reliance on membership in the City of God: "A man, I, am the remote circumference, the skirt, the thin suburb or frontier post of God," he wrote in 1836, "but go inward & I find the ocean; I lose my individuality in its waves" (*JMN*, 5, 177). The heart of the self-reliant pilgrim's City of God was not self-interest, but selfless love. "Let us be lovers and servants of that which is just," Emerson argued, "and straightway every man becomes a centre of a holy and beneficent republic" (*W*, 10, 353).

12. Emerson used this journal passage in his essay on "The Method of Nature" (*W*, 1, 205).

On the basis of an insistence that the City of God was a community of love, Emerson could begin to search in the earthly realm of the City of Man for pieces and foreshadowings of the Celestial City. By sharing in the love of God, finite individuals made possible a communion with each other. "No love without sympathy," Emerson believed. "Minds must be alike. All love a seeking in another what is like self. . . . If we both love God we shall be wholly alike & wholly love each other" (*JMN*, 3, 260–61). For this reason he could argue in a letter to Margaret Fuller in 1840 that friendship "is the best of all external experiences, we pray toward it as to the holy city" (*L*, 2, 344). He often stressed that he did not consider this human community of saints to be physically unified. "Most persons," he said in 1835, "exist to us merely or chiefly in relations of time & space. Those whom we love, whom we venerate, or whom we serve, exist to us independently of these relations" (*JMN*, 5, 61). This stress on a community of inner ties led him to argue in a late lecture on "The Scholar" that "the society of lettered men is a university which does not bound itself within the walls of one cloister or college, but gathers in the distant and solitary student into its strictest amity" (*W*, 10, 261). It was the hope of finding such a community of true pilgrims that justified a pilgrimage that seemed at times painfully solitary. "We walk alone in the world," he recognized in his essay "Friendship."

> Friends such as we desire are dreams and fables. But a sublime hope cheers ever the faithful heart, that elsewhere, in other regions of the universal power, souls are now acting, enduring and daring, which can love us and which we can love. . . . By persisting in your path . . . you draw to you the first-born of the world,—those rare pil-

grims whereof only one or two wander in nature at once, and before whom the vulgar great show as spectres and shadows merely. (*W*, 2, 213)

Such communities of love were for Emerson primary evidence for believing in an affirmative conclusion to the drama of pilgrimage. "In moments when our own faith wavers when we are disturbed with melancholy doubts," he argued in 1828, "the unfailing refuge of the mind is in that little honoured number of good men & women among our friends whose probity is our anchor that like a squadron of angels gather on the mount before us and send out from their seraph faces courage & light into our hearts. Ten good men would save Sodom & five or six good men are our examples, our evidences, and the pillars that we lean on" (*JMN*, 3, 131–32).[13]

Emerson recognized that it was difficult for the finite prophet to determine precisely who were the citizens of this holy community on earth and how extensive this community was. At his most conservative, he could follow traditional Augustinian and, more specifically, Puritan theology in asserting

13. Paul in *Emerson's Angle of Vision*, pp. 185–90, discusses briefly Emerson's hopes that Concord might become an ideal community, but he does not stress sufficiently Emerson's examination of the meaning and possibilities of "inner" community. In a letter to Margaret Fuller in 1840, Emerson commented, "The 'Community' has that attraction for me that it may bring friends together conveniently & satisfactorily. But perhaps old towns & old houses may learn that art one of these days, under the kingdom of the New Spirit" (*L*, 2, 364). Relevant to Emerson's communal hopes, though neither deal with him specifically, are Arthur E. Bestor, Jr., *Backwoods Utopias: The Sectarian and Owenite Phases of Communitarian Socialism in America, 1663–1829* (Philadelphia, 1950), and Kaul, *The American Vision.* See also the suggestive, though overly simplified, study of the image of "home" in Allen Guttmann, "Images of Value and the Sense of the Past," *New England Quarterly*, 35 (1962), 3–26.

that this city of saints was limited in number. Thus at times he could find the hope of "salvation" only in the prophets themselves—his American scholars and poets. It had been his prejudice since boyhood, he admitted in his 1838 lecture "Literary Ethics," "that a scholar is the favorite of Heaven and earth, the excellency of his country, the happiest of men. His duties lead him directly into the holy ground where other men's aspirations only point" (*W*, *1*, 155). As late as 1860 he argued that, as the "prophet" of Heaven, "the true scholar is the Church" and "belongs to a superior society" (*W*, *10*, 242–49). In his most optimistic moments, however, Emerson attacked religious exclusionists who reserved the possibilities of salvation for only a few of the human race.[14] One of the great hopes of his life was that mankind, "in search of a religion," would move from a "Jewish cultus"—a narrow conception of a Chosen People—toward a "Divine or . . . truly Human" faith (*W*, *11*, 392).[15] As early as his Unitarian ministry, he was arguing this cosmopolitan form of the Christian drama. All mankind, he believed, might be included in the "great company of pilgrims" (*Y*, 138). By 1834, he was urging a Transcendental version of this drama: "Democracy has its root in the Sacred truth that every man hath in him the divine Reason or that though few men since the creation of the world live according to the dictates of Reason, yet all men

14. "We are in a transition," Emerson said in the concluding lecture of a series in 1843 on "New England," "from that Jewish Idea before which the Ages were driven like sifted snows, which all the literatures of the world . . . have tingled with, to a more human & universal thought, namely, to a perception of the Universal preference of the law in all action & passion, which we were wont to suppose had its special resorts, & its darling men" (Houghton manuscript 199.4).

15. Cf. Emerson's comments on various forms of Cultus in his Divinity School Address (*W*, *1*, 128, 149–50).

are created capable of doing so. That is the equality & the only equality of all men" (*JMN*, 4, 357).[16]

Emerson's belief in the radical equality and hence radical community of all men's souls was a crucial meeting point for the inner City of God and the external City of the West. He was pushing the Christian drama toward such a connection when, in 1836, he quoted St. Augustine's "sublime ejaculation" to truth: "And yet, as rich as thy furniture is, O City of God! thy gates stand always open, free to all comers. For thy immoveable Wealth needs no guard, the Exchequer of Light and Truth is secure against all thievish attempts, and the treasures of Wisdom, though common to all, can yet be rifled and carried away by none" (*EL*, 1, 383). Emerson was not affirming the metaphorically walled Celestial City of the medieval Christian or its "exclusionist" externalization in the Puritan's own City on a Hill; he was arguing for an "open" City of divine spaciousness. "The doors of heaven," he argued in 1831, "may be flung as wide as human freedom—no man can enter but the good man, for when the bad man shall see them there is no beauty that he should desire them. Like must be joined to like" (*JMN*, 3, 273). As a divinely cosmopolitan metropolis, however, the City of God took an expansive view of what constituted goodness. "Heaven is large," Emerson argued in his essay "Spiritual Laws," "and affords space for all modes of love and fortitude" (*W*, 2, 162).[17]

16. "Every man by God's arrangements whilst he ministers & receives influence from all others," Emerson argued in 1829, "is absolutely imperially free. When I look at the rainbow I find myself the centre of its arch. But so are you; & so is the man that sees it a mile from both of us. So also the globe is round, & every man therefore stands on the top" (*JMN*, 3, 168).

17. Thoreau was making similar individualistic use of the metaphor of the City of God when he advised a friend to "let nothing come

Only because all human beings—and hence all Americans—were potentially citizens of an inward City of God could Emerson believe in the usefulness of discussing his nation's people as being saints on a communal pilgrimage toward a "Western" City on a Hill. "We see the enlargement of religious truths in its effects," he said in a sermon delivered several times during the middle 1830s, while he was most under the spell of an optimistic Transcendental individualism. "In the place of unsupported virtues of solitary individuals that sparkle in the darkness of antiquity . . . the nations of the globe are brought together by pacific and equitable commerce; liberal humane Christian associations are correcting the manners and relieving the sufferings of vast masses of men" (*Y*, 197–98). He was referring not only to the internal but to the external possibilities of the pilgrimage when, in 1831, he argued that "A community of Christians would be a field of splendid occasions, exciting recollections, purposes; grand characters & epical situations that would leave the loftiest fiction . . . far beneath it" (*JMN*, 3, 248). "Let us hope infinitely," he wrote a friend in 1839, "& accustom ourselves to the reflection that the true Fall of man is the disesteem of man; the true Redemption selftrust; the growth of character is only the enlargement of this, & year by year as we come to our stature we shall inherit not only forms & churches & communities but earth and heaven" (*L*, 2, 213).

Because of this hope Emerson could express occasional impatience with modern saints who dissipated their personal resources in escapist rebellions against urbanizing America. "I read Napoleon's memoirs lately," he remarked in 1844, "&

---

between you and the light. Respect men as brothers only. When you travel to the celestial city, carry no letter of introduction. When you knock, ask to see God—none of the servants" (*Correspondence*, p. 216).

could not help grudging to Europe that grand executive faculty which in this vast empty Eden of ours with so many fine theories & so many white-robed candidates, might consolidate, organize, & put into action, so much" (*L*, 3, 268). A national City on a Hill, he believed, could never substitute for the individual's City of God, but it could be a highly desirable consequence of that redemptive vision. As his reading in history had taught him, "Sacred cities, to which a periodical religious pilgrimage was enjoined" tended "to invigorate the national bond" (*W*, 2, 22). Speaking out of the solitary prophet's vision that all men were bound on a communal pilgrimage, even when their external civilization did not reflect it, he could "say like the republicans, Citoyen! Citoyenne! to whatever venerable or enchanting form moves in the vast city of God" (*L*, 2, 82).

If the pilgrim's path of the Romantic prophet led through solitude, it could also lead through external nature—an especially appropriate path for any American facing an undeveloped continent. Truth, Emerson argued in his late essay "The Scholar," was to be found "on the great highways of Nature, which were before the Appian Way, and which all souls must travel" (*W*, 10, 285). For all the Romantic implications of this natural highway, it was also a well-worn path on the landscape of the traditional Christian drama. Having fallen from an Edenic garden into a "wilderness" experience—the psychological and moral foundations of the City of Man—Adam and his sons had faced the task of setting out on a renewed "quest for paradise." One version of this quest was that of Christian primitivism, which looked for a return to the original Eden of simple innocence. Equally as influential—and probably more important for Emerson—was the version supported by the Christian believers in a fortunate fall, which differentiated between the paradise lost and the paradise to be regained.[18] If sinning man had fallen from a blessed garden, saved man could in at least metaphorical terms regain a divine City. In the cosmology of the Middle Ages, the original Garden of Eden, though attached as a remote suburb to the City of God, was actually suspended between that City and the wilderness of degenerate matter and therefore was vulnerable to devilish assault. The Eden of the redeemed soul was more secure, however. Because of Christ's victory over Satan, as Milton argued in Book IV of *Paradise Regained,*

> though that seat of earthly bliss be fail'd
> A fairer Paradise is founded
> For Adam and his chosen Sons. (ll. 613–15)

Paradise regained was not located somewhere between the Celestial City and imperfect earth. It was an organic part of the Celestial City, protected by the walls of that City from encroachments from the wilderness. "Zion's garden," as the New England poet Edward Taylor had stated in affirming the central strain of the Christian urban tradition, was merely one aspect of Zion. The major metaphor was not Paradise but the City of God:

> Would God I in that Golden City were,
> With Jaspers Walld, all garnisht, and made swash,
> With Pretious Stones, whose Gates, are Pearles most
> cleare

18. If the problem of an original fall from innocence has its own characteristic literary modes—e.g. the adolescent's initiation into adult experience—the problem of a fortunate fall often is treated literarily through some form of a "pilgrimage." An interesting recent work on the literary problems of *felix culpa* is Herbert Weisinger, *Tragedy and the Paradox of the Fortunate Fall* (East Lansing, Mich., 1953).

> And Streets Pure Gold, like to transparent Glass,
> That my dull Soule might be inflamde to see
> How Saints and Angells ravisht are in Glee.[19]

Despite his attraction to the myths of Christian primitivism, Emerson found a doctrine of *felix culpa* more useful for his purposes. At its most heavenly, American nature was not merely rural; it was a divine park within an urban Heaven. In the harmonious relationship of the Celestial City and its Heavenly Paradise, in fact, might be found a religious analogue to the relationship of the City of the West and its hinterland.

In charting the pilgrim's path to the Heavenly City through nature, Emerson had as a point of departure the traditional metaphorical association of Heaven with the starry sky. In April 1827, when returning from an attempt to recover his health in Florida, he stopped in Charleston and there experienced one of the earliest of his periodic releases of personal energy and optimism—his psychological equivalent of salvation. "The night is fine," he wrote;

> the stars shed down their severe influences upon me, and I feel a joy in my solitude that the merriment of vulgar society can never communicate. There is a pleasure in the thought that the particular tone of my mind at this moment may be new in the Universe; that the emotions of this hour may be peculiar & unexampled in the whole eternity of moral being. I lead a new life. I occupy new ground in the world of spirits, untenanted before. I commence a career of thought & action which is expanding before me into a distant & dazzling infinity. Strange

19. Donald E. Stanford, ed., *The Poems of Edward Taylor* (New Haven, 1960), p. 38.

> thoughts start up like angels in my way & beckon me onward. I doubt not I tread on the highway that leads to Divinity. (*JMN*, 3, 78)

To a maturing Emerson, the stars came habitually to symbolize his desire for a divine angle of vision from which the City of Man could be seen in its flux and imperfection.[20] In a lecture on "The Naturalist" in 1834 he argued that since "in cities we are in danger of forgetting our relation to the planet and the system," the stars were useful in "looking down from their far and solemn heights into every narrow and deep lane, forcibly admonishing the eye that by chance catches their beam of higher relations than he ordinarily remembers" (*EL*, 1, 76). When Emerson recast this passage for inclusion in the opening section of *Nature*, he related it even more explicitly to the Christian drama: "Seen in the streets of cities, how great they are! If the stars should appear one night in a thousand years, how would men believe and adore; and preserve for many generations the remembrance of the city of God which had been shown! But every night come out these envoys of beauty, and light the universe with their admonishing smile" (*W*, 1, 7).[21]

Emerson's metaphorical linking of the stars and the Celestial City, however, was not merely based on the conventions of Christian rhetoric. It was increasingly aimed at converting this rhetoric into a strategy for realizing his own Romantic aims. As a young minister asserting that "the as-

20. See Paul, *Emerson's Angle of Vision*, pp. 80–84.

21. Cf. Thoreau's complaint in 1840 that "we look up to the gilded battlements of the eternal city, and are contented to be suburban dwellers outside the walls" (*Journals*, 1, 171). Emerson's reference to the nightly returning stars indicates his increasing emphasis on an immanent Creator rather than on the Enlightenment's First Cause.

pects of the heavens" revealed God and that the Bible must be read "by the light of nature" (*Y*, 170–71), he had remained fairly comfortably in the general liberal tendencies of post-Newtonian Christianity.[22] By the time of his resignation as minister of the Second Unitarian Church of Boston, however, he had moved beyond even this tentative liberal compromise with orthodox Puritanism and was arguing that nature was a better and truer interpretation of the Christian drama than was the Bible. In a sermon on astronomy he argued that, in the natural universe, "there is no ungoverned orb, no loose pin, no lawless particle through all the heights and depths of the city of God" (*Y*, 176), and in his journal for 1831 he pointed to the implications of this belief for a prophet just beginning a Romantic pilgrimage: "Nothing done at random. No accidents in nature. You go out of a city & come to social disorder & wilderness, never get out of God's city—order order everywhere. morals paramount. equality of number of the sexes. proportion of vegetable & animal life" (*JMN*, 3, 311–12).

To the City of Man, nonhuman nature represented "social disorder & wilderness." To the prophetic pilgrim, however, nature's usefulness lay precisely in its representation of values other than those of fallen man. In contrast to nature, Emerson argued in 1841,

> the town has to offer—Persons, that strange magical, flattering, inspiring disappointing creation. Ah me! if those were fixtures & could only act where they were, I suppose no grove of oaks or of palms—no mountain-

22. For a background to this linking of God and nature in Protestant thought, see two books by Ernest L. Tuveson: *Millennium and Utopia: A Study in the Background of the Idea of Progress* (Berkeley, 1949), esp. Chaps. 3 and 4, and *The Imagination as a Means of*

> brook or vast sunny seabeach would have the power to detain a pilgrim. But sometimes when we see the person in town we find that his angel in the woods was better. (*L*, 2, 396)

As early as 1824 he was borrowing the eighteenth-century's rhetoric of the sublime to suggest nature's value as a contrast to the City of Man:

> He who frequents these scenes where Nature discloses her magnificence to silence & solitude, will have his mind occupied often by strains of thought of a peculiarly solemn tone. . . . The pilgrim who retires hither wonders how his heart, could ever cleave so mightily to the world whose deafening tumult he has left behind. What are temples & towered cities to him? He has come to a sweeter & more desireable creation. When his eye reaches upward by the sides of the piled rocks to the grassy summit, he feels that the magnificence of man is quelled & subdued here. (*JMN*, 2, 236)

Contrasting man and nature was not an end in itself, however. By humbling the prophet, nature was providing the basis for his redemptive pilgrimage. Like the Jewish nation's forty-year errand in a God-created wilderness, the pilgrim might find nature both a means of liberation from the moral wilderness of a falsely civilized "Egypt" and a means of testing and purifying himself in preparation for entering a Prom-

---

Grace: Locke and the Aesthetics of Romanticism (Berkeley, 1960), esp. Chap. 3. Also useful are Carl Becker, *The Heavenly City of the Eighteenth-Century Philosophers* (New Haven, 1932), and Marjorie Hope Nicolson, *Mountain Gloom and Mountain Glory: The Development of the Aesthetics of the Infinite* (Ithaca, 1959).

ised Land and building a New Jerusalem.[23] On a sunset stroll with his brother Charles in 1835, Emerson was moved to view the woods as the church "of a divine Artist," with "beautiful Gothic arches . . . & cathedral windows as of stained glass formed by the interlaced branches against the grey & gold of the western sky" (*JMN*, 5, 109). Seen by the appropriately "westward" vision of the prophetic pilgrim, nature's "palace of magic" (*J*, 5, 58) became the grounds for affirming the holiest of human possibilities. As Emerson argued in his second "Nature" essay:

> Nature is loved by what is best in us. It is loved as the city of God, although, or rather because there is no citizen. The sunset is unlike anything that is underneath it: it wants men. And the beauty of nature must always seem unreal and mocking, until the landscape has human figures that are as good as itself. If there were good men, there would never be this rapture in nature. . . . The critics who complain of the sickly separation of the beauty of nature from the thing to be done, must consider that our hunting for the picturesque is inseparable from our protest against false society. Man is fallen; na-

23. Thoreau's famous essay, "Walking," is structured largely around this theme: "For every walk," he argues, "is a sort of crusade, preached by some Peter the Hermit in us, to go forth and reconquer this Holy Land from the hands of the Infidels." But the frustration of the idealist in being unable to find this vision realized in actual American society often led to the conversion of the Christian drama into a satiric device. In Melville's *Confidence Man* the president of the Black Rapids Coal Company attempts to sell a college student some water-lots in "the New Jerusalem"—"the new and thriving city, so called, in northern Minnesota . . . originally founded . . . by two fugitives, who had swum over naked from the opposite shore" (*Works, 12*, 65–66). Significantly, the student rejects this opportunity and chooses instead to invest in the Black Rapids Coal Company.

> ture is erect, and serves as a differential thermometer, detecting the presence or absence of the divine sentiment in man. By fault of our dulness or selfishness we are looking up to nature, but when we are convalescent, nature will look up to us. (*W*, 3, 178)

Seen in divine perspective, the noblest parts of the City of Man were not a chaotic moral wilderness but the "suburbs and extremities of nature" (*W*, *1*, 111). As a "hundred-gated Thebes" (*W*, *12*, 29), the natural world offered the pilgrim magnificent entrances into God's Metropolis and the promise that man's own city might be redeemed. In reaffirming the role of his prophets as New Cosmopolitans—"no longer strangers and pilgrims in a traditionary globe" (*W*, 2, 194)—Emerson could argue that the redeemed man "is at home in markets, in senates, in battles . . . & learns to look at sea & land, at nations & globes as the moveables & furniture of the City of God."[24]

In light of Emerson's strategic manipulation of the ambiguous meanings of "society" and "solitude," "wilderness" and "civilization," in the interest of an optimistic drama of pilgrimage, his criticism of Thoreau's use of a similar strategy is revealing in its implicit awareness of the limits of such rhetorical maneuvers. When in 1843 Thoreau sent him "A Winter Walk" for inclusion in the *Dial,* Emerson reacted strongly in his journal:

> Henry Thoreau sends me a paper with the old fault of unlimited contradiction. The trick of his rhetoric is soon learned: it consists in substituting for the obvious word and thought its diametrical antagonist. He praises wild

24. "Home," the second lecture in a series on "Human Life," first delivered in 1838 (Houghton manuscript 197.11).

> mountains and winter forests for their domestic air; snow and ice for their warmth; villagers and wood-choppers for their urbanity, and the wilderness for resembling Rome and Paris. With the constant inclination to dispraise cities and civilization, he yet can find no way to know woods and woodsmen except by paralleling them with towns and townsmen. Channing declared the piece is excellent: but it makes me nervous and wretched to read it, with all its merits. (*J*, 6, 440–41)

Two weeks later Emerson expressed the same objection in a letter to Thoreau,[25] and he thought enough of his opinion to air it publicly in his memorial tribute of 1862 (*W*, *10*, 479).

Emerson saw at least two major problems in such rhetorical strategy. First, he recognized that such manipulation of metaphors became too easily a pointless rhetorical game with no redemptive possibilities. If the prophet played the game too irresponsibly, he risked dissevering himself from any truly creative verbal communion with his fellow pilgrims. "The angels are so enamored of the language that is spoken in heaven," Emerson argued in his essay "Intellect," "that they will not distort their lips with the hissing and unmusical dialects of men, but speak their own, whether there be any who understand it or not" (*W*, 2, 347). When the prophet pretended to speak like an angel, he ran the risk of not speaking at all to men. The second problem was the reverse of this: in trying to use the imperfect language of the City of Man, the prophet faced the continual frustration of being unable to describe the City of God to the satisfaction of the angels. "The aim of the author is not to tell truth—that he cannot do, but

25. Thoreau, *Correspondence*, p. 137.

to suggest it," Emerson said in 1835, at the outset of his own literary career.

> He has only approximated it himself, & hence his cumbrous embarrassed speech: he uses many words, hoping that one, if not another, will bring you as near to the fact as he is. For language itself is young & unformed. In heaven it will be, as Sampson Reed said, "one with things." Now, there are many things that refuse to be recorded,—perhaps the larger half. The unsaid part is the best of every discourse. (*JMN*, 5, 51)

Nevertheless, the problems of such a strategy were less compelling to Emerson than its virtues, especially in comparison to the alternative literary means that writers of his day were using to keep alive the Christian urban drama in nineteenth-century America. On one hand, religious spokesmen for Puritanism and evangelical Protestantism were attempting to hold to a traditional literal interpretation of the drama and were therefore failing to speak directly enough to the leaders of their age and their nation. As a poet, Emerson could appreciate the integrity of such literalism. "I listen without impatience," he said in 1834 of a Bostonian minister's sermon, "because though the whole is literally false, it is really true; only he speaks Parables which I translate as he goes" (*JMN*, 4, 319–20).[26] He realized, however, that many of his fellow Americans could not respond to such traditionalism; it disregarded "the capital secret" of the prophet's profession,

26. Similarly, Emerson could appreciate interpretations of scripture by the Swedenborgians: "the interpretation of the passages is doubtless wholly false. . . . But the sentiment . . . is nevertheless true & eternal" (*JMN*, 3, 165–66). See Emerson's essay on Swedenborg in *Representative Men*, and Paul, *Emerson's Angle of Vision*, pp. 62–70.

"namely, to convert life into truth" (*W*, *1*, 138), to infuse contemporary experience with religious significance. On the other hand, most of the attempts to bring the Christian drama "up-to-date" suffered from the reverse defect—an inability to convert eternal truth into more than a rationalization of contemporary actuality. Christianity, he argued in 1831, was

> in some respects better understood & more consistent & more divine when preached to a barbarous nation. For it stands in such striking contrast to the system it would replace that here is no danger of their being anywhere confounded. . . . When the whole world *Christizes* the Christian finds a shelter for his sins which before he had not. Once if he had sinned it would have been paganism. Now it is only what this Christian world doth, & so he does not lose caste. Nay in the general sympathy the partisans of the world & of Christ often change sides & the man of this world argues the cause of Christian love so long as it does not hurt his worthy interest & the Christian in poor extenuation of his own compliances strives to wrest the truth into a seeming sanction of the customs of the day. (*JMN*, *3*, 287)

Working between these two unsatisfactory alternatives, Thoreau had, in *Walden*, used the difficult strategy of rhetorical contradiction to build a figurative City on a Hill.[27] Emer-

27. In building his metaphorical version of a Holy City at Walden, Thoreau characteristically redefined common terms: "I have thought that Walden Pond would be a good place for business . . . it is a good port and a good foundation. No Neva marshes to be filled; though you must everywhere build on piles of your own driving" (*Walden*, Chap. 1). While living there he wrote in his journal: "Here I know I am in good company; here is the world, its centre and metropolis" (*Journal*, *1*, 365).

son's application of this strategy was for a similar end. "There is nothing small or mean to the soul," he wrote in 1841.

> It derives as grand a joy from symbolizing the Godhead or his universe under the form of a moth or a gnat as of a Lord of Hosts. Must I call the heaven and the earth a maypole and country fair with booths, or an anthill, or an old coat, in order to give you the shock of pleasure which the imagination loves and the sense of spiritual greatness? (*J*, 6, 18)

Emerson's "nervous and wretched" reaction to Thoreau's rhetoric was actually only a hair's breadth away from the "shock of pleasure" that he wished his own manipulation of metaphors to convey. This "shock of pleasure," in fact, was the psychological equivalent of religious conversion—the event that gave motivation to the pilgrimage itself. Emerson was anxious in the name of "spiritual greatness" to liberate himself and his society from the literalism of traditional literary interpretations of the Christian drama and from the flaccid clichés of contemporary interpretations of this drama. By placing the metaphors traditionally connected with the pilgrimage into new and even startling contexts, he was attempting to suggest those elements of the City of God that might be found in America's City of Man.

In his constant search for "a Redeemer of the human mind" (*W*, 12, 332), therefore, Emerson had come by the 1840s to treat the poet as the most hopeful example of the prophetic pilgrim. As he described him, the poet embodied the major features of Augustine's or Bunyan's saint. In 1843 he argued that artists and scholars "live in the world as strangers in their own house" (*W*, 12, 400). In the Bunyanesque "mire" and "slough" of contemporary life, their faith in the redemptive power of poetry was "a lonely faith, a lonely protest in the uproar of atheism" (*W*, *8*, 74). Because of his struggle not only with values but with words, the poet's goal was an especially demanding one. "The maker of a sentence," Emerson declared in 1834, "launches out into the infinite & builds a road into Chaos & old Night" (*JMN*, *4*, 363). The "wilderness" through which the poet's path lay was not merely that of the immoral City of Man but that of nature's "alien world; a world not yet subdued by the thought" (*W*, *1*, 168). In trying to subdue this painful experience to a beautiful and affirmative thought, the poet was undergoing his own special purgatory. "Mediator, Mediation," Emerson complained in a weary moment in 1851. "There is nothing else; there is no Immediate known to us. . . . The Judgment Day is in reality the past. We have all been judged, and we have judged all. We would gladly think highly of Nature and Life, but what a country-muster, what a Vanity-Fair full of noise, squibs and egg-pop it is" (*J*, *8*, 243–44). To redeem the Vanity Fairs of nature and man for the purposes of holy art was an ambitious task which demanded "an asceticism . . . as only the hardihood and devotion of the scholar himself can enforce" (*W*, *1*, 176).

This need of the poet to "lead the impossible right life," to "keep the road to Heaven, though it lead through Bedlam" did not always rest easily on Emerson's shoulders. "It is lucky for the peace of Boston & all honest cities," he wrote Margaret Fuller in 1843, "that the scholars & the religious generally are such puny bodies; if they had any vigour answerable to their perception, they would start aside every day from expectation & their own prescription, and destroy the peace of all burgesses. For me," he added pessimistically, "I have only impulse enough to brood now & then on the conditions favorable to thought & life, but not enough yet to make me either a pirate or poet" (*L*, 3, 229–30). But it was precisely because the conditions for poetic sainthood were so severe that the City of Man's need for them was so great. Redacting a Bunyanesque metaphor, Emerson argued in his essay "The Transcendentalist" that "In our Mechanic's Fair, there must be not only bridges, ploughs, carpenters' planes, and baking troughs, but also some few finer instruments" (*W*, *1*, 358). Because of his hope that among the Transcendentalists were to be found at least a few of these "finer instruments" of poetic perception, Emerson was willing to defend their antisocial tendencies: "Let them obey the Genius then most when . . . he seems to lead into uninhabitable deserts of thought and life; for the path which the hero travels alone is the highway of health and benefit to mankind" (*W*, *1*, 357–58). Only by such a painful path could the poet attain "the mountain of vision" (*W*, *10*, 287)—an aesthetic Pisgah or Zion from which the Cities of the Plains might be evaluated and hopefully redeemed by a divine perspective. Like the path of Dante or Bunyan's Christian, the poet's road was painful because the City of God was so high,[28] but the vision at the top of the mount was well worth the climb—a vision of beauty, freedom, and love. "Why do we seek this lurking beauty in skies, in poems, in drawings," Emerson asked in 1838. "Ah! because there we are safe,

28. Height, of course, along with light, was a central traditional attribute to the City of God. As Cooper observed, "habit has taught us to imagine that 'the path to heaven' lies upward" (*Excursions in Italy*, *1*, 238). It is no wonder that William Bradford despaired when he first saw the bleak Massachusetts shore. In the midst of a flat and hostile wilderness, his band of pilgrims could not, "as it were, go up to the top of Pisgah, to view from the wilderness a more goodly country to feed their hopes" (*Of Plymouth Plantation, 1620–1647*, ed. Samuel Eliot Morison [New York, 1952], p. 62).

there we neither sicken nor die. I think we fly to Beauty as an asylum from the terrors of finite nature. We are made immortal by this kiss, by the contemplation of beauty" (*J*, 4, 467). In the kingdom of the poet's affirmative vision lay the "cities of refuge to which we can one day flee if the worst come to the worst" (*J*, 5, 120–21).

The great works of art, believed Emerson, reflected both this mountaintop experience of the poet and the path by which he had reached the summit. At its finest, poetry was not only a "holy place" (*W*, 3, 14) but "the shadow of a passing traveller" (*W*, 2, 289). In both senses it was a "Holy Writ" (*W*, 10, 269), a guide to other potential pilgrims. Like the Old Testament prophets, the poet could predict the downfall of the City of Man in the name of the City of God; he could "shove all usurpers from their chairs by electrifying mankind with the right tone, long wished for, never heard. The true center thus appearing, all false centres are suddenly superseded, and grass grows in the Capitol" (*J*, 7, 207–08). But the prediction of destruction, like the defense of solitude or the escape to nature, was strategic rather than final. Like the Puritan's jeremiad, the poet's threat of Hell was a prelude to a conditional promise of Heaven. "The aim of writers is to tame the Holy Ghost, and produce it as a show to the city," Emerson noted in 1845. "But the sole terms on which the Infinite will come to cities is the surrender of cities to its will" (*J*, 7, 16). While a young ministerial student, he had been intrigued by the biblical reminder that "when a dread of impending vengeance had cleansed the corruptions of Ninevah, that dread was taken away because its end was accomplished. . . . God knew that they would repent & therefore knew that he should not destroy the city" (*JMN*, 2, 87). The ultimate purpose of the great poet's art was, like the Christian drama of pilgrimage, not destructive but affirmative. Literature, Emerson argued, could open "a secret door . . . that may lead to Parnassus" (*J*, 7, 297). The pilgrim could find the best books to be "bridges or ships" to carry him "safely over dark morasses and barren oceans, into the heart of sacred cities, into palaces and temples" (*W*, 7, 192). In a spiritual sense, all the most creative art was an attempt to create in beauty a symbol of an eternal City. Through his artistic efforts, the poet liberated his and other men's imaginations for communion in a Romantic City on a Hill. "When we once in our writing come out into the free air of thought," Emerson argued in 1839, "we seem to be assured that nothing is easier than to continue this communication at pleasure indefinitely. Up, down, around, the kingdom of thought has no enclosures, but the Muse makes us free of her city" (*J*, 5, 323).

As Emerson moved further away from his days as minister and from his first radically Transcendental enthusiasm, his use of the Christian urban drama underwent modification. As he increasingly read the Bible and its Christian interpreters for literary interest rather than for theological insights, his use of the elements of pilgrimage became less explicit. City of God, for example, rarely appears as a metaphor in Emerson's writings after the early 1840s. The disappearance of this term also indicates a concurrent tendency of his thought—a decline of his most apocalyptic hopes for himself and his world. In admitting that both his pilgrimage toward the Celestial City in himself and his nation's search for a City on a Hill were much more difficult and even more frustrating than he had hoped they would be, Emerson fell back to an extent on his Puritan heritage and began to give more honest attention to the actual pilgrim's progress through the City of

Man than to the heavenly goal that he still believed eventually awaited this lonely traveler. A striking example of these tendencies is "Experience," one of Emerson's most compelling essays. Published in his second series of *Essays* in 1844 (*W*, 3, 43–86), it represents not only his attempt as prophet to make his personal experience relevant to the larger dilemmas of human existence but also his attempt as poet to find ways of satisfactorily organizing these dilemmas into a cohesive literary structure.[29]

At its most explicit level, the essay is organized by a sequential presentation of seven "lords of life" that Emerson believes rule human experience—"Illusion, Temperament, Succession, Surface, Surprise, Reality, Subjectiveness" (p. 82). By themselves, however, these lords do not give the essay a dramatic coherence. In fact, this explicit scheme of organization seems loose and unwieldy. Emerson does not devote himself wholeheartedly to any one lord at any one time but intermixes the major section on each lord with subsidiary references to other lords. In fact, various lords seem so closely interrelated that they become on occasion mistakable for one another. "I dare not assume to give their order," Emerson states, "but I name them as I find them in my way" (p. 83). However, the qualifying "in my way" indicates what is really the essay's most compelling structural device—the metaphor of travel. "Experience" is primarily about movement itself, particularly about the movement of the individual human mind through a finite, temporal world. The lords of life are

29. The most detailed analysis of "Experience" to date is in Bishop, *Emerson on the Soul*, pp. 193–201. Bishop's analysis, however, covers only the first two-thirds of the essay and is not interested in its structure or metaphorical strategy. He follows basically the interpretation suggested by Whicher in *Freedom and Fate*, pp. 111–22.

"threads on the loom of time" (pp. 82–83). Whatever else it may do, the essay represents Emerson's attempt to convert the aimless movement of a soul caught by an implicit City of Man into a purposeful pilgrimage of redemption.

In becoming a pilgrimage, this movement also becomes metaphorically westward. It is as if the narrator were starting out, like Columbus (whom Emerson mentions twice in the essay), from the shores of an "experienced" Europe that he has long and painfully confronted and facing the challenge of an "ocean" experience in the hopes of arriving at a psychologically new, because unexplored, Western land. The lords of life become the metaphorical fixtures of a Bunyanesque landscape, and the prophet's task is to learn to treat them not as a Vanity Fair, a Slough of Despond, and a Giant Despair, but as a Great-heart, an innocent Patience, and a range of Delectable Mountains. Unlike much of Bunyan's landscape, however, the lords of Emerson's experience are not immobile.

> The lords of life, the lords of life—
> I saw them pass . . .
> Some to see, some to be guessed,
> They marched from east to west. (p. 43)

The westering pilgrim is, so to speak, going the way of these lords of experience. Whether he likes their company or not, he must learn to accept them as guides who will lead him out of a City of Destruction and toward a Celestial City.

The opening paragraph of "Experience"—like most of the first two sections on Illusion (pp. 45–50) and Temperament (pp. 50–55)—dramatizes the plight of a fallen world that "is almost all custom and gross sense" (p. 47). In this City of Man the narrator can find initially only an experience of meaningless motion. "Where do we find ourselves?" he asks. "In a series of which we do not know the extremes, and believe that it has none. We wake and find ourselves on a stair; there are stairs below us, which we seem to have ascended; there are stairs above us, many a one, which go upward and out of sight" (p. 45). Because the Cains of this fallen world—and Emerson identifies himself provisionally with this group—"lack the affirmative principle" (p. 45), even the redemptive possibilities of upward direction seem illusory: "We are like millers on the lower levels of a stream, when the factories above them have exhausted the water. We too fancy that the upper people must have raised their dams" (p. 46). Psychologically speaking, this damming up of the individual's creative spirit is the cause or at least the sign of his "damned" state. The second paragraph extends the metaphor of travel to describe the agonies of a soul without personal faith who sees only in others the possibilities of meaningful pilgrimage: "Every ship is a romantic object, except that we sail in. Embark and the horizon quits our vessel and hangs on every other sail in the horizon" (p. 46). All true pilgrims must cross this metaphorical Atlantic, and the narrator grieves over his inner inability to maneuver this path: "An innavigable sea washes with silent waves between us and the things we aim at and converse with" (p. 48). In this state even pain proves unredemptive and cannot "carry me one step into real nature" (p. 49). Such a feeling is equivalent to life in Dis. "Nothing is left us now but death. We look to that with a grim satisfaction, saying, There at least is reality that will not dodge us" (p. 49).

Since damnation is associated with an inner incapacity for faith, Emerson appropriately moves to a consideration of that "prison of glass," Temperament, "the iron wire on which the beads [of illusion] are strung" (p. 50). By offering a psychological or naturalistic version of hell, he can comment wryly on traditional Christian versions of this state: "I knew a witty physician who found the creed in the biliary duct, and used to affirm that if there was a disease in the liver, the man became a Calvinist, and if that organ was sound, he became a Unitarian" (p. 51). Significantly the metaphorical equivalent of Temperament is not progressive but circular movement: "a certain uniform tune which the revolving barrel of the music-box must play" (p. 52). To accept Temperament as the ruling experience or lord of life is to affirm the Slough of Despond and the City of Destruction: "On this platform one lives in a sty of sensualism, and would soon come to suicide" (p. 54).

At this point in the essay, Emerson throws off the garb of Cain that he has assumed provisionally and reveals his desire to believe himself a true pilgrim. He shows the reader the first sign that he is among the saved number—his possession of faith in the power of creative freedom.

> But it is impossible that the creative power should exclude itself. . . . The intellect, seeker of absolute truth, or the heart, lover of absolute good, intervenes for our succor, and at one whisper of these high powers we awake from ineffectual struggles with this nightmare. We hurl it into its own hell, and cannot again contract ourselves to so base a state. (pp. 54–55)

This affirmation of possible salvation begins slowly; the narrator-pilgrim is still dishearteningly close to Dis, still aware of the hellish meanings that can be read into experience. Yet he becomes increasingly willing to affirm the heavenly meanings that may lie at the end of his reverent exploration.

Thus the movement of the third lord of life, Succession (pp. 55–58), is not the self-defeating materialistic revolution of Illusion. In this section movement begins to work toward a higher purpose: "health of the body consists in circulation, and sanity of mind in variety or facility of association. We need change of objects" (p. 55). The emerging pilgrim returns to the metaphor of an ocean again, but this time the inability to journey lies not in the narrator but in others. "Our friends . . . stand on the brink of the ocean of thought and power, but they never take the single step that would bring them there" (pp. 56–57). For the narrator, circularity has begun to assume a more hopeful form than it had at the outset of the essay. "It needs the whole society," argues Emerson, "to give the symmetry we need. The parti-colored wheel must revolve very fast to appear white. . . . Like a bird which alights nowhere, but hops perpetually from bough to bough, is the Power which abides in no man and in no woman, but for a moment speaks from this one, and for another moment from that one" (pp. 57–58). In fact, experience itself begins to assume a redemptive force. Theory alone will not launch the pilgrim on his metaphorically westward journey. "A political orator," Emerson remarks, "wittily compared our party promises to western roads, which opened stately enough . . . but soon became narrower and narrower and ended in a squirrel-track and ran up a tree" (pp. 58–59).

The next section, on the lord of Surface, adds to the theoretical possibilities of pilgrimage the need for the pilgrim's personal example of concrete action. "We live amid surfaces," he argues, "and the true art of life is to skate well on them" (p. 59). One way of keeping the westward road from ending in a squirrel-track is to accept the value of all the road's features—"to find the journey's end in every step of the road, to live the greatest number of good hours" (p. 60). As an instinctive rather than intellectual ability, this power is an outgrowth of the divine side of Temperament; like Jonathan Edward's divine and supernatural light, it is thus a more accurate sign of salvation than the ability to reason theoretically on salvation. "What help from thought?" Emerson asks. "Life is not dialectics. . . . Intellectual tasting of life will not supersede muscular activity. . . . Life is not intellectual or critical, but sturdy. Its chief good is for well-mixed people who can enjoy what they find, without question" (p. 59).

Mere uncritical action in or movement through external nature, however, cannot satisfy the prophetic pilgrim for long. The external natural world is not a sufficient guide for the human imagination. "Nature, as we know her," says Emerson, "is no saint." Its processes are not "direct" but dialectical, and its fluctuations make it difficult for the pilgrim to keep to the balanced "mixture of power and form" that is the sign and secret of a saved life. In nature "Everything runs to excess; every good quality is noxious if unmixed, and, to carry the danger to the edge of ruin, nature causes each man's peculiarity to superabound" (pp. 65–66). Though "Everything good is on the highway," this road sets definite limits for the pilgrim. "The middle region of our being is the temperate zone. We may climb into the thin and cold realm of pure geometry and lifeless science, or sink into that of sensation. Between these extremes is the equator of life, of thought, of spirit, of poetry,—a narrow belt" (p. 62). Hence we have the difficulty of being a true pilgrim: "A man is a golden impossibility. The line he must walk is a hair's breadth" (p. 66).

Emerson's enumeration of the dangers to the pilgrim of a dialectical interpretation of experience, however, is merely a prelude to his affirmation of the divine possibilities of dialectical movement. If man is caught by natural undulations, it is often for his own ultimate good. He begins to redefine the nature of this "natural" fate in his section on Surprise (pp. 67–70). Even as early as the section on Surface, he stated that "I accept the clangor and jangle of contrary tendencies" (p. 62). This acceptance is predicated on his faith that such dialectical interaction is (at least psychologically and artistically) the means by which the divine tendency of the "middle" road is made possible. Dialectical surprise—or what Emerson calls an "angel-whispering"—gives strong hints of the divine power that motivates the pilgrimage: "Power keeps quite another road than the turnpikes of choice and will; namely the subterranean and invisible tunnels and channels of life" (p. 67). Surprise points to the dialectical basis of the imagination itself: "the chemical and ethereal agents are undulatory and alternate; and the mind goes antagonizing on, and never prospers but by fits" (p. 68). These dialectical powers are a sign not of damnation but of the potential for salvation. "The most attractive class of people," Emerson argues, "are those who are powerful obliquely and not by direct stroke" (p. 68). Significantly, he refers to "the newness" created by the imagination's surprising spontaneities, in a biblical reference to Luke 17:20, for example, as "the kingdom that cometh without observation" (p. 68). Ultimately, the hellish implications of the dichotomies of freedom and fate, power and form, are transcended by the prophet's dialectical vision of a divine force that embodies them all: "Every man is an impossibility until he is born; every thing impossible until we see a success. The ardors of piety agree at last with coldest scepticism—that nothing is of us or of our works—that all is of God" (p. 69).

To affirm the existence of a progressive God is to advance the pilgrim substantially along his road. Appropriately, therefore, Emerson now finds in his path the lord of Reality (pp. 70–75)—that great father of all the other lords of life. This Reality is no longer merely the present-tense actuality of Surface. Having taken on the religious force of spontaneity, it becomes a term for the ideal end of the pilgrim's journey. At this point in his pilgrimage, the prophet feels hopeful enough to argue that one divine will structures all the dialectical diversities of human experience. "Life is hereby melted into an expectation or a religion. Underneath the inharmonious and trivial particulars, is a musical perfection; the Ideal journeying always with us, the heaven without rent or seam" (pp. 70–71). With such a faith—a faith reflecting the renewed creative powers of an imagination that was formerly without hope—the pilgrim nears the end of his imaginative journey:

> Do but observe the mode of our illumination. When I converse with a profound mind, or if at any time being alone I have good thoughts . . . I am at first apprised of my vicinity to a new and excellent region of life. By persisting to read or to think, this region gives further sign of itself, as it were in flashes of light, in sudden discoveries of its profound beauty and repose, as if the clouds that covered it parted at intervals and showed the approaching traveller the inland mountains, with the tranquil eternal meadows spread at their base. . . . But every insight from this realm of thought is felt as initial and promises a sequel. . . . I clap my hands in infantine joy and amazement before the first opening to me of this august magnificence, old with the love and homage of innumerable ages, young with the life of life, the sunbright Mecca of the desert. And what a future it opens! I feel a new heart beating with the love of the new beauty.

> I am ready to die out of nature and be born again into this new yet unapproachable America I have found in the West. (pp. 71–72)

The sudden heavenly experience the pilgrim discovers is not that static "Eastern" one of a primitive Eden regained; it is a dynamic, open experience, metaphorically Western in spirit. Reborn out of a hopeless empiricism, he is ready—at least in imagination—to enter the Celestial City in its guise as a "sun-bright Mecca" of the West. As fellow pilgrims do likewise, a spiritual community of hopeful saints will be formed, a "commonwealth of friendship and wisdom" (p. 74). It is significant that Emerson concludes this section on Reality by an extended glorification of the divinely affirmative possibilities of man's dialectical experiences. "Suffice it for the joy of the universe," he says, "that we have not arrived at a wall, but at interminable oceans. Our life seems not present so much as prospective. . . . Our greatness is always in a tendency or direction, not in an action. It is for us to believe in the rule, not in the exception" (pp. 73–74).

Once he has "experienced" exhilarating faith in the existence of a real if "unapproachable" City of God, the pilgrim can accept in good faith all the other lords of experience, however painful. Emerson shows this acceptance in his presentation of the final lord, Subjectiveness (pp. 75–80). In some ways this lord represents a spiraling back to the lord of Illusion, but now seen from the viewpoint of the saved rather than the damned imagination. Emerson reminds us of this kinship in the opening sentences of the section: "It is very unhappy, but too late to be helped, the discovery we have made that we exist. That discovery is called the Fall of Man. Ever afterwards we suspect our instruments. We have learned that we do not see directly, but mediately" (p. 75). He now introduces an element explicitly missing from the initial attitude toward Illusion. Whereas in that first section he complained that "we have no superfluity of spirit for new creation" (p. 45), he now suggests that "perhaps these subject-lenses have a creative power; perhaps there are no objects. . . . Nature, art, persons, letters, religions, objects, successively tumble in, and God is but one of its ideas. Nature and literature are subjective phenomena; every evil and every good thing is a shadow which we cast" (p. 76). Since the pilgrim has learned to believe in his salvation, this subjectivity has become not a damnable fate but a source of personal hope—an indication of the creative potential of the pilgrimage itself.

The pilgrim is able to salvage hope from the wilderness of finite experience because of his faith that God is "the native of these bleak rocks" (p. 81). Far from preventing the pilgrimage, subjectivity becomes the imagination's means of saving the possibility of pilgrimage from the pessimistic temptations of modern experience. "Saints are sad," Emerson says, "because they behold sin . . . from the point of view of the conscience, and not of the intellect. . . . The intellect names it shade, absence of light, and no essence. The conscience must feel it as essence, essential evil. This it is not; it has an objective existence, but no subjective" (p. 79). Only by believing in the divine possibilities of subjectivity can the imagination transform its solipsistic dramas into a path toward salvation: "A subject and an object—it takes so much to make the galvanic circuit complete" (p. 80).

The lords of life have accompanied the pilgrim for the full length of his journey. In doing so, they prevent him from finally attaining permanently the Celestial City. Rather, they make the pilgrim aware that "the irreconcilableness of the two spheres" of his experience, inner and outer, is the rule rather than the exception (p. 82). "I know," admits Emerson in the concluding section of the essay, "that the world I converse with in the city and in the farms, is not the world I think. I observe that difference, and shall observe it. One day I shall know the value and law of this discrepance" (pp. 84–85). His acceptance of the lords of life has come to rest on his belief that man's divine possibilities lie in his power to find imaginative pleasure in the dramas of experience, even when they pain his conscience and confuse his understanding. In doing so, he becomes in at least an inner sense the ruler rather than the pawn of his lords. "All I know is reception; I am and I have. . . . I worship with wonder the great Fortune. My reception has been so large, that I am not annoyed by receiving this or that superabundantly. I say to the Genius, if he will pardon the proverb, *In for a mill, in for a million* (pp. 83–84). If Emerson's experience remains, like *Pilgrim's Progress*, a "dream," it has become at least a hopeful dream: "far be from me the despair which prejudges the law by a paltry empiricism; since there never was a right endeavor but it succeeded. Patience and patience, we shall win at the last" (p. 85). The pilgrim Emerson finds ultimately that he must judge experience qualitatively rather than quantitatively; one experience of the divine, however fleeting, becomes a balance for a million ordinary experiences. In the subjective "solitude to which every man is always returning," the fallen, time-bound pilgrim finds a "sanity and revelations which in his passage into new worlds he will carry with him" (p. 85). Only because of these fragmentary glimpses of the City of God can an Emerson caught in the City of Man shore up his courage enough to conclude hopefully: "Never mind the ridicule, never mind the defeat; up again, old heart . . . there is victory yet for all justice; and the true romance which the world exists to realize will be the transformation of genius into practical power" (pp. 85–86).

Emerson could never find a full measure of this practical power. By the 1860s, as the firmament of his own life and thought began to shrink to a tent, his personal striving after a Celestial City reduced itself to a hope for better Boston clubs. If one could only "find at No. 2000 Tremont Street what scholars were abroad after the morning studies were ended," he said in a late essay, "Boston would shine as the New Jerusalem in his eyes" (*W*, 7, 244). But such concessions to increasing age and experience do not mar the importance of his earlier experimentation with the elements of the Christian drama. A partly liberated son of New England Puritanism and a preacher turned Transcendental poet, Emerson found this drama a useful tool for expressing his own brand of Romantic prophecy. By liberating the Christian's Celestial City—and hence the entire Christian pilgrimage—from its specifically theological context, he and his contemporary writers were able to keep alive a traditionally powerful series of metaphors as strategic literary implements—ones that not only could criticize earth-bound man for his failings but could challenge him hopefully to continue to direct his life toward an elusive and ultimately ineffable vision of the ideal.

4. The City of Man

We came out to Europe to learn what man can,—what is the uttermost which social man has yet done. (JMN, 4, 74)

Then the Friar Bernard went home swiftly with other thoughts than he brought, saying, "This way of life is wrong, yet these Romans, whom I prayed God to destroy, are lovers, they are lovers; what can I do?" (W, 1, 316)

I seem to have been driven away from Rome by unseen Angel with sword or whip for nothing would have served me so well & dearly as Rome. (L, 4, 461)

If Emerson's prophetic stance led him to measure actual civilization by comparing it, in a redacted Christian drama, to a figurative and Romantically oriented City of God—to a vision of ideal truth, goodness, and beauty—his stance as historian led him more characteristically to measure contemporary society by comparing it dramatically to what the City of Man—a metaphor for all human history, both urban and nonurban—had been in the past and what it actually could or probably would be in the future. The two points of view merged momentarily during Emerson's period of Transcendental radicalism, when his personal brand of apocalyptic hopes, feeding on the rising revivalistic fervor of his era, proclaimed that the imperfect American society of the 1830s might, through individual regeneration of its members, become an earthly New Jerusalem. The clouds of natural, social, and psychological experience rapidly obscured this vision of perfectibility, however, and Emerson had to struggle as best he could for the remainder of his life with an admission that the City of Man, except for brief flashes in the imaginations of individual men of faith, might never be more than a makeshift, provincial outpost of the City of God. Dreaming in the 1830s of an eternal City beyond time or at least unaffected by time, he was forced by experience to give much of his intellectual labor to men participating in, bound by, and subject to history.

We do an injustice to Emerson's thought, however, if we treat his admission of the human (as distinct from the eternal) significance of the City of Man as primarily an admission of the defeat of his Romantic dreams of transcendental glory. To do so is to neglect the continuity of his thought as it developed out of his early education during the first quarter of the nineteenth century. Whatever impact Transcendental Romanticism had on Emerson's view of the City of Man in history, it did not uproot an equally fundamental way of looking at that City—a perspective derived from the metaphors and dramatics of classical literature.

The strength of the classical tradition in America at the beginning of the nineteenth century is a phenomenon increasingly well documented. The Greek and Roman classics (often in English translations) had constituted a major element in the education and libraries of America's eighteenth-century leaders, and the same was certainly true of Emerson and his contemporaries. In addition, after the first part of the eighteenth century the writings of European neoclassicists and English Augustans had begun to circulate widely in America, not only as books but in newspapers and periodicals. If the assigned reading of Emerson's college days included few of the neoclassicists, such writers were nevertheless considered essential extracurricular matter. His reading of Greek and Roman literature decreased somewhat after the 1820s, with the exception of Plutarch and a few other favorites, but he kept in touch with the metaphors and themes of this literature through his lifelong reading in the neoclassicists.[1]

Detailed familiarity with classical literature, of course, was not as broadly based in the American population as was active acquaintance with the Bible. At its more restricted levels, neoclassical and classical art and literature functioned in the America of Emerson's youth as the proper education of a gentleman, as matter for polite conversation, and as the best means of imitating the fashions of London and the Continent. In its more generalized manifestations, however, the classical tradition—at least as cultural metaphor if not as literature—found a broader and potentially more dynamic application to America. A wedge for using classical rhetoric for political aims had been formed by Puritans themselves, as they began to replace biblical metaphors with classical metaphors in order to justify their enterprise. The pedantic and vacillating Cotton Mather could call Harvard by the biblical name Kirjath-Sepher, the City of Books, and in the same breath call the college's president, Charles Chauncy, "the American Cadmus."[2] By the middle of the eighteenth century, some American liberals, while rejecting the Calvinists' New Jerusalem, found a back door to the heavenly City and accepted its major components of height, light, and order under a new Roman name in their own vision of American society. Charles San-

1. See Rusk's introduction to the *Letters*, *1*, xxxi–xxxii. Much of Emerson's classical reading is indicated in Edmund G. Berry, *Emerson's Plutarch* (Cambridge, Mass., 1961).

2. Quoted in George H. Williams, *Wilderness and Paradise in Biblical Thought* (New York, 1962), p. 144.

ford has even suggested that Benjamin Franklin's autobiography can be read as a secularized *Pilgrim's Progress*, with Philadelphia as a neoclassic City on a Hill.[3]

By the end of the eighteenth century, American culture on both the popular and educated levels was looking to the classical tradition to justify and dramatize the nationalistic and idealistic aspirations of a new republic. If American society in its drawing-room tendencies turned to Petrarchan lyrics, neoclassical pastorals, and the social commentaries of both the Roman and English Augustans, it turned in its nationalistic tendencies to classical and neoclassical epic, history, political theory, and public architecture. From the term "Senate" to the designs that Jefferson proposed for the capitol of Washington came encouragement to America to think of itself as a New Rome—not the Rome of Catholicism, despotism, and corruption, but a freshly emerging empire, full of both Athenian culture and Roman vigor, simplicity and grandeur, grace and justice, artistic achievement and economic expansion. The American adaptation of the classical urban metaphors is closely related to America's conception of its own historical movement. This adaptation can be traced as it moved up the developing Hudson River, giving rhetorical status to the towns of Troy, Rome, Athens, and Syracuse, and as it carried such names across the Appalachians into literally every state admitted to the Union after 1800. Cincinnati and Lexington were highly representative in their rival claims to the title of "Athens of the West." The original states had already named most of their major towns before the surge of neoclassicism, but they also indulged in dreams of a Westernized version of classical grandeur. The title of Athens was ap-

3. Charles L. Sanford, *The Quest for Paradise: Europe and the American Moral Imagination* (Urbana, Ill., 1961), pp. 123–25.

plied before the end of the eighteenth century to Boston, Philadelphia, and Charleston, and New York mounted a heady campaign to gain recognition as the major American Rome.[4]

Henry Nash Smith has indicated convincingly that in the nineteenth century another dream grew up beside the dream of Rome and the "westward course of empire." He argues that while the nation's empire builders were treating the American continent primarily as a "passage to India," other thinkers were asserting that America's own internal development was to be primarily that of a "garden."[5] Many of Smith's own citations, however, show implicitly that even the dream of a New Rome, for all its imperialistic manifestations, looked primarily not toward expansion of the American nation beyond its Pacific terminus but toward internal development of its own continental resources. In nineteenth-century popular thought, the dreams of an urban empire and an agrarian nation—of a Rome and Arcadia—developed side by side in a neoclassical version of the thesis of the City of the West. Relatively few Americans sensed any major conflict between these two visions, any more than they sensed the many ambiguities within each vision itself. To most Americans, the image of a New Rome referred to both the total continental empire and to the growing urban capitals of that empire. Rhetorically as well as historically, the Capital and

4. Walter R. Agard, "Classics on the Midwest Frontier," *Classical Journal*, 51 (1951), 103–04, lists popular classical names for Midwestern towns; a scanning of the index of any detailed atlas of the United States will reveal the same phenomenon in every state. See also George R. Stewart, *Names on the Land: A Historical Account of Place-Naming in the United States* (Cambridge, Mass., 1958).

5. Henry Nash Smith, *Virgin Land: The American West as Symbol and Myth* (Cambridge, Mass., 1950), esp. Chaps. 1, 2, and 11.

the Continent were to reinforce each other. Emerson was participating in a national sentiment when he wrote in 1822 that

> there is everything in America's favour, to one who puts faith in these proverbial prophecies of the Westward progress of the Car of Empire. . . . Aloof from the contagion during the long progress of [other nations'] decline America hath ample interval to lay deep & solid foundations for the greatness of the New World. . . . Here the new Romes are growing. (*JMN*, 2, 72)[6]

As Emerson's comment implies, the dream of actualizing a New Rome was evident in more than the pamphlets of shrewd speculators or the rhetoric of enthusiastic boosters of individual cities. It captured the imaginations of American writers who were searching for a national literature. The dream had been implicit as early as the Virgilian opening to Cotton Mather's *Magnalia*, and by the end of the century Phillip Freneau, Joel Barlow, and many others had painted in imitative verse a splashy vision of a rising American Empire that would be both holy and, in the best sense, Roman. Although Washington Irving, in his *Knickerbocker History of New York*, satirized good-naturedly the epic pretensions of both his native city and his nation (drawing heavily on classical allusion and literary precedents in order to do so), his *Astoria* and biography of George Washington showed him re-

6. Emerson concluded a poem on "East and West," written in 1822, with the following quatrain:

> And to the West shall Empire come
> Amid our mountains, stall his steeds.
> Here Glory find his final home
> And Grandeur write immortal deeds. (*JMN*, 1, 352)

sponding as well to the dream of empire. The classical dream, even if in widely varying forms, was one to which America's artists were as committed as its politicians.[7]

Widespread application of classical metaphors to American culture created problems for the serious artist similar to those involved in the popular use of the Christian urban drama. In the course of popular redaction, for example, diverse and even disparate elements of the classical world were lumped indiscriminately together. Namers of new towns often seemed unaware of any functional differences among the actual ancient capitals from which they drew their appellations; it was enough that such capitals connoted Romantic grandeur and high culture. If adoption of classical metaphor in prerevolutionary America had indicated basically the imitation by a province of the styles current in its European metropolis, nineteenth-century usage of both Hellenistic and Roman figures sprang in addition from a vaguely Romantic impulse.[8]

Popular Romantics in America did not really protest against neoclassical precepts, as had many European Ro-

7. Interesting comments on American writers' imitation and adaptation of classical metaphors can be found in Spencer, *The Quest for Nationality,* esp. pp. 17–24. Relevant aspects of Freneau, Barlow, and other early nationalistic poets are discussed in Leon Howard, *The Connecticut Wits* (Chicago, 1943).

8. Talbot F. Hamlin, *Greek Revival Architecture in America* (London, 1944), argues persuasively that the best American architecture of the early nineteenth century was able to combine a desire for "grandeur" and national expansion, symbolized by a Roman style, with a desire for simplicity, purity, and "democratic" ideals, symbolized by a Grecian style. From this combination, Hamlin believes, Americans were able to achieve a happy and unique "national" style. He also notes, however, that when such an emerging eclecticism was carried to extremes, especially in the matter of external detail, it hurt more than aided the development of American architecture. Much the same might be said of American literature during that period.

mantics, but rather grafted various Romantic modes of literature and architecture *onto* that neoclassicism.[9] Such grafting was symbolized by Thomas Coles' painting, "The Artist's Dream," with its mixture of Grecian, Roman, Egyptian, and Gothic styles. But eclectic redaction of classical metaphors and conventions in popular usage created a serious artistic problem. If eclecticism offered the American writer potential "liberation" from bondage to the English Augustan variety of literary neoclassicism, it also produced the dangers of potentially chaotic symbols and rhetorical terms that might be used for ignoble as well as noble purposes.[10] Because of gen-

9. Howard Mumford Jones, in *Ideas in America* (Cambridge, Mass., 1944), pp. 122–23, argues that whereas European Romantics revolted against a decadent classicism, American Romantics associated American classicism with the American Revolution and therefore treated it as a liberating tradition. See also Robert E. Spiller, "Critical Standards in the American Romantic Movement," *College English, 8* (1947), 344–52.

10. Emerson himself at times could redefine such terms strategically. In 1842 he argued that "this much agitated question of the Classic and Romantic" was "not a question of times, nor of forms, but of methods"; he asserted that "the Classic is creative and the Romantic is aggregative; that the Greek in the Christian Germany would have built a Cathedral; and that the Romantic in our time builds a Parthenon Custom House" (*J*, 6, 231–32). Note Melville's similar satirization of American Philhellenism in *Redburn* (*Works*, 5, 190–91). Hawthorne, however, suggested that America's use of classical rather than Gothic forms was based on literary as well as materialistic considerations. Standing in the Forum of Rome, the narrator of *The Marble Faun* feels that

> the events of Roman history, and Roman life itself, appear not so distant as the Gothic ages which succeeded them. . . . If we remember these medieval times, they look further off than the Augustan age. The reason may be, that the old Roman literature survives, and creates for us an intimacy with the classic ages, which we have no means of forming with the subsequent ones. (*Works*, 6, 194–95)

eral popular acceptance of vaguely defined classical metaphors, an American writer or orator might apply ingenuously to a respectable American institution a classical figure whose traditional content made other Americans feel it unworthy of the new application. Arguing against imposition of the metaphor of Rome onto American civilization, Thoreau could assert that "New England, at least, is not based on any Roman ruins."[11] On the other hand, American rhetoricians might borrow a truly noble figure from the classical past to praise or justify a contemporary institution that other Americans felt of little worth. Abolitionists became aware of this danger by the 1850s when they heard George Fitzhugh and other Southerners justify slavery as Athenian. Both the applications and the protests, however, indicated the ambiguity of such metaphors as they were inherited by nineteenth-century American literature.

The ambiguities of classical urban metaphors were not merely products of indiscriminate modern usage. They were an inherent part of the classical tradition itself. For one thing, no unqualifiedly ideal term existed in the classical tradition. In the Christian urban drama, the City of God stood at the unquestioned center of ultimate value, but classical literature's major metropolis, Rome, was generally accepted, for all its glory, as an imperfect City of Man. If some of its European adherents had attempted to picture Rome as approaching the status of a New Jerusalem, other European writers had found in its shadows the hue of Dis. Augustine himself, for all his love of what was to become in nineteenth-century travel guides the "Eternal City," set down a more negative pattern of interpretation—that of Rome as the major earthly symbol of Cain's City, founded on murder (Romulus' slaying of Remus), ruled

11. Thoreau, *Journals*, 4, 276.

by oppressive force, and doomed to destruction.[12] Such a double perspective on Rome intrigued Europe for centuries after the fall of the actual Empire, and it proved equally fascinating to American artists of Emerson's day growing up on Virgil, Gibbon, and *Childe Harold.* Rome's double destiny—its rise and fall, its heavenly pretensions and hellish connections—made it the central dramatic problem of classical literature.

The central city in the classical drama was involved in another ambiguity to which the City of God was not subject—that produced by time. Rome was subject to history and thus to change. Therefore, there existed not "one Rome" in classical and neoclassical literature, but many. As Emerson himself noted in a sermon in 1829,

> That which bears the same name and stands in the same place is not always the same thing. There has been a large town in Italy called Rome for now near twenty-five hundred years but it could only be a child that [would] think and speak alike of the Etrurian village and the city of the consuls and the city of the emperors and the city of the barbarians and the city of the Popes and the city of artists. (Y, 54)

Hawthorne made much the same point in *The Marble Faun,* as he described the "threefold antiquity" of Rome. His admission that "we know not how to characterize, in any accordant and compatible terms, the Rome that lies before us" pointed to the artistic difficulties inherent in interpreting a phenomenon whose very involvement in time made it a symbol of ambiguity.[13]

Because of the ambiguities of the terms involved in the

12. Augustine, *City of God,* Bk. 15, Pt. 5.
13. Hawthorne, *Works,* 6, 19–20, 135.

classical tradition, the various dramatic dialogues in which Rome participated (with a pastoral ideal, with a mythic past, with a barbaric threat, etc.) did not tend as easily toward the melodramatic as did the dramatics of the Christian tradition. Rather, the elements of the Roman dialogues tended to modify each other—to move less often toward polarization than toward ironic tension and internal complexity. Though the metaphors of the central Christian drama could allow Emerson and his contemporaries to hint at a Transcendental Ideal, the metaphors of the drama of Rome might allow, by their very ambiguity, a more subtle interpretation of the City of Man. The "problem of Rome," Emerson realized, was a problem not only of the classical world but of the modern world. In interpreting America and the City of the West as a new manifestation of the City of Man, he and his contemporary American writers faced both a historical and an artistic problem. Involved was not only the course of American development, but the relevance of classical metaphor to that development. As in his use of the Christian urban drama, Emerson needed to test not only his modern world by means of classical metaphors—an exercise for which many precedents existed in the neoclassical literature of Europe—but also the adequacy of these metaphors to interpret and guide the modern world. Analyzing the New Romes of history, he was led inevitably to discuss the place of the New Romes in literary art.

As numerous scholars have noted, Emerson inherited the eighteenth-century debate between the theories of cyclical history and progressive history. These theories form the two basic dramatic structures for his attitude toward classical civilization and its successors. His early journals show him attempting continually to make sense of America's own development in the light of both poles of the debate and, at the same time, to discover if American history might cast any light on the validity of either theory. "We judge of the value of every portion of history," he wrote in 1822 at the age of nineteen, "by its usefulness in application to our own and other times. Can we learn from the greatness, or the disasters it recounts, how to mould our own governments, in order to ensure the benefits and avoid the faults of the nation we see? —then history is valuable" (*JMN*, *1*, 82–83).

Raised on a strong dose of Gibbon,[14] young Emerson often found the lessons of the past symbolized most conveniently in the rise and fall of Rome. "I am answerable," he said in 1826, "for whatever wisdom I can glean from the wisdom of Rome; for whatever counsel I can extract from the death of so many heroes & the decline of so many nations" (*JMN*, 3, 22). The lesson taught by Rome often seemed too dark for Emerson's comfort (*JMN*, 2, 164), since it implied that man's movement through time was governed by a series of vicious historical cycles. As he read Gibbon's recounting of Italy after the fall of the Empire, he was depressed by the impression that "each year is a disastrous repetition of tyranny, revolu-

14. Philip L. Nicoloff's argument in *Emerson on Race and History* (New York, 1961), p. 93, that eighteenth-century historians had almost no effect on Emerson's historical theories must be qualified; Nicoloff, like others, places too much emphasis on the classical sources of Emerson's attitudes toward history and Rome. Gibbon, Emerson once argued, "will carry the reader through 1400 years of time. He cannot spare Gibbon . . . though never profound, his book is one of the conveniences of civilization, like the new railroad from ocean to ocean" (*W*, 7, 205). This "connecting" quality of Gibbon is also emphasized in Emerson's journal for 1833: "Splendid bridge from the new world to the old built by Gibbon" (*JMN*, 4, 221). He was intensely interested in making his own historical commentaries serve this bridging function—to provide a relevant lesson for the modern world.

tion, & bloodshed, until the eye is lost in the hopeless confusion wherein nothing predominates but the names of War, Faction, Misery" (*JMN*, *1*, 83). If, as he argued in 1822, "new Romes" were growing in America "& the Genius of man is brooding over the wide boundaries of infant empires," a cyclical view of the historical drama demanded that in America also "are to be played over again the bloody games of human ambition, bigotry, & revenge & the stupendous Drama of the passions to be repeated" (*JMN*, 2, 72). Though young Emerson was not entirely happy with such a conclusion, he was fascinated with the tragic drama.[15]

In the face of the dark lessons contained in the fall of Rome, young Emerson showed his liberal inheritance in a continuing and intense wish to find in American development an opportunity to break out of the cyclical patterns of the past —to draw an upwardly progressive tangent to the more characteristic, self-defeating cycles of civilized history.[16] Whether he rationalized the duality of historical movement in terms of the "principle of Contrast" (*JMN*, *1*, 60) or in terms of his later belief in "compensation," he was continually searching for ways to mitigate the cyclical doctrine's application to the

15. In 1826 Emerson noted, "Few things need more philosophy than the study of history. For it is not easy or safe to look long on these turning wheels, lest we grow giddy" (*J*, 2, 127). Compare Cooper's cyclical attitude toward history; in *Excursions in Italy* he argues that "the prosperity that is founded on violence contains the principle of its own destruction" (2, 289). See Jones, *O Strange New World*, Chap. 10, and Perry Miller, *Errand into the Wilderness* (Cambridge, Mass., 1956), Chap. 10.

16. In *The House of the Seven Gables*, Clifford expresses a variation on this progressive hope: "All human progress is in a circle; or to use a more accurate and beautiful figure, in an ascending spiral curve. . . . The past is but a course and sensual prophecy of the present and the future" (Hawthorne, *Works*, 3, 308).

future of America. At the very least, he attempted to soften the doctrine by stressing the creative aspects of the historical cycle. Calling Rome a "fabled Phoenix" (*JMN*, *1*, 236), he could argue that, if Time "demolished Rome," it also saw to it that "from the ruins of Rome many nations rose" (*JMN*, *1*, 243). At his most optimistic, young Emerson believed that out of the very processes of cyclical history would emerge forces that would make cyclical history itself no longer inevitable. Using a metaphor almost religious in implication, he expressed hope, after reading Gibbon, that "the sufferings of Florence, of Pisa, of Genoa, and of Rome may prevent the necessity of the after repetition of similar suffering, and the bloody sacrifice once made, may be made for the world" (*JMN*, *1*, 84). As a young historian looking at the moral lesson presented by Rome, he followed many of his generation in urging that man's free will was the primary determining factor in the rising and falling of civilization. The young American nation's historical perspective made it "answerable for whatever wisdom" it could gain from the past—answerable because it was a "free" nation. Its very perspective on the past was a tool of freedom that made America an "experiment which begins with infinite advantages" (*JMN*, 2, 76–77). By bringing intellectual order out of the seeming chaos and confusion of the previous Romes of history, the American historian was giving his nation a fighting chance. By means of the lessons he recorded, Americans might erect a New Rome that would not fall.

Young Emerson's attitudes toward Rome as a moral lesson, however, were not always identical to his attitudes toward Rome as a subject for art. There existed in him a tendency toward a Byronic melancholy—toward that Weltschmertz felt by so many young Romantic artists of the early nineteenth century. This tendency expressed itself not only in the self-consciously dramatic qualities of Emerson's introspective writing but in the external subjects with which he chose to deal. If the moralist in him protested against the necessity of applying a cyclical pattern to American development, the latent Romantic poet in him found the downward slope of the cycle a temptingly fascinating subject for contemplation. The history of virtue, he asserted in 1822, was "less interesting" than the history of vice. If the darker side of the past "leaves a melancholy impression on the mind," he argued, "the mere succession of imposing images produces a pleasure which counter-balances the disagreeable effect of the facts themselves" (*JMN*, 2, 90). Though the study and portrayal of the darker aspects of man's development gave much "moral pain," they also gave undeniable "intellectual pleasure" (*JMN*, 2, 178–79). The pain was the price the moral artist knew he must pay for remaining true to his artistic desire to portray the imperfect City of Man.

That young Emerson was sometimes willing to pay the price was indicated as early as 1821, when he noted in his journal that "Destruction of a city" might make a fine subject for a poem (*JMN*, 1, 55). Using Rome as a suitable subject, he actually experimented with this theme in several early poems. His early journals also contained dozens of prose passages that dwelled with melancholy pleasure over the drama of risings and fallings in past empires and cities.[17] Though

17. In 1820 Emerson wrote a long poem dealing melodramatically with the decline of the Roman Empire (*JMN*, 1, 235–42), and in 1822 he wrote three stanzas on the "Fall of the Senate" (*JMN*, 1, 136). His early poem "The Grave," which obviously imitates Bryant's "Thanatopsis," begins: "Can thy gates shut, Oh City of the Dead!" (*JMN*, 1, 72–73). For examples of his early prose comments on the dramatic decline of empire, see *JMN*, 1, 6, 15, 111–12; *JMN*, 2, 105; and Y, 112.

his temperament would not allow him to explore the dark shadows of history as deeply as did Hawthorne or Melville, he nevertheless continued to admit that such shadows were not only morally enlightening but even aesthetically desirable. In 1837, at the height of his Transcendental assertiveness, he watched the economic depression that raged around him with the eye not only of a moral prophet but of a poet: "The black times have a great scientific value. It is an epoch so critical a philosopher would not miss. As I would willingly carry myself to be played on at Faneuil Hall by the stormy winds & strong fingers of the enraged Boston so is this era more rich in the central tones than many languid centuries" (*JMN*, 5, 332–33).

A related observation, however, was written fifteen years earlier on July 3 as Emerson contemplated the fact that "to-morrow is the birthday of our pride." The observation indicated that a further problem was involved in the relationship of historical development and artistic expression:

> Will it not be dreadful to discover that this experiment made by America, to ascertain if men can govern themselves—does not succeed? that too much knowledge, & too much liberty makes them mad. Still we ourselves shall have the melancholy consolation of that magnanimous proverb—"the world will last our day," & also, in that prophetic glory familiar to your countrymen, we will seek to believe that its corruption & decay shall be splendid with literature & the arts, to the latest time—splendid as the late day of Athens & Rome. (*L*, 1, 121)[18]

18. Cf. Hawthorne's remark in *The Marble Faun* that "there is reason to suspect that a people are waning to decay and ruin the moment that their life becomes fascinating either in the poet's imagination or the painter's eye" (*W*, 6, 340–41).

Implied, perhaps unconsciously, was a crucial connection between art and decay. Part of this connection had been drawn, of course, by an entire generation of hunters for the picturesque, who felt that art and artful history might evoke the color of a destructively immoral civilization even while condemning that civilization. Emerson's statement probed potentially deeper, however—not only into the aesthetic and moral reactions of the nineteenth-century observer of such history, but into the very mainsprings of the past. What, for example, was the historical source of artistic creativity? Did the ability to create great art arise out of the moral progress of civilization, or did it spring from the very "seeds of decay" that had created the downward movements in civilization's cyclical development? "In old cities of old nations," Emerson reflected in 1822, "the importunity of temptation becomes tremendous. Virtue grows cold & solitary while vice solicits with the syren [sic] voice of taste, & literature, of fashion, & genius" (*JMN*, *I*, 155). If Emerson fervently wished to enlist history in the cause of morality, he also wished to see art committed to the same cause. His early reading in Gibbon and others was thus a harsh education, for it showed him that such connections were more easily hoped for than actually found in the past record of mankind. If America were to progress morally and materially and artistically, it would have to learn the "lesson of Rome" radically better than had any other nation in human history. As young Emerson grew toward Transcendental manhood, he became increasingly aware that in his roles of prophet and poet he must learn and teach that lesson to his fellow Americans.

Emerson's youthful formulation of such problems formed an intellectual and literary background against which he placed actual experience when he visited Europe in 1833.

Having just passed through what Whicher has called his "first crisis"—a crisis in which universal decay had seemed personified in the death of his wife Ellen and in which received opinions such as those contained in Unitarian dogma became unsatisfactory answers to his increasingly insistent questions—he was ready to find new ground on which to explore the problems of history and art, and his European trip made such new ground available. But we must not consider only what he found in Europe; we must remember also the intellectual baggage he took on his trip. If many of his earlier opinions were modified by contact with the actual Europe, the actuality was also interpreted through the medium of these opinions. The traveler Emerson's initial interpretation of the problem of Rome was a literary one, based on his earlier reading of poetry, history, and philosophy.

The literary education that formed Emerson's preconceptions of Europe was perhaps the most important element shared by nearly all Americans who traveled to Europe before the middle of the nineteenth century. Whether Americans went abroad to toy casually with the pleasures of the "picturesque" associations of a decaying past, or whether they traveled for more serious and creative reasons, the books they had read before leaving America influenced their view of Europe. As Cooper suggested, "the American who goes to Europe finds his great pleasure, at first, in hunting up the memorials of the past . . . and is burning with the desire to gaze at objects of which he has often read."[19] Hundreds of ordinary American tourists, raised on the standards of taste proclaimed by Gilpin and others, searched *Childe Harold* and John Murray's *Handbooks for Travellers* uncritically for guides as to what was picturesque and what was not, dredging out of

19. Cooper, *Gleanings in France*, p. 57.

themselves responses of melancholy and sublime elation suggested as appropriate by these handbooks.[20]

A minority of more critically minded compatriots, however, felt compelled not only to test Europe by means of its image in conventional and more sophisticated literature, but to test that literature in terms of their own European experience. In fact, one of the major subjects of the best American writing on Europe was the disparity between the book on Europe and the actual experience of Europe. As Cooper faithfully juxtaposed his guidebooks' descriptions of Europe as "sublime," "pittoresque," and "beau" against what he himself observed, he became increasingly disgusted by the conventional rhetoric of these books. He wished to make independent, not derivative, judgments. Hawthorne complained that, in England, "every point of beauty is so well known, and has been described so much, that one must need look through other peoples' eyes; and feels as if he were looking at a picture rather than a reality." Melville, in *Redburn,* devoted a long section to exploring the inadequacies of his hero's guidebook to Liverpool in the face of Redburn's actual experience of the modern city.[21] Redburn's final advice to himself, "hereafter follow your nose through Liverpool," was advice that

20. In 1836 Emerson called the Fourth Canto of *Childe Harold* "the best guidebook to the traveller who visits Venice, Florence, and Rome" (*EL,* 1, 374). While in Rome in 1833 he had asserted that "Italy is Byron's debtor, and I think no one knows how fine a poet he is who has not seen the subjects of his verse" (*JMN,* 4, 165).

21. Cooper, *Excursions in Switzerland,* 1, 35, and *Excursions in Italy,* 1, 288–89, and passim; Hawthorne, *English Notebooks,* p. 156; Melville, *Works,* 5, Chaps. 27–41. William H. Gilman, in *Melville's Early Life and "Redburn"* (New York, 1951), argues on p. 187 and elsewhere that the inadequacy of Redburn's guidebook indicates Melville's belief that the past was inadequate as an interpreter of present experience.

made sense to Emerson and others of Melville's contemporaries. If their initial literary experiences had wrapped a "romantic haze" around European antiquity, their personal observations of Europe suggested a reality more complex, more dangerous, and more stimulating than any sublime or merely picturesque spectacle. Like the experiences of Hawthorne and Melville, Emerson's confrontation of the actual Rome modified and enriched his understanding of what that city "meant" in the context of history and art. It also allowed him to consider the precise nature of the literature that had interpreted Rome to him. By exploring the problem of Rome as a concrete historical phenomenon, he found himself also exploring what it meant to be a poet.[22]

Emerson's reading in Gibbon, Byron, and others had prepared him to find an interesting spectacle of a decayed Rome —a decay all the more poignant because of the heights from which he believed Rome had fallen. In 1820 he had expressed a rather romanticized conception of such heights:

> If power could make men happy the ancient great Roman citizens ought to have been the happiest of subjects. . . . Oh it was worth their factions & their fears to live in that agony of high excitement, those tremendous strivings for power, enjoying the more than mortal grandeur of Roman glory! Since those mighty times there has been no man of whom it might be said that he stood forth like a Consul of Rome as proud as all earth's crowded honours could render a man! (*JMN*, *I*, 20–21)

22. A provocative essay by Anthony Winner, "Adjustment, Tragic Humanism and Italy," *Studi Americani*, 7 (1961), 322, suggests that "the American dream of Italy merely projects against a foreign background images of fear and hope which serve to suggest the dreamer's private necessity."

In 1833, with perhaps a more sophisticated conception of a Roman glory now lost, Emerson traveled to Italy with a double purpose. On one hand, he was prepared to read in a decayed Rome the moral lesson that he believed history taught, but he was also looking for the aesthetic implications of such decayed grandeur. His treatment of Syracuse in his journals is a good example of his double purpose. From a moral standpoint, the city seemed to him an apt illustration "of great things turned to vile uses" (*JMN*, 4, 124). But describe such "vile uses" as he might—women washing in the city's famous public fountain, the innumerable beggars, the magnificent aqueduct now turning a small grist mill—the general tone of his descriptions indicated a predisposition for the picturesque quality of such melancholy scenes. Syracuse was, from first view, "a beautiful sad sight," an epitome of "sad solitude" (*JMN*, 4, 123, 131). "Still, melancholy, old metropolis!" he wrote near the end of his three-day visit in the city; "under the moon, last eve, how wan & grey it looked" (*JMN*, 4, 126).

Emerson moved on to Naples with the same double interest. Although he asserted "I won't be imposed upon by a name" and proclaimed his "simple human rights of seeing & of judging" Naples and the rest of Italy for himself (*JMN*, 4, 141), his judgments of that city exhibited a fairly traditional emphasis on decayed grandeur and the picturesque. As at Syracuse, he moaned that "the effect of every Antiquity" in Naples was "spoiled by the contrast of ridiculous or pitiful circumstances" (*JMN*, 4, 142). Naples' antiquities were "to what base uses turned" (*JMN*, 4, 146). More characteristic of his tone, however, was his melancholy description of "the woes of this great city" (*JMN*, 4, 145). One of Emerson's major objections to Naples seemed to be not so much its melancholy effects as its physical discomforts—his loneliness and coldness there, his gloomy hotel rooms, and the lack of good coffee. He wished to indulge in sentimental melancholy from an aloof aesthetic distance, and the reality of Naples in 1833 provided too many distractions (*L*, *1*, 370). It was in the context of such a complaint that he wrote his brother, "I go to see old Rome, not new" (*L*, *1*, 368).

Emerson thus clearly intended to examine the aesthetic aspect of old Rome as well as its moral lessons. Arriving during the pre-Easter festivities and remaining until most other Easter tourists had departed, he reveled in a Rome whose artistic and architectural glory could now show itself only in a context where "all is ruinous" (*JMN*, *4*, 160). On April 13 he observed, "It is a graceful termination to so much glory that Rome now in her fallen state should be the metropolis of the arts" (*JMN*, *4*, 159). Rome displayed not only that curious combination of decay and beauty which intrigued the early nineteenth century, but also the problem that such beauty seemed to have emerged from and almost because of the decay. The lessons of politics, empire, and immorality sometimes assumed secondary importance as Emerson contemplated Rome's position as a storehouse for all the art of a cyclical past (*JMN*, *4*, 158). One could wander through the Vatican, he felt, "till the eye was dazzled & glutted with this triumph of the arts." To his journal he confided:

> Go & see it, whoever you are. It is the wealth of the civilized world. It is a contribution from all ages & nations of what is more rich & rare. He who has not seen it does not know what beautiful stones there are in the planet, & much less what exquisite art has accomplished on their

> hard sides for Greek & Roman luxury. . . . It is vain to refuse to admire. You must in spite of yourself. It is magnificent. (*JMN*, *4*, 150)[23]

What could be said of the Vatican could be said of Rome as a whole. At night the city was a unique and overwhelming aesthetic experience: "how faery beautiful! An Arabian Nights' tale" (*JMN*, *4*, 156). If Rome was a lesson in the consequences of immorality, it was also an important education in the creation and contemplation of art—an object not only for the ethical mind but for the Romantic imagination. To Emerson Rome was a "very good & instructive" city, where he could "grow wiser by the day, & by the hour."

> Here are the manifest footprints of the nations & the ages. Here is the town of centuries, the capital of the ancient & of the modern world. All is large, magnificent, secular, & the treasury of the arts is evidently the contribution of the whole civilized world. . . . It is a grand town, & works mightily upon the senses & upon the soul. It fashions my dreams even, & all night I visit Vaticans. . . . I lie down at night enriched by the contemplation of great objects. . . . Ah great great Rome! it is a majestic city, & satisfies this craving imagination. (*L*, *1*, 372–74)

Despite his "stubborn faith that the elements of man's intellectual & moral life abound everywhere for all" and that "a man may be trained in a barnyard who shall measure with Scipio," Emerson felt obliged to admit to his brother that "the idea of Rome nothing else but Rome can supply" (*L*, *1*, 379). Though he might bemoan the negative aspects of civilized

23. See Cooper's ecstatic entrance to Rome in *Excursions in Italy*, 2, 76–84.

history that he felt Rome epitomized, he could never escape the belief that such negative aspects had contributed both to the creation of a city of beautiful forms and to the city's possibilities as a metaphor for noble beauty.

In the years following his visit to Rome, the Emerson who contended that "traveling is a fool's paradise" and that "there is no history, only biography" seemed at times to feel guilty for admitting that he still admired his Roman experiences and still was fascinated by "the idea of Rome." "In my weak hours," he wrote in 1838, "I look fondly to Europe and think how glady I would live in Florence and Rome. In my manly hours, I defy these leanings, these lingering looks *behind,* these flesh-pots of Egypt, and feel that my duty is my place and that the merrymen of circumstance should follow as they might" (*J*, 5, 100–01). The very fervor of the protest against Rome and Europe indicated the strong hold of the objects of protest on Emerson's sensibilities; it pointed up a tension often arising in his thought between the concept of moral "duty" and the vision of aesthetic beauty. Two decades after his first trip to Europe he wrote to a friend, "How gladly I would help you see London, which you like not alone! How gladly go to Paris & to Rome[.] I seem to have been driven away from Rome by unseen Angel with sword or whip for nothing would have served me so well & dearly as Rome" (*L*, 4, 461).

Equally bittersweet was Emerson's letter to the traveling Margaret Fuller, written from Concord in 1847. After complaining about the sterility and blindness of American culture, he turned his thoughts to Margaret's own experiences:

> And now Rome is keeping its old promise to your eyes & mind, Rome which has always kept its promise, & which

> *like Nature* has that elasticity of application to all measures of spirit. These millennial cities in their immense accumulations of human works find it easy to impress the imagination by gradually dropping one piece after another of whim blunder & absurdity,—hay stubble & bladders,—until nothing but necessity and geometry remains. But is not life too short & the history of Rome too long, than that an American should hurry through its streets & ways, & never open Plutarch or Livy, much less Horace or Cicero? Ah must we walk proudly too in Rome, & say, But we are Americans & have no Roman affairs? (*L*, 3, 400–01; my italics)

To speak of a Rome as full of imaginative possibility as nature itself—and of the American Adam's loss as well as gain when he asserted his independence of such a past—certainly placed the "problem of Rome" in a crucial position in Emerson's thought. For all his Romantic Hellenism, which tended to portray Greece as a hero and Rome as a villain, Emerson might also use Rome itself as a counterpart of the Romantic imagination. Though he often praised the simplicity, organic naturalness, and even stoic virtue of ancient Greece, something about the idea of Rome satisfied his dramatic imagination as the idea of Greece could not. It seems likely that even when his use of the "Greek strategy" reached its height in his most fervent period of Transcendental assertion, it was qualified by the powerful idea of Rome—an idea that had fascinated him ever since his college days. Rome meant history. Rome meant civilization and society. Rome meant art. It was a synecdoche for the best and worst in the City of Man. The internal complexities and ambiguities of such components of the idea of Rome were not a handicap to its use; rather, they were a stimulus. Once Emerson had visited Rome, he knew that no responsible artist could escape the necessity of coming to terms with both ancient Rome and the New Romes of the modern world.

If Emerson entered Rome wishing "to see old Rome, not new" (*L*, *1*, 368), he concluded his visit on a different note. After writing his brother William about the glories of "this venerable old egg shell," he added, "But I hate to be in Rome & know nothing of present Rome which much excites my curiosity" (*L*, *1*, 379, 381). The desire to see "present Rome" was not a disparagement of the old. Rather, it was an emerging sense of the importance of knowing the way in which the old functioned in a new context—the way in which the idea of Rome might be applicable to and significant for the modern world. Without stretching reality too uncomfortably, we may conveniently treat Emerson's travels in 1833 from Italy to France and then to England as a symbolic movement from the old Rome to the new Romes that had emerged with modern Europe.

In 1833 Emerson was only partly aware of any such movement. Arriving in Paris in June, he found "that in leaving Italy I had left forever that air of antiquity & history which her towns possess & in coming hither had come to a loud modern New York of a place" (*JMN*, *4*, 197). Though he spent a profitable month in Paris and admitted that he was probably only "walking on the crust," he felt that "it is not [desirable] to me" (*L*, *1*, 388). "Paris, all modern," he said, "cannot compare with Rome or with Florence, whose glory is departed or departing" (*L*, *1*, 386). His first visit to London was also a surface approach, based on predispositions established by his literary training. "We know London so well in books & pictures

& maps & traditions," he noted on his arrival, "that I saw nothing surprizing in this passage up the Thames" (*JMN*, *4*, 204). In "sauntering in London streets," he "felt much like an English boy on his first visit from the country,—the names were so familiar and the things so new, yet tallying so well with their pictures" (*J*, *3*, 229–30).[24] His initial acquaintance with London was too hurried to give him time to examine the city in detail. In any case, the closeness of his impressive Italian experiences did not allow him the perspective he would need in order to make effective application of such experiences to the problems presented by modern London.

By the time of Emerson's return to Europe in 1847, however, he had gained the perspective necessary to apply the concept of a "new Rome" to Europe, just as he had already begun to apply the term to America. For all his interest in the problem of Europe as a whole, he did not lump Europe's parts together indiscriminately. He was still interested in the peculiar characteristics of various European cities and, when opportunity allowed him to escape briefly to France after his English lectures, wrote a great deal about the difference between Paris and London. He stated that, for pure personal pleasure, he preferred the French to the British capital. Still, as a historian, he felt that the differences between these and other European cities were in some senses less significant than their similarities. However diverse, European cities rep-

24. In 1822 Emerson had defended religion's affirmation of spiritual reality by appealing to the "idea" of London: "We are continually compelled to act upon faith and having heard from a third, tenth, or twentieth mouth that there is a city called London we send thither our merchandise without ever dreaming how madly we act upon a report which may be a fable" (*JMN*, *1*, *142*). In *Our Old Home* Hawthorne said that his early reading "had made London the dream-city of my youth" (*Works*, *7*, 256).

resented a set of common problems. These problems were not only urban; they pointed to European history as a whole. As Emerson noted in his journal shortly after his return from England, "Europe concentrates itself into a capital. He has not seen Europe who has not seen its cities" (*J*, 8, 45).

If many of the European capitals were representative of the "meaning" of modern Europe, London was the most logical choice for a writer who wished to bring the idea of Rome as up to date as possible, to make the idea as relevant as possible to the problem of American history and American literature. A number of factors could account for Emerson's interest in London. For one thing, it had been the home and working ground of many of the scholars and artists whom he had read and admired. As early as 1825 he had noted that "Newton removed to London not to be made Mintmaster to Queene Anne but because a court collects a city & this can furnish the facilities of books & instruments & above all of kindred society which science demands" (*JMN*, 2, 311–12). By the late 1830s this sense of London as the home of the man of imagination was personalized for Emerson by his developing friendship and correspondence with Carlyle. Carlyle's letters were filled with the sense of modern London and with the importance of the city as a lesson. In 1835 he reminded Emerson that "this monstrous London has taught me several things during the past year; for if its Wisdom be of the most *un*instructive ever heard of by that name of wisdom, its Folly abounds with lessons,—which one ought to learn" (*Corr*, 135). It was Carlyle who reminded Emerson of the specific lessons London might teach an American. In the spring of 1847, a few months before Emerson sailed for England, the craggy Briton pointed out to his American friend that "London is properly *your* Mother City too,—verily you have about as much to do with it, in spite of Polk and Q. Victory, as I [have]!" (*Corr*, 423).[25] Emerson certainly could not escape the fact he had recognized as early as his 1833 trip to England—"that it is the most resembling country to America which the world contains" (*JMN*, *4*, 81). By exploring England and London, he believed he was in many ways exploring America.

When he visited London, therefore, in the spring of 1848, at the conclusion of his lecture tour in England's provincial cities, Emerson did so with a much firmer and more clearly articulated purpose than he had possessed in 1833. From London he wrote to a friend, confirming his characteristic criticism of travel, that "few men are fit for it, and one ought to be supported by a commanding motive to save it from being a long impertinence" (*L*, *4*, 31). In 1848 Emerson had this sort of "commanding motive." It is important to remember that he did not come to London initially to lecture, though that formed his basic reason for visiting other areas of England.[26] He came to London to observe and explore. As early as November 1837 he was becoming impatient to see the "brilliant spectacles" and "very desirable persons" of London "after I have fulfilled my northern engagements" (*L*, *3*, 428). In fact, London figured so heavily in his purpose that

25. Cf. Emerson's comment in 1832: "Our upstart antiquities hide themselves like little children between the knees of such a fatherly place as London" (*JMN*, *4*, 34). His high consciousness of his European experiences as "lessons" is shown in his comment in 1833, while in London: "I thank the great God who has led me through this European scene[,] this last schoolroom in which he has pleased to instruct me" (*JMN*, *4*, 78).

26. Once in London, Emerson was finally persuaded by friends to lecture there. See Townsend Scudder, "Emerson in London and the London Lectures," *American Literature*, 8 (1936), 22–36. Also useful is Scudder. "A Chronological List of Emerson's Lectures on His British Tour of 1847–1848," *PMLA*, 51 (1936), 243–48.

he refused to comment on England as a whole until he had seen its metropolitan capital. "Though I have seen so many towns & cities," he wrote his mother, "I am not entitled yet to know or say anything, whilst I move up & down in these obscure districts so far from London" (*L*, 4, 6). With such motives, Emerson found the capital much more than the "very dull city" (*JMN*, 4, 414) of his 1833 visit. After less than a week in the city he wrote his wife:

> The most wonderful thing I see is this London . . . the centre of the world[.] the "nation in brick"; the immense masses of life of power of wealth, and the effect upon the men of running in & out amidst the play of this vast machinery, the effect to keep them tense & silent, and to mind every man his own,—it is all very entertaining, I assure you. I think sometimes that it would well become me to sit here a good while, and study London mainly, and the wide variety of classes, that, like so many nations, are dwelling here together. I have many good thoughts, many insights, as I go up & down. (*L*, 4, 35)

After Emerson had been in London for a month he complained to a friend that "the days in London are too short for all that is to be done in them . . . I hope I shall yet have something to show for my London experience" (*L*, 4, 59).

By the time he left England Emerson had a great deal to show—in many pages of letters and in dozens of passages in his journals. But the profits of his trip were embodied in their most coherent form in *English Traits* (1856), the product of his visits, journals, and eight years' contemplation of the "London experience." If the book is structured as has been suggested by Emerson's theories of history and racial development, London itself is a crucial symbol of these theories. *Eng-*

lish Traits, in fact, is also organized around a pervading sense of the growth and influence of London.

The book begins with a chapter recounting Emerson's first trip to England. This first chapter rises above mere narrative only when he tells of his first meeting with Carlyle. Carlyle is living on a farm in the Scottish Highlands, but already Emerson senses that this writer's significance must be treated in the context of London. The Scotsman is "as absolute a man of the world, unknown and exiled on that hill-farm, as if holding on his own terms what is best in London" (*W*, 5, 15). Carlyle "was already turning his eyes toward London with a scholar's appreciation. London is the heart of the world, he said" (p. 18).[27] Emerson's eyes also begin to move in the direction of that metropolis. In the third chapter, "Land," as the outline of Emerson's analysis begins to take shape, London assumes a central position in a nation that is the center of the modern world:

> England resembles a ship in its shape, and if it were one, its best admiral could not have worked it or anchored it in a more judicious or effective position. Sir John Herschel said, "London is the centre of the terrene globe." The shopkeeping nation, to use a shop word, has a *good stand*. The old Venetians pleased themselves with the flattery that Venice was in 45°, midway between the poles and the line; as if that were an imperial centrality. Long of old, the Greeks fancied Delphi the navel of the earth, in their favorite mode of fabling the earth to be an animal. The Jews believed Jerusalem to be the centre. I have seen a kratometric chart designed to show that the

27. Cf. *JMN*, 4, 219–21. All page references to *English Traits* are from Vol. 5 of the *Works*.

> city of Philadelphia was in the same thermic belt, and by inference in the same belt of empire, as the cities of Athens, Rome and London. It was drawn by a patriotic Philadelphian, and was examined with pleasure, under his showing, by the inhabitants of Chestnut Street. But when carried to Charleston, to New Orleans and to Boston, it somehow failed to convince the ingenious scholars of all those capitals.
>
> But England is anchored at the side of Europe, and right in the heart of the modern world. (pp. 40–41)

In Chapter Four, Emerson stresses even more explicitly the actual and symbolic importance of London to his study of this "heart" of the world: "What we think of when we talk of English traits really narrows itself to a small district. It excludes Ireland and Scotland and Wales, and reduces itself at last to London, that is, to those who come and go thither" (p. 52).

Having established London's centrality, Emerson, in Chapter Five, establishes its pervasive influence:

> The nation sits in the immense city they have builded, a London extended into every man's mind, though he live in Van Dieman's Land or Capetown. . . . The modern world is theirs. They have made and make it day by day. The commercial relations of the world are so intimately drawn to London, that every dollar on earth contributes to the strength of the English government. (p. 92)

Though London's power is partly economic, partly political, and partly cultural, such power is most basically psychological—"a London extended into every man's mind," wherever he may live. The English "have made the island a thoroughfare, and London a shop, a law-court, a record-office, and scientific bureau, inviting to strangers; a sanctuary to refugees of every political and religious opinion; and such a city that almost every active man, in any nation, finds himself at one time or other forced to visit it" (pp. 92–93).

The image of London as an inescapable magnet is emphasized throughout *English Traits*. Emerson reminds the reader in Chapter Ten that "the wealth of London determines prices all over the globe. All things precious, or useful, or amusing, or intoxicating, are sucked into this commerce and floated to London" (pp. 162–63). But London's force is centrifugal as well as centripetal; the English "trample on nationalities to reproduce London and Londoners in Europe and Asia" (p. 254) much as Americans were reproducing Westerners and cities of the West across the American landscape. Looking for types of this assimilative force as it works through both concentration and expansion, Emerson calls the London *Times* a symbol of London and the modern city—a dynamic cosmos of many elements (p. 263). Whatever tendencies in modern history, whether good or bad, are implied by nineteenth-century England, they receive their strongest expression in the "whirlpool" of London.[28]

As Emerson analyzes the structure, historical basis, and future implications of this dynamic cosmos of modern London, a duality of attitude begins to assert itself—the same duality that had governed his early reading of history and his treatment of Rome. On one hand, he treats England and its metropolis as merely a new example of cyclical history. In the political and economic processes that make London func-

28. Note Cooper's comment in *Gleanings in England*, p. 106, that "eternal movement" was one of the major characteristics of London. Hawthorne's and Melville's descriptions of London also emphasize this quality of lively power.

tion are the same "seeds" of decay that caused the decline of all ancient nations—the forces of selfishness, complacent materialism, and narrowness of vision. Characteristically, Emerson had earlier looked closely for signs of such latent decay in the areas of both society and art. One possible sign was the growing social and economic unrest in Britain. For many years, he had followed with interest the periodic depressions of the British economy, and his youthful belief that "Britain treads with fear upon an unsound & perilous footing[,] burning with flame to an unknown extent" (*JMN, 1*, 127) seemed at least partly confirmed in the many protests by English labor against the oppressive conditions in industrial England.[29] In *English Traits*, he also examines a possible decline of British force in its artists' loss of a sense of "ideal beauty," exemplified by the nineteenth-century writers' denial of "the expansive element which creates literature" (p. 245).

On the other hand, Emerson also finds much in contemporary England to support the side of his mind that fervently wishes to discover progress in history. Artistic quality and economic crises notwithstanding, industrial England was growing—if only materially—at an almost frightening speed. Some English towns, Emerson had written his wife in 1847, "are growing almost at the rate of American towns, and, in Lancashire, will by & by meet, & make a city as big as and bigger than London, and London is filling up Middlesex. The mechanical might & organizations it is oppressive to behold" (*L*, 3, 452–53). Though the extreme moralist in Emerson wished

29. While in England in 1847 and 1848, for example, Emerson showed a great interest in the Chartist movement and even attended a meeting of a group of Chartists in London (*J*, 7, 414; *L*, 4, 34–35). See *L*, 3, 442–43, for an example of Emerson's discussion of the poverty, suffering, and evil he observed while in industrial England.

to see materialism inherently self-defeating in the course of history, the "problem of London" did not offer any obvious empirical answer to the seeming conflict between moral and material history. As a professing Romantic poet, he was torn between his desire to treat London as an imperfect symbol of a divine Idea and his fascination with London as a brilliant, though often fearsome, set of facts. The "London experience," like the "idea of Rome," was fascinating, dangerous, and unavoidable, and he was continually oscillating between his sense of the danger to the moral historian and his interest in the poetic aspects of that danger. *English Traits* shows, if imperfectly, both sides of these tensions within his thought.

Since most recent scholars have stressed Emerson's criticisms of nineteenth-century England, they have underestimated the other pole of his opinions. Representative of these scholars is Philip Nicoloff, whose useful study of *English Traits* argues that the concluding section of Emerson's book is increasingly pessimistic in tone. By the time Emerson wrote *English Traits*, argues Nicoloff, he had accepted an "organic" version of cyclical history and had adapted "the general principle of ameliorative evolution" to a theory of spirally progressive history. British power had been based on the hybrid vigor of an assimilating Saxonism, and the decline of this racial vigor would also cause the decline of the political, economic, and cultural strength of the British nation—a strength that the new "American race" seemed to be inheriting. Emerson believed, says Nicoloff, that at the middle of the nineteenth century England was approaching its old age and that the future of its life and literature could only be "effete and barren." The English of Emerson's day "were little more than helpless spectators at their own catastrophe. They had not been betrayed by their particular nature (there existed no better in the world), but by a debilitating necessity which worked irresistibly on all organic life." According to Nicoloff, Emerson identified the peak period of British "health" as occurring in the Elizabethan Age, when physical vigor was harnessed to the purposes of religious idealism. England's decline was shown in the splitting apart of the racial mind and the racial body. Nicoloff cites as proof Emerson's conclusion that nineteenth-century England contained "two nations," "two complexions, or two styles of mind,—the perceptive class, and the practical class . . . one in hopeless minorities; the other in huge masses." Paraphrasing Emerson, Nicoloff states what he believes to be the basic theme of *English Traits:* "Through the sometime accord but now perpetual discord of these two nations was to be read the history of the English states."[30] In Nicoloff's interpretation of Emerson's work, such discord meant the ultimate decline of the British nation.

Unfortunately, Nicoloff's paraphrase is imprecise, and this imprecision is symptomatic of his misreading of an important aspect of Emerson's attitudes toward mid-century England. In the quotation cited by Nicoloff, Emerson did not refer to the "history" but to the "power" of the British state, implying that this power was not only in the past but was also a part of the present Britain. Emerson's actual remarks deserve to be quoted more fully:

> The two complexions, or two styles of mind—the perceptive class, and the practical finality class,—are *ever* in counterpoise, interacting mutually: one in hopeless minorities; the other in huge masses; one studious, contemplative, *experimenting;* the other, the ungrateful pupil, scornful of the source whilst availing itself of the

30. Nicoloff, *Emerson on Race and History,* pp. 223, 233.

> knowledge for gain; these two nations, of genius and of animal force, *though* the first consist of only a dozen souls and the second of twenty millions, *forever* by their discord and their accord yield the power of the English State. (p. 260; my italics)

Imaginative genius, implies Emerson, has always been in a numerical minority—as much during the period of England's literary "flowering" as during the nineteenth century. The very interaction between the genius and utilitarian indicates the continuing rather than the declining power of the British nation. British genius has merely chosen different channels of expression at different points in history—poetry and drama in the Elizabethan Age, historical writing in the eighteenth century, and reformist writing in the nineteenth century.

Emerson had often criticized the particular channels in which the imaginative energies of a genius like Carlyle ran in contemporary England, but he did not deny the force of such genius. In *English Traits* he complains that "the essays, the fiction and the poetry of the day have . . . municipal limits" (p. 246)—that is, are limited by the attitudes dominant in London—but he also realizes that such "limits" are not at all narrow. Having explored London himself, he was well aware of the interest that such a dynamic metropolis could hold for the artistic genius.[31] If London had been less dynamic, it would have been less interesting, and genius would have searched for other channels of expression. If the artist became too enamored with the material values implicit in the London experience, he might become corrupted and his latent

31. See *Corr,* 145, 151, and *J,* 7, 442. In *English Traits* Emerson wrote that "the range of nations from which London draws, and the steep contrasts of condition, create the picturesque in society, as broken country makes picturesque landscape" (*W,* 5, 114).

idealism misdirected. But the existence of such danger was an argument for rather than against the continuing vigor of London.

Emerson had noted in his journal Marx's contention that "the classes and the races too weak to master the new conditions of life must give way" (*J*, 8, 351), and Nicoloff cites this as evidence that Emerson saw the British nation as a whole giving way to the better-adapting American nation.[32] In fact, however, Emerson's discussion in *English Traits* stresses the ways in which such "selective evolution" was occurring within the confines of England itself. "It is not a final race," he argues, "but a race with a future" (p. 67), and the future need not be found only in America. Though he realizes that "the Middle Ages still lurk in the streets of London" (p. 109), he is also pleased "by that uncorrupt youth in the face of manhood, which is daily seen in the streets" of that same city (p. 66).

Certain segments of England, it is true, were disappearing because they lacked adaptability to modern conditions, but other, better-adapting segments were replacing them. Though the traditional British aristocracy was becoming effete, a new and vigorous "natural aristocracy" was taking its place. The Church of England's loss of popular support was not due merely to a growth of materialism but also to a genuine religious spirit that was searching for more iconoclastic channels. Though the traditional holders of wealth in Britain had become timid and complacent, the new "creators" of wealth were aggressive to the point of being oppressive. The "new" Englishman was in many ways a rather materialistic version of Emerson's "self-reliant" man—"an island himself,

32. Nicoloff, p. 126.

safe, tranquil, incommunicable" (p. 105)—and the polish of such a man is not effete, but a hardy expression of his self-reliance. "Every man in this polished country," Emerson notes, "consults only his convenience, as much as a solitary pioneer in Wisconsin" (p. 105). The best Englishmen were still pioneers in the nineteenth century, and even when Emerson criticizes the channels in which they worked, he does not criticize the underlying pioneer spirit or doubt its existence. In its most modern tendencies, London itself was a "Western" city in the metaphorical sense of that term—just as all cities on the frontier of history were Western in spirit.

It was the very existence of so many dynamic individualists, so many "Westerners," in modern Britain that created many of the tensions Emerson discusses in *English Traits*. He treats these tensions basically not as a sign of decay but as a sign of continuing life. The vital part of England is not a safe, timid world, but a world of continuing risks and dangers.[33] "A proof of the energy of the British people," he argues, "is the highly artificial construction of the whole fabric," and he stresses that Britain's tensions are at the very base of this national energy: "Bacon said, 'Rome was a state not subject to paradoxes;' but England subsists by antagonisms and contradictions" (pp. 93–94). This nineteenth-century "Rome" seemed to depend for its vitality on the same tensions that destroyed the ancient Rome. If this is true, then history is more than cyclical, and society is learning gradually through time to cope with, though not resolve, the conflicts it has created.

33. In London in 1848 Emerson noted: "One goes from show to show, dines out, and *lives in extremes*. Electric sparks six feet long; light is polarized; Grisi sings; Rothschild is your banker; Owen and Faraday lecture; Macaulay talks; Soyer cooks. Is there not an economy in coming where thus all the dependence is on the *first men of their kind?*" (*J*, 7, 406–07; my italics). Cf. *J*, 8, 362, 374, 520.

For all its many continuing inadequacies and ignoble actions, contemporary English history indicated the growth of the free mind of mankind. When Emerson argued in 1853, as he was writing *English Traits*, that "England can only fall by suicide" (*J*, *8*, 464), he was pointing not only to the real dangers the modern nation faced but to its continuing power to choose its fate. As he reminds his readers near the conclusion of the book, "only the English race can be trusted with freedom,—freedom which is double-edged and dangerous to any but the wise and robust" (p. 304). For all their "pagan" or brutish qualities (pp. 280, 304–05), the new emerging leaders of the core of Britain seemed capable of meeting the economic and social crises of their day. Despite Emerson's qualifications—his sense of the "drag of inertia" by the British past (p. 305)—he sees England "in her old age, not decrepit, but young and still daring to believe in her power of endurance and expansion" (p. 313).[34]

England is thus a Rome with a difference—a New Rome that can appeal to the poet not because of a decayed past but because of a dangerously exciting present and a fascinatingly undetermined future. The major danger to this New Rome—this Europe-based, westward-looking city—is not the "inertia" of the past, but the misuse of its new power by irresponsible individualism. England can not die of organic old age; its death can come only through the free will's destructive application of its own enlarged freedom. The conclusion of *English*

34. In 1848 Emerson wrote Margaret Fuller from London: "I leave England with an increased respect for the Englishman. His stuff or substance seems to be the best of the world. I forgive him all his pride. My respect is the more generous that I have no sympathy with him, only an admiration" (*L*, *4*, 62). Interesting in comparison is Cooper's reference to England as "a country that all respect, but few love" (*Gleanings in England*, p. 394).

Traits is one toward which the entire book has been building: "England is the best of actual nations. It is no ideal framework, it is an old pile built in different ages, with repairs, additions and makeshift; but you see the poor best you have got. London is the epitome of our times, and the Rome of to-day" (p. 299).[35] London symbolizes the entire development of human history up to the middle of the nineteenth century. If Emerson wished to chart the future potential of America, he needed to start not by denying the problem of Rome as it had been updated in the problem of London, but by mutually testing this problem and the American context. In London were found in all their complexities not only the sins and destructive elements of the City of Man, but also its creative potentials. The drama of London, like the drama of Rome, was both a lesson for America and a legitimate subject for the American artist ultimately concerned with his own Western cities. *English Traits* affirms both the lesson and the subject.

Emerson's metaphorical application of the problematic dramas of Rome and New Romes to American development was an important component of his search for a usable past. Only in his most radical statements of individualistic idealism did he deny the reality or relevance of the past. Even during the late 1830s, one of his major concerns was history. In the same year, 1836, that he called for an "original relation to the

35. Hawthorne, in *Our Old Home*, also compared the English to "the old Romans" and said that for all London's imperfections "the world has nothing better." Speaking of Rome and London, he argued that "as long as either of those two great cities shall exist, the cities of the Past and of the Present, a man's native soil may crumble beneath his feet without leaving him altogether homeless upon earth" (*Works*, 7, 256–57). See B. Bernard Cohen, "Emerson and Hawthorne on England," *Boston Public Library Quarterly*, 9 (1937), 73–85.

universe" (*W*, 1, 3) in *Nature*, he also gave a series of twelve lectures entitled "The Philosophy of History." The major tension in these lectures—between a tendency to deny external history any ultimate teleological status and a recognition of external history as a "lesson"—reflected Emerson's desire to help the individual escape from the limitations of the past. It also reflected an admission more characteristic of his work as a whole—that the individual as *human* being can assert his individuality only within the context and drama of history.[36] Emerson's concept of usable history, like similar concepts of other modern historians, was an attempt to find a workable compromise between the claims of the individual soul and the claims of the social past. Though the past was relevant to the present, the precise degree and manner of relevance might vary significantly, depending on the specific aspects of the past being studied and the specific aspects of the present to which they were applied. Through a cautious use of the past and a cautious participation in its dramas, the new individual might assert both his individuality and his continuity with history.

The same double potential might hold true for a new nation. To the extent that American development was radically unique (and to the extent that human history was thus noncyclical), the "idea of Rome" had only limited applicability to that development. As Emerson stated in his essay "History" (1841):

> I am ashamed to see what a shallow village tale our so-called History is. How many times we must say Rome, and Paris, and Constantinople! What does Rome know of rat and lizard? What are Olympiads and Consulates

36. These lectures are now conveniently reprinted in *EL*, 2, 1–188.

> to these neighboring systems of being? Nay, what food or experience or succor have they for the Esquimaux seal-hunter, for Kanàka in his canoe, for the fisherman, the stevedore, the porter? (*W*, 2, 40)

To the extent, however, that American history was merely cyclical—merely perpetuated the past weaknesses and sins of mankind—Rome became equally (because indifferently) as useful a metaphorical basis as any other. "Yes," Emerson mused in 1851 in one of his skeptical moods,

> History is a vanishing allegory, and repeats itself to tediousness, a thousand and a million times. The Rape of the Sabines is perpetual, and the fairest Sabine virgins are every day pounced upon by rough, victorious Romans, masquerading under mere New Hampshire and Vermont and Boston names, as Webster, Choate, Thayer, Bigelow, or other obscurity. (*J*, 8, 251–52).

Between these two polar attitudes lay a spectrum of attitudes concerning the relevance of the Roman drama to the American experience.

Since Emerson, along with his and previous generations, tended to treat cyclical history as indicative of human imperfection, he often applied the term "Rome" to America when he wished to criticize those elements in American development that he felt were the same as those that had destroyed Rome. Attacking American materialism, for example, in a journal passage of 1839 on the "Dangers of Commerce," he argued that "this invasion of Nature by Trade with its Money, its Credit, its Steam, its Railroad, threatens to upset the balance of man, and establish a new, universal Monarchy more tyrannical than Babylon or Rome" (*J*, 5, 285). On the other hand, aware that the complex idea of Rome also contained admirable qualities, Emerson applied the term at times to qualities that he admired in America. In an 1834 journal passage tracing the creative work of divine providence in contemporary civilization, he noted that "a ship, a locomotive, a cotton factory is a wonder until we see how these Romes were not built in a day, but part suggested part & complexity became simplicity" (*JMN*, *4*, 285). He claimed, while discussing the glories of American nature at the Cape Ann seashore, that "here are twenty Romes and Ninevahs and Karnacs in ruins together" (*J*, *9*, 55), and he referred to the woods around Concord as a "leafy Rome" (*W*, *9*, 43).

This internalization of the metaphor of Rome even led Emerson to disregard the imperfect aspects of actual Rome and to play instead with the term's possibilities as a metaphor for the morally ideal. In the poem "Written in Rome" in 1833 Emerson advised the reader to "Obey the nobler impulse; that is Rome" (*W*, *9*, 397). In the same essay in which he had criticized Roman history as a "shallow village tale," he allowed the term to serve as a metaphor for man's broadest transcendental possibilities:

> In old Rome the public roads beginning at the Forum proceeded north, south, east, west, to the centre of every province of the empire, making each market-town of Persia, Spain, and Britain pervious to the soldiers of the capital; so out of the human heart go . . . highways to the heart of every object in nature, to reduce it under the dominion of man. (*W*, 2, 36)[37]

37. Cf. a passage in Thoreau's journal for 1838 entitled "Every Man is a Roman Forum." "In me is the forum," he argues, "out of which go the Appian and Sacred Ways, and a thousand beside, to the ends of the world" (*Journals*, 1, 84).

Believing that the good and beautiful might survive the weeding-out process of history's selective evolution, "so that the antiquities and permanent things in each city are good and fine" (*J*, 6, 250),[38] Emerson as poet might pursue a similar selective borrowing from the nobler aspects of Rome and Europe's New Rome—and from their dramas—in order to challenge his own nation to greater achievement.[39] If Americans were sons of the perpetually creating Over-Soul and thus New Adams, they were also sons of Rome and Europe. They need not imitate the mistakes of the earthly father in order to show an instinctive and natural respect and even affection for his moments of wisdom and true achievement.[40] Americans need not deny Rome; they need only select which parts

38. In 1836, while praising the Marine Railway, the United States Bank, and the Bunker Hill Monument as "perfectly genuine works of the times, "Emerson attempted to balance the demands of the moment and the demands of ultimate value: "You must exercise your genius in some form that has essential life now; do something that is proper to the hour & cannot but be done. But what is once done well, lasts forever. As the gladiator, the Apollo, the Parthenon, the Iliad" (*JMN*, 5, 150).

39. Many such comparisons of Rome and America occur in the literature of the American Renaissance. See Melville's discussion in *Mardi* of Vivenza as a new Romara (*Works*, 4, 239–41). Borrowing from the legend of Romulus and Remus, Thoreau argued that "America is the she-wolf of to-day, and the children of exhausted Europe exposed on her uninhabited and savage shores are the Romulus and Remus who, having derived new life and vigor from her breast, have founded a new Rome in the West" (*Journals*, 2, 151).

40. In a lecture in 1835 Emerson argued that "the American character is only the English character exaggerated" and that "the features of the English genius both good and bad, have, in the greater freedom of our institutions, become more prominent" (*EL*, 1, 233). In a lecture in 1842 he asserted that New England represented the best aspect of the Mother Country: "The New England of today the England of the Future it is here" ("New England"—Houghton manuscript 199.4).

of its foundations they too would build upon, need only decide which elements of its dramas they would adapt to their own roles. The very act of selection was an act both of homage to and liberation from the past. As Emerson pointed out in his sermon "The Genuine Man," which he delivered at least thirteen times between 1832 and 1837, America might accept with gratitude the "useful and elegant arts" of the Romes of history—not as an end, but as a necessary base upon which America might "out-Rome" Rome. "It seems to be left to us to commence the best of all works. . . . To us has been committed by Providence the higher and holier work of forming *men*, true and entire men" (*Y*, 180).

In searching for a dramatic matrix in which the tension between America's sense of obligation to the past and its sense of a special destiny might be resolved, Emerson turned to his own nation's domestic past. It is a scholarly truism that Hawthorne, Bancroft, and many others among his contemporaries explored the possibilities of such a dramatic resolution. Few recent students of Emerson, however, with the possible exception of Rusk, have noted adequately his interest in the American past. It is highly significant that, shortly before calling in *Nature* for an original relation to experience, he spent several weeks of serious work to prepare the "Historical Discourse" which he delivered on September 12, 1835, at the celebration of Concord's second centennial.[41] In an important

41. This speech is printed in *W*, *11*, 27–48. Rusk argues that it "was probably the greatest effort Emerson ever made at gathering and checking facts in the manner of a scholar, with the possible exception of his more deliberate preparation for the writng of his book on England many years later" (*Life*, 221). Emerson's sources included seven volumes of the Concord Town records, Mather's *Magnalia Christi Americana*, many Puritan works, and a local history of Concord (*L*, *1*, 455, and *W*, *11*, 552–71). George H. Callcott, "Historians in Early

sense Emerson's extensive research into New England's history in preparation for the speech was intimately bound to his subsequent cry for an American Scholar who was both original and comprehensive—both an Adam and a Cosmopolitan. "Our ears shall not be deaf to the voice of the time," he stated in the opening remarks of the "Discourse." "We will review the deeds of our fathers, and pass that just verdict on them we expect from posterity on our own" (*W*, *11*, 29). Emerson's speech was in part an embodiment of his belief that man's human (as distinct from divine) originality sprang only out of a sense of continuity with the past. "We should give to our being what permanence we can," he argued; "we should recall the Past, and expect the Future" (p. 30). His "Historical Discourse" was an attempt to exercise his role as poetic historian—to interpret the "rich, historical past" (*J*, 6, 480) in such a way as to allow the present to use it creatively in achieving a lastingly progressive future.

Emerson's treatment of Concord's history, like his treatment of many other problems, can be illuminated by watching the way his friend Thoreau pushed the same technique to its extreme. Thoreau argued in *Walden* that he had traveled far in Concord, and his journals and other works became an elaborate attempt to justify this contention.[42] If Concord was a microcosm of the world, both in space and in time, then Thoreau knew he must find—or create—all major aspects of that world within the bounds of his local community. His rhetori-

Nineteenth-Century America," *New England Quarterly*, 32 (1959), 501–02, indicates the large number of local histories written during this period.

42. In addition to Paul, *The Shores of America*, the most useful analysis of the landscape of Thoreau's inner journeys is Perry Miller's provocative introduction to *Consciousness in Concord: The Text of Thoreau's Hitherto "Lost Journal," 1840–1841* (Boston, 1958).

cal answer to this problem was to argue that "Concord . . . is my Rome, and its people . . . are my Romans." He asserted at moments that "New England, at least, is not based on any Roman ruins. We have not to lay the foundations of our houses in the ashes of a former civilization." But after denying to America a foreign past, he felt obliged to create a domestic past as weighty as the non-American. Thus, he searched the cellar-holes near Concord for American "antiquities"; such decay, he argued, "is the decline and fall of the Roman Empire." He urged that "two hundred years" of "antiquity" "is nearly as good as two thousand to our imagination," since it carried the American mind "back to the days of aborigines and the Pilgrims; beyond the limits of oral testimony, to history which begins already to be enamelled with a gloss of fable." By equating his own life's span and thus his own memory with recorded history—a psychological technique smacking of Transcendental egotism—Thoreau could refer to Walden Pond as "one of the most ancient scenes stamped on the tablets of my memory, the oriental Asiatic valley of the world, whence so many races and inventions have gone forth in recent times."[43]

After creating such a nobly imagined "past," both mythic in origin and "civilized" in development, Thoreau had no hesitation in referring to his hut at Walden as "centre and metropolis" of the world, in calling Concord "a rural Venice," or in praising the Lexington and Concord of Revolutionary days in terms of the grandest metaphors of the classical urban tradition:

43. Thoreau, *Correspondence*, p. 94; *Journals*, 6, 276; 2, 158–59; 13, 16; 1, 380–81. For Thoreau's interest in New England history, see Lawrence Willson, "Another View of the Pilgrims," *New England Quarterly* 34 (1961), 160–77.

Ye were the Grecian cities then,
 Then Romes of modern birth,
Where the New England husbandmen
 Have shown a Roman worth.

Whatever the moral merits of their original referents, such metaphors were useful to him in challenging his fellow citizens in Concord not to imitate Athens and Rome in every external sense, but to look inside themselves for the same divine resources that had created the best inner aspects of those two classical empires. Thoreau was not looking for a past for antiquarians; he was searching for a usable past for himself and for his fellow Americans in Concord. "Rome and Romans are commonly a piece of rhetoric," he once complained. History, like literature, was without value unless applied creatively to the problems of the present.[44]

Engaging in such creative updating, Thoreau could refer to Varro's writings on agriculture as the Roman's "*New England Farmer,* the very manual those Roman farmers read, speaking . . . as if Rome were still the mistress of the world, —as fresh as a dripping dishcloth from a Roman kitchen." The idea of Rome was still "fresh" because Concord could use it. For this reason Thoreau advocated strongly that his community establish a library to buy those "works of art, journals and books, and scientific instruments" that might be of value to the American present and future. Such purchases "would educate the village, elevate its tone of thought, and, if it alone improved these opportunities, easily make it the centre of civilization in the known world, put us on a level as to opportunities at once with London and Arcadia, and secure us a culture at once superior to both." As he elaborated this plea

44. Thoreau, *Journals,* 1, 365; 2, 444; *Collected Poems,* pp. 8, 34.

in *Walden,* he added a significant reminder: "To act collectively is according to the spirit of our institutions. . . . Instead of noblemen, let us have noble villages of men." For all his rhetorical anarchism, Thoreau recognized the way in which the individual and community could support each other—the community providing resources for the individual's education and the individual using his education creatively and thus benefiting (even if indirectly) the entire community. History, he felt, was to be read in terms of the interaction of the individual and the community. Conflict of the two resulted in cyclical history. In their cooperation lay the only lasting basis for progressive history.[45]

The same poles of individual freedom and communal unity structured Emerson's "Historical Discourse" at Concord. Emerson's treatment of Concord, like Thoreau's, emphasizes the town's possible role as a microcosm. In the broadest sense, Concord's history seems to trace the outlines of mankind's total development through time. In a more specific sense, it represents what Emerson believes to be the major tendencies of American history. The pattern he traces in the "Discourse" is neither a stultifying cycle nor an easily upward line. It is rather a spiral that reflects both the failures and the successes of what Emerson terms the "experiment" at Concord. He introduces a group of freedom-loving individualists, Puritan "nonconformists," and brings them as pilgrims to a spot of land "not to be reached without a painful and dangerous journey through an uninterrupted wilderness." Then he watches them as they struggle to found a community that will live up to its name in the face of inhibiting ties to the past (including psychological ties, the most inhibiting of all), threats from the natural wilderness, and disintegrating forces emerging from

45. Thoreau, *Journals,* 2, 444; 3, 25–26; *Walden,* Chap. 3.

the very individualism that prompted the town's founding. The history of Concord, as Emerson interprets it, is an experiment to determine whether mankind can in fact balance communal peace and individualism, "concord" and freedom.

During Concord's first period of growth, says Emerson, its individual citizens worked through democratic processes to support the community's laws, and the community in turn gave the individuals opportunities symbolized by the "freeholds" into which the corporate land holdings were divided. The individuals' sense of personal power in the community was balanced by their sense of duty to and love for that community:

> Its settlers, whilst they were exploring their granted and natural rights and determining the power of the magistrates, were united by personal affection. . . . For the first time, men examined the power of the chief whom they loved and revered. For the first time, the ideal social compact was real. The bands of love and reverence held fast the little state, whilst they untied the great cords of authority to examine their soundness and learn on what wheels they ran. (p. 45)

Under such a balancing of individual and community needs, the town's history becomes a creative drama, and the early town records are "a certificate of the progress of the Saxon race," "a lesson of humanity and love" (p. 50).

The first major setback to the progressive historical drama of Concord, as Emerson interprets it, occurred during King Phillip's War. He explicitly points to the "moral" reason for the setback—the unwillingness of Concord to include American nature in its definition of "community." "The worst feature in the history of those years," he argues, was "that no man spake for the Indian. . . . It is the misfortune of Concord to have permitted a disgraceful outrage upon the friendly Indians settled within its limits" (p. 61). After tracing this brief downturn in the spiral of Concord's development, Emerson can "turn gladly to the progress of our civil history" (p. 62). He pictures a second upward movement lasting for an even longer period than the first: "From the beginning to the middle of the eighteenth century, our records indicate no interruption of the tranquility of the inhabitants, either in church or in civil affairs" (p. 64).

The next test of Concord's progress occurred during the American Revolution, when the principle of individualism found itself in armed conflict with an English community that no longer supported such individualism. Concord declined momentarily into poverty and debt after the war—the cost, Emerson believes, of any conflict between community and individual freedom—but such a decline was only temporary because of Concord's determination to balance within itself both poles of historical force in an open-ended dialectical drama. Emerson stresses that "whilst the town had its own full share of the public distress, it was very far from desiring relief at the cost of order and law" (p. 81). The Revolutionary War had not been fought only because of the farmers' "thirst for liberty" (p. 72); it was also a reaffirmation of the ideal of dynamic order implicit in the founding of Concord. This process of combining freedom creatively with order occurred with the town's acceptance in 1788 of the new Constitution of the United States. "This event closed the whole series of important public events in which this town played a part. From that time to the present hour, this town has made a slow but constant progress in population and wealth, and the arts of peace" (p. 82).

Concord's history had thus been characterized by increasingly shorter "declines" in development and by increasingly longer periods of rising. Surely, Emerson implies, this pattern indicates the spirally progressive pattern possible in a community learning to live in accordance with higher ideals than mere materialistic gain. "For the most part," he argues, "the town has deserved the name it wears" (p. 83). Though Concord's rate of physical growth had slowed by 1835, Emerson prefers to think this slowing was due to the fact that the youth of Concord were emigrating in order to plant small Concords throughout America. They did this because the truest "meaning" of Concord was psychological and moral. In these senses, Concord—the best part of the American past in its desire to balance freedom and order, progress and stability, change and continuity—was *becoming* America, or rather, America was becoming a truly "United" States, a national "Concord."

Because he believed this interpretation of Concord's history, Emerson could "feel some unwillingness to quit the remembrance of the past. With all the hope of the new," he states, "I feel that we are leaving the old. Every moment carries us farther from the two great epochs of public principle, the Planting, and the Revolution of the colony" (p. 85). For all his stress on the importance of the future, Emerson had no intention of forgetting the usable, because noble, past. This past was made not only for individual heroes or scholars but also for the community as a whole: "those who fill a space in the world's history . . . are borne forward, as it were, by the weight of thousands whom they lead" (p. 86). Concord, like Rome, is not perfect, but it is understood best, believes Emerson, when treated as an example of the *process* of human striving for both individual and communal perfection. Carefully he closes his address on a note of reverence: "The acknowledgment of the Supreme Being exalts the history of this people. It brought the fathers hither. In a war of principle, it delivered their sons. And so long as a spark of this faith survives among the children's children so shall the name of Concord be honest and venerable" (p. 86).

Emerson added a note to his original remarks on Concord nearly thirty-two years later when, on April 19, 1867, he spoke at the dedication of the soldier's monument in Concord. The town had just participated in a new and crucial "epoch of public principle," the Civil War, and in his speech Emerson attempted both to relate the recent event to past events and to relate his town specifically to the towns of America. "This day," he said, "is in Concord doubly our calendar day, as being the anniversary of the invasion of the town by British troops in 1775, and of the departure of the company of volunteers for Washington in 1861. . . . Every other town and city has its own heroes and memorial days." He was proud "that the heroes of old and of recent date, who made and kept America *free* and *united* [my italics], were not rare or solitary growths, but sporadic over vast tracts of the Republic," and he was certain "that the virtues we are met to honor were directed on aims which command the sympathy of every loyal American citizen, were exerted for the protection of our common country, and aided its triumph" (*W*, *11*, 349–50).

Emerson treated the new soldier's monument, a granite obelisk, as a symbol both specific and universal; "the roots of the events it appropriately marks," he said, "are in the heart of the universe." He described the obelisk in terms of significant religious metaphors adapted to his own purposes:

> The art of the architect and the sense of the town have made these dumb stones speak; have, if I may borrow the

> old language of the church, converted these elements from a secular to a sacred and spiritual use; have made them look to the past and the future; have given them a meaning for the imagination and the heart. . . . 'Tis certain that a plain stone like this, standing on such memories, having no reference to utilities, but only to the grand instincts of the civil and moral man, mixes with surrounding nature,—day by day with the changing seasons, by night the stars roll over it gladly,—becomes a sentiment, a poet, a prophet, an orator, to every townsman and passenger, an altar where the noble youth shall in all time come to make his secret vows. (*W*, *11*, 351)

Out of the American wilderness and the wilderness of chaotic war had emerged a "sacred and spiritual symbol"—a reminder to both Concordians and Americans of their continuing holy errand into the wilderness, of their continuing attempt to enlist the support of the City of Man in building an earthly imitation of the City of God. The obelisk was a symbol rooted deeply in both nature and history, but, "standing on such memories," it also enjoyed an "original" relation to the universe. Looking both "to the past and the future," it symbolized both continuity and change, tradition and progress. It was a figurative Pisgah on that pilgrimage that structured both Emerson's sense of history and his sense of the artistic process —"an altar where the noble youth shall in all time come to make his secret vows."

By treating the obelisk as an artistic symbol both of history and of an ongoing religious sentiment, a humanly created holy spot for the community and the individual, Emerson could portray Concord and its fellow northern towns as being collectively in the Civil War a holy Rome, a psychologically defined City of the West that was also a New Jerusalem on the march:

> As cities of men are the first effects of civilization, and are also instantly causes of more civilization, so armies, which are only wandering cities, generate a vast heat, and lift the spirit of the soldiers who compose them to the boiling point. The armies mustered in the North were as much missionaries to the mind of the country as they were carriers of material force, and had the advantage of carrying whither they marched a higher civilization. (*W*, 11, 355)

Despite his many doubts and qualifications, Emerson continued to hope that moral and material progress were compatible, and that the American artist might remain true to the reality of the latter while asserting the ideals of the former. The American had dual citizenship, and Emerson wished to believe that in the American context at least he need be disloyal to neither. Along with other dreamers of the American dream, he continued to confront painful historical experience with the assertion that a nation striving to become a New Rome might also become a holy City in the best of all possible Western empires.

❦ 5. The Organic City

And what they call their city way
Is not their way, but hers. (W, 9, 225)

Man was not made to live in a swamp, but a frog. If God meant him to live in a swamp, he would have made him a frog. (J, 9, 153)

The Indian cheer, the frosty skies,
Rear purer wits, inventive eyes,—
Eyes that frame cities where none be,
And hands that stablish what these see. (W, 9, 63–64)

In *Nature,* Emerson challenged each individual to experience "an original relation to the universe" (*W,* 1, 3). Often during his active literary career he also urged human society as a whole to do the same. If the imperfect City of Man were to become more like the City of God, it needed to ally itself more closely with the forces animating and governing the universe. Urban civilization—especially any civilization hoping to become an ideal City of the West—needed to relate itself more creatively to those aspects of the universe that were not urban. To Emerson, the city's need to wed itself to "nature" was a social counterpart of the individual's need to unite the "me" to the "not-me."

Such a task was by no means simple for either the individual or the society, as centuries of human history had indicated—and as Adam and Eve's expulsion from the Garden of Eden has asserted in archetypal metaphor. By the nineteenth century, in fact, new historical developments had complicated the task both of reconciling man and nature and of expressing artistically any vision of reconciliation. The introduction of the complex machine powered by other than direct human force and the growth of the huge industrial city forced thinkers and artists to reexamine the implications of the traditional dualism of urban and nonurban, and such reexamination produced not only some of the best art of the nineteenth century but also some of the most anguished. Paul Ginestier, in a brilliant study, has argued that

> one of the essential characteristics of the machine age is precisely the imposition of a mechanical rhythm upon the *laissez-faire* of the organic periods in which man was closer to his origins. One of the great factors of today's poetical creation results from the conflicts and problems of adjustment which have developed out of the superimposition of a metallic rhythm upon the psychic rhythm.[1]

In nineteenth-century European literature this increasing sense of tension between the "metallic" and the "psychic," the mechanical and the organic, the artificial and the natural, often led to pessimism both as to the direction of society's development and as to the artist's status in that society. As Francis D. Klingender has noted, Mary Shelley's creation of Frankenstein's monster in 1817 expressed a common fear "that

1. Paul Ginestier, *The Poet and the Machine,* trans. Martin B. Friedman (Chapel Hill, N.C., 1961), p. 15. Part of the modern argument that the machine is "impersonal" is based, of course, on a fear of the increasingly indirect relationship of the individual's efforts and the product he produces (or, increasingly, merely helps to produce).

science might cease to be the willing slave of man and become instead his master and destroyer."[2] In the Romantic artist's eyes, "the city-dweller became a type of the man isolated not only from his fellows, but from those forms of nature which might lead him to a Transcendental sense of unity with the universe."[3] Though such artists might live in actual industrial cities, they increasingly devoted themselves, Frank Kermode contends, to a Romantic "image" that was "other" than the city and to "the substitution of organicism for mechanistic modes of thinking about works of art."[4]

American Romantics felt this heady wind of disillusion as it swept to them across the Atlantic, and to an extent they responded to the European artist's elaborate pose of alienation from the modern city. Poe's "Man in the Crowd," the nightmarish New York of Melville's *Pierre*, and the dead New York of Hawthorne's "New Adam and Eve" all indicated ways in which "urban" experience was hostile to "natural" experience. In comparison to the central strain of European Romanticism, however, American Romanticism tended to soften and even blur the distinction between the urban and the natural. To many European Romantics the city was at best a necessary purgatory, at worst a killing inferno, but rarely did they conceive the city and nature as anything but inevitably and constitutionally opposed. American Romanticism, however, though often admitting the *fact* of such a dichotomy, at the same time denied its inevitability or necessity.

Emerson himself was one of the chief proponents of rec-

2. Francis D. Klingender, *Art and the Industrial Revolution* (London, 1947), p. 103.

3. R. A. Foakes, *The Romantic Assertion*, p. 47. For a treatment of the symbolic qualities of the city, see also W. H. Auden, *The Enchafed Flood; or the Romantic Iconography of the Sea* (New York, 1950).

4. Kermode, *Romantic Image*, pp. 4–5, 43.

onciliation. In his roles of historian and prophet he urged rapprochement in two areas. First, he wished to see the physical city become more creatively related to its natural hinterland and more internally "natural" or "organic." Second, he wanted to find ways by which the poet might integrate the growing industrial city into an artistic work that professed to embody organic principles. Whether dealing with the industrial city itself or with the artistic treatment of that city, he tended to accept a dichotomy of city and nature not as a conclusion, but as a point of departure—as the beginning of a potential dialectical or dramatic movement toward "organic" reconciliation.

No discussion of Emerson's efforts at reconciliation can be very profitable unless we recognize the complexities of two key Emersonian terms, "nature" and "organic." Arthur O. Lovejoy's important study should remind us of the many shifting and even conflicting meanings of "nature" as that term reached the nineteenth century.[5] Many of these meanings are found in Emerson's writings. An excellent recent study by Paul Lauter justly cautions us to be sensitive to the shifting aspects of Emerson's vocabulary and points usefully to the reasons for the fluidity of his language. At his best, Emerson tended to treat the many meanings of "nature" less as truth than as strategic metaphors—as devices for reconciliation. When weakest, the strategy seems merely semantic juggling, but at its most successful, however, it at least appears to give the reconciliation of urban and nonurban worlds a basis in reality.[6]

5. Arthur O. Lovejoy, "'Nature' as Aesthetic Norm," in *Essays in the History of Ideas* (Baltimore, 1948).

6. Charles R. Metzger, in *Emerson and Greenough: Pioneers of a Transcendental Esthetic* (Berkeley, 1954), pp. 35–36, argues that in

Uneasy with the ambiguities of "nature," a number of recent scholars have put more weight on the term "organic," especially as Emerson applied it to his art but also as he applied it to the physical environment. That term, however, also embodies several denotations. Vivian Hopkins points to some of these meanings by listing three that are relevant to Emerson's writing:

> In its simplest sense, organic form states that a work of art derives excellence from its resemblance to natural objects. . . . The principle of imitation enters into this conception, though Emerson and Coleridge are reluctant to admit it—partly because they had developed "organic form" to supplant "imitation," a term which neoclassical usage had crusted with artificiality. . . .
>
> The second and more subtle definition of organic form is the development of details in a work according to one controlling purpose, so that the whole presents a union of integrated parts. . . .
>
> A third sense of the term appears in a work's being judged organic if it produces upon the observer an impression similar to that caused by nature's works.[7]

Emerson's works "*nature* means variously man, not-man, not-society, out-of-doors, essence, universe, and God; and thus, unfortunately, in failing to distinguish his one use of the term from another Emerson not only expanded his conception but also confused his exposition." Paul Lauter, however, in "Truth and Nature: Emerson's Use of Two Complex Words, "*ELH*, 27 (1960), 66–85, argues that "Emerson risks, or more correctly, *courts* confusion of these traditional senses of *nature*, subordinating discrete meanings to the larger rhetorical purpose: namely, to associate, even to equate the created world with the creator, to manipulate the reader into viewing the physical universe as directly the product, as the part and article of God as Creator" (p. 81).

7. Hopkins, *Spires of Form*, pp. 66–80.

Though Hopkins' definitions raise unanswered questions, they at least suggest that "organic" can be applied to the three major foci of the creative process—to the created object itself, to the creator in the act of creation, and to the observer in the act of perceiving the created object.

All definitions of "organic," however, force us back to the problem of what Emerson meant by "nature." For the purposes of this discussion, three of his uses of the term are especially relevant: nature as the objects and processes not created by human beings; nature as the synonym for "essence," an object (especially, a human) being most "natural" when most nearly corresponding to its own type or essential character; and nature as the underlying spiritual force that animates the universe. At his most Transcendentally assertive, Emerson argued that all three varieties of nature were identical or at least inherently complementary. By being true to his own nature, man might experience the same influx of spiritual power that also animated the nonhuman portion of the finite physical world. In his less Transcendental moments, however, Emerson admitted that there seemed to be a discrepancy between "natural" processes, human behavior, and spiritual purpose. Finite man, as a creator both of physical cities and of urban art, faced the complex and difficult task of making his product "organic" in three sometimes conflicting senses: as an imitation of the processes discernible in his natural environment, as an expression of innate human needs and feelings, and as an expression (spontaneous if possible, conscious if necessary) of spiritual ideals. Emerson's attempt to reconcile the industrial city to organic nature and to organic art involved much more than a mere affirmation of farming or gardens or woodland walks or contemplation of the stars. It involved centrally his exploration of what he meant by "human nature." In the equation of human experience, God and nature were givens, even if unfathomed. Man himself was the major variable, and Emerson's search for the organic city was at base an attempt to solve for this human variable.

Some recent scholars, notably Sherman Paul, have given substantial weight to Emerson's well-known distinction between the city and the country in a journal passage for 1839:

> The City delights the Understanding. It is made up of finites: short, sharp, mathematical lines, all calculable. It is full of varieties, of successions, of contrivances. The Country, on the contrary, offers an unbroken horizon, the monotony of an endless road, of vast uniform plains, of distant mountains, the melancholy of uniform and infinite vegetation; the objects on the road are few and worthless, the eye is invited ever to the horizon and the clouds. It is the school of the Reason. (*J*, 5, 310–11)

Underemphasizing the complex tone of this passage, Paul has cited it as an indication that Emerson stressed an inevitable dichotomy between the artificial urban environment and the organic environment of surrounding country.[8] Certainly, Emerson recognized that the gap between actual cities and their hinterlands constituted *one* aspect of experience. Such a recognition lay behind his statement that "the values of Boston are artificial values . . . whilst the values of Maine are primary

8. The passage, for example, contains a number of ambiguities. Emerson's use of "delights" conveys at least some positive connotations; neither "finites" nor "varieties" implies totally negative meanings, though both terms signify transcendental limitations. Conversely, "monotony," "uniform," "melancholy," and "few" imply that the natural setting has a negative as well as a positive function for Emerson's poetic aims. See Paul, *Emerson's Angle of Vision,* p. 82.

and necessary" (*J*, *8*, 166). To the extent that the city's objects and activities were merely mechanical, arithmetically accumulative, and manipulative, they produced an "artificial" product explicitly opposed to the organic products of rural nature (*W*, *12*, 178–79).[9] This artificiality was often embedded in the writings of artists who lived in the mechanical city. "Pope and Johnson and Addison," Emerson complained in 1837, "write as if they had never seen the face of the country but had only read of trees & rivers in books" (*JMN*, 5, 348).[10]

Of this dichotomy, a major symbol was the wall. As noted earlier, American writers might treat the city wall as a positive symbol of unity, order, and protection, or as a restricting agent. To the extent that they espoused an organic theory of art and value, they might also let the wall suggest the sharp split between an urban and nonurban environment. To American writers traveling abroad one of the most striking aspects of European cities was their surrounding walls. Even more interesting, however, is the American writers' imposition of similarly enclosing walls onto American cities whose gridiron patterns made such walls only metaphorically possible.[11] Em-

9. Emerson often referred to New York and other cities as "a world of surfaces" (e.g. *J*, *6*, 165). Paris, he argued in 1854, was a world of "numerical order" and "superficial analysis" ("France or Urbanity"—Houghton manuscript 202.4). See Melville's distinction between the city and country in *Pierre*, Chap. 1, or his description of London in *Israel Potter* as an environment where "no speck of any green thing was seen" (*Works*, *11*, 212).

10. Robert Spiller suggestively contrasts the rhythms of eighteenth century life (the closed couplet) with the "open-minded" and flowing rhythm of American life after the Revolution ("The American Literary Dilemma and Edgar Allan Poe," pp. 9–10).

11. Cooper commented that "this practice of cutting off a town like a cheese-paring is very common on the continent" (*Residence in France*, *1*, 210). Melville called the walls of Jerusalem an "arbitrary

erson constantly described the streets of American cities as artificial canyons whose walls symbolized the unnatural restrictions placed by civilization on natural man. In 1833 he asserted optimistically that "the walls of cities and their artificial modes of life have not yet tamed the savage in us" (*EL*, *1*, 46). In a more pessimistic mood he argued that

> the inhabitants of cities pay a high tax for their social advantages, their increased civilization, in their exclusion from the sight of the unlimited glory of the earth. Imprisoned in streets of brick and stone, in tainted air and hot and dusty corners, they only get glimpses . . . of the face of the green pastoral earth which the great Father of all is now adorning with matchless beauty as one wide garden. (*Y*, 39)

To the extent that such artificial walls held firm, whether metaphorically or literally, the dichotomy between mechanical city and organic hinterland was static rather than dynamic, unfortunate rather than tragic. Threatened by or unhappy with the urban routine, the urban worker or poet might escape to external nature and there "be aired & *insulated* in the fields" (*L*, *1*, 411).[12] Neither the city nor the natural hinterland, however, were static. Both were full of movement, and

---

limitation & prescription of things" (*Journal, 1856–57*, pp. 139, 150). Note his striking use of walls as a symbol in "Bartleby the Scrivener." Thoreau, in *Walden*, called Boston a walled city and pointed in contrast to his hut where "unfenced nature" reached up "to your very sills" (Chaps. 1 and 14).

12. In 1837 Emerson wrote, "Being a lover of solitude I went to live in the country seventeen miles from Boston, & there the northwest wind with all his snows took me in charge & defended me from all company in winter, & the hills & sand-banks that intervened between me & the city, kept guard in summer" (*JMN*, 5, 283).

in moving they inevitably interacted. The dynamic interaction of opposing forces was bound to produce conflict, and, to the extent that urban and natural forces were polar opposites, such conflict could lead only to destruction. When meeting in the same physical arena, either mechanical processes would destroy the natural or natural forces would obliterate the work of man—and perhaps man himself.

To Emerson and contemporary American writers, the dynamic mechanical city of both modernizing Europe and developing America often seemed to be showing greater force than nature and to be turning its hinterland into an "emasculated country," in Thoreau's term, leaving only "a maimed and imperfect nature."[13] Many of the medieval walled cities of Europe had industrialized and "overflowed the girdle" that once restrained their growth. The result, especially in industrial England, was a growing number of "mushroom" towns with "straggling suburbs," which were "denaturalizing" the countryside at an increasingly rapid rate and imposing the "cold plan" of a gridiron of streets and buildings upon older random growths. While traveling through a number of England's industrial towns, Hawthorne was repulsed by "their heaps of refuse matter from the furnace, which seems to be the only kind of stuff which Nature cannot take back to herself and resolve into the elements when man has thrown it aside."[14] Like Hawthorne, Emerson was both impressed and somewhat frightened by the "mechanical might" of the grow-

13. Thoreau complained that "almost all our improvements, so called, tend to convert the country into the town" (*Journals, 14,* 57). Cf. *Journals,* 6, 108, and *11,* 78–79.

14. Hawthorne, *English Notebooks,* pp. 128–29, 200; Cooper, *Gleanings in England,* pp. 189–91; *A Residence in France, 1,* 210; *Gleanings in France,* p. 72. Note Melville's use, in "The Encantadas," of a "city lot" of cinders as a symbol of desolation and sterility.

ing English towns. The British railroad seemed to him a "cannonball" which had "machinized [sic] the world" (*L*, 3, 452–53). He wrote Thoreau that "everything centralizes, in this magnificent machine which England is. Manufacturer for the world she is become or becoming one complete tool or engine in herself." Like his contemporaries, he was very sensitive to the destructive potential of such industrialization. "This invasion of Nature by Trade," he argued in 1839, threatened to "establish a new, universal Monarchy more tyrannical than Babylon or Rome" (*J*, 5, 285).[15]

Whatever was happening in Europe, the mechanical invasion of nature by the burgeoning industrial cities of America caused particular anxiety among those American Romantics who wished to see their nation's civilization develop in harmony with rather than in opposition to the continent's organic hinterland. As Hawthorne watched the rapid growth of towns along the Erie Canal and anticipated the time when "the wondrous stream may flow between two continuous lines of buildings, through one thronged street, from Buffalo to Albany," he also noted that "the wild nature of America" was being driven out of its accustomed strongholds "by the encroachments of civilized man." He suggested that a useful sketch might be written about "the devouring of the old country residences by the overgrown monster of a city."[16] In "I

15. Thoreau, *Correspondence*, p. 194. In *White Jacket* Melville found a striking symbol for the tyrannical aspects of urban civilization in its invasion of nature (both external and human)—the cruising man-of-war. Throughout the novel the *Neversink* is compared to "a city afloat," a "lofty, walled, and garrisoned town" that embodies all the professions, processes, and dangers of a modern metropolis still governed by a medieval mentality.

16. Hawthorne, *Works*, 2, 484–85, 492–93; *American Notebooks*, p. 99.

and My Chimney," Melville noted critically that the "large rivalry in building tall houses" had caused the economically oriented cities to encroach not only on horizontal nature but on the very air above them.[17] And Emerson watched with mixed feelings "the endless procession of wagons" creeping by his home at Concord, carrying manufactured goods from Boston to "all the towns of New Hampshire & Vermont" and "to every cabin in the hills" (*JMN*, 5, 296–97). As the expanding railroad system "made Massachusetts Boston," he began to wonder if this expanding urban influence were not also imposing a "hard shallow fruitless worldliness" on the hinterland (*L*, 3, 215).

When most pessimistic, Emerson and his contemporaries felt that natural forces would be degraded if they made misguided attempts to find some sort of working compromise with the mechanical might of the radically aggressive city. Nature could retaliate adequately, they sometimes feared, only by destroying the city. As Thoreau put it, "Artificial, denaturalized persons cannot handle nature without being poisoned." In fact, he argued satanically that nature should declare war on the city, and in *Walden* he compared timber being hauled by rail to Boston to "long battering-rams going twenty miles an hour against the city's walls."[18] Perhaps the era's most powerful metaphor for nature's spontaneous destruction of the aggressive city was the sinking of the Pequod in *Moby Dick*, but similar images occurred to other American

17. Melville, *Complete Stories*, pp. 375–76. Hawthorne recognized a similar encroachment when he visited Sheffield, England; "the famous town of razors and penknives" was "enveloped in a cloud of its own diffusing" (*Works*, 7, 171). Compare Dickens' description of Coketown from a distance in *Hard Times*, Bk. III, Chap. 6.

18. Thoreau, *Journals*, 8, 448–49; *Walden*, Chap. 4.

writers. Poe described destruction of the walled city by disease in "The Masque of the Red Death" and by "gravity" in "The Fall of the House of Usher." The most common form of destruction, however, was a manifestation of what might be called the conflagratory imagination. Hawthorne recurred time and again to the modern city's destruction by fire, and Melville twice threatened the medieval ship-city of *White-Jacket* with a similar fate.[19] Emerson at various times pointed to the destruction of cities by a wide range of natural forces —floods, earthquakes, volcanoes, disease, and fire.[20] His desire to depopulate and "leave the cities void" (*W*, 9, 229) by emigrations was merely a more humane way of allowing natural force to destroy urbanism as a way of life.

Such an extreme position was less characteristic of Emerson, however, than a more creative attitude. Between the polar fear of a ruthlessly aggressive industrial city and the polar reaction that described an apocalyptically avenging nature lay a spectrum of possible attitudes and strategies of reconciliation. As both social observer and prophetic poet, Emerson primarily wished to convert the modern city to "organic" purposes and to ally it to its natural environment without denying the importance and even the necessity of the city. In fact, an organically oriented city might reaffirm and augment the creative role of civilization by reflecting and stimulating humanity's moral and spiritual development. It is not

19. See Hawthorne's "Fire Worship," "The Devil in Manuscript," "Old News," "The New Adam and Eve," and "Earth's Holocaust." Fire is also a central challenge to the Pequod and to Ahab in Chap. 119 of *Moby Dick*.

20. E.g. Y, 112. In his essay "Circles" Emerson remarked, "Beware when God lets loose a thinker on this planet. Then all things are at risk. It is as when a conflagration has broken out in a great city, and no man knows what is safe, or where it will end" (*W*, 2, 308).

really surprising that, in an era that witnessed the development of "garden cemeteries" and the beginnings of agitation for a Central Park in New York, Emerson too should have looked for ways in which nature could be introduced into the city in a manner acceptable to nature, man, and God.[21]

A first step toward "naturalizing" the physical city might take the form of bringing in individual natural objects. The presence of plants, especially as gardens and parks, appealed to Emerson's sensibilities. In a sermon in 1829 he argued that even in imprisoning streets of brick and stone "something of the mighty process of vegetation forces itself on every human eye. The grass springs up between the pavements at our feet and the poplar and the elm send out as vigorous and as graceful branches to shade and to fan the town as in their native forest" (*Y*, 39).[22] In a lecture in 1833 he praised the Jardin des Plantes in Paris for its ability to educate an urban audience in "natural philosophy" (*EL*, 1, 7–10). While on a Western tour in 1863, he admired Salt Lake City for being a "hab-

21. For discussions of the use of "green forms" in nineteenth-century cities, see Lewis Mumford, *The City in History: Its Origins, Its Transformations, and Its Prospects* (New York, 1961), pp. 474–78, and *The Brown Decades* (New York, 1931), Chap. 2; Christopher Tunnard, *The City of Man* (New York, 1953), Chap. 8; and Ruth Huth, *Nature and the American: Three Centuries of Changing Attitudes* (Berkeley, 1957), pp. 57–69.

22. Traveling Americans were often impressed with the public and private gardens of European cities. Note, however, the special use Hawthorne makes of the walled urban garden in "Rappaccini's Daughter" and the somewhat ironic way in which Melville describes London's "Paradise of Bachelors." Thoreau, as usual, pushed the concept of a garden city to its rhetorical extreme and treated the elms of Concord as "old citizens" of the town (*Journals*, 8, 131–40). "Each town should have a park," he argued in 1859, "or rather a primitive forest . . . for instruction and recreation. Let us keep New York *new*, preserving all the advantages of living in the country" (*Journals*, 12, 387).

itable garden" (*J*, 9, 540). Part of his program for natural urban renewal was expressed in the poem "Art":

> On the city's paved street
> Plant gardens lined with lilacs sweet;
> Let spouting fountains cool the air,
> Singing in the sun-baked square. (*W*, 9, 277)

Another element of nature, water, could also function creatively in an urban environment. Personifying that element in his lecture "Water" in 1834, Emerson reminded his listeners that "we have set him to cleanse our cities. . . . He washes away the filth of cities and continents" (*EL*, *1*, 51–52). The morally educative force of water seemed plain to him as he wrote his wife in 1843 about a fountain he had seen that day in New York:

> The city itself is an animating spectacle with its beautiful fountain in the Park . . . I cannot look at it enough as I pass. By moonlight & in sunshine & in summer as they say it has finer finest aspects & moods. . . . It says to the newsboy who roars "Morning Herald, New Era, Tribune, Sun, Aurora," all day to every passenger through the Park, "I am Kuhleborn: I am the Great Power of Water come from distant mountains to tell you, dear little cit, that you are a mountaineer too, and it is the love of home that allures your eyes to me." (*L*, 3, 145)[23]

Air and light might also pour into the city, urging it out of a merely artificial routine. In his poem "The World-Soul," Em-

23. Hawthorne, in *The Marble Faun,* stressed that the ancient mossy fountains still brought water into a decayed Rome (*Works*, 6, 53–54). In "Sketches from Memory" he described the water of the Erie Canal as the fertilizing agent and organic source of the towns along its banks (*Works*, 2, 484–85).

erson was happy that the "crimson morning flames into / The fopperies of the town" (*W*, 9, 17). If the civilized world were merely "an immense Boston or Hannover Street with mountains of ordinary women, trains & trains of mean, leathern men all immovably bounded," such "mountains of rubbish" might nevertheless "reflect the morning sun & the evening star" (*L*, 4, 376).[24]

But the mere introduction of natural objects into the modern city was often not sufficient to modify substantially its mechanical routines. Rather than transforming the urban mechanism, natural processes ran the danger of being harnessed for mechanical purposes. Though "every house" might be, as Emerson put it, "a quotation out of all forests and mines and stone quarries" (*W*, 4, 42), such man-made quotations might turn out to be artificial rather than organic statements. Thoreau believed that cranberries, lumber, bark, and ice often lost something vital when "translated" into urban environments. Hawthorne realized that even natural air and light lost their purity on entering the industrial city and intermingling with "the all-pervading smoke" and "sable snow-flakes of bituminous coal."[25] Rather than water's cleaning the city, the city might soil the entering water. The fountain Arethusa, noted Emerson during his visit to ancient Syracuse in 1833,

24. In an unusually optimistic mood Thoreau asked the reader of his poem "Our Country" to "see Boston, Baltimore, and New York stand / Fair in the sunshine of the eastern sea" (*Collected Poems*, p. 134). Hawthorne saw a redeeming symbol in a "streak of sunshine journeying through the prisoner's cell" (*American Notebooks*, p. 97); in the character of a human sunbeam, Phoebe, he attempted to bring a similar redemption to the House of the Seven Gables.

25. Thoreau, *Journals*, 6, 88, and *Walden*, Chap. 16; Hawthorne, *Works*, 7, 326–27. Nevertheless Thoreau wished to believe that the water of Walden would help purify "the sweltering inhabitants of Charleston and New Orleans, of Madras and Bombay and Calcutta."

served "as one great washing tub to fifty or sixty women who were polluting it with all the filthy clothes of the city" (*JMN*, *4*, 125). Even when physical nature seemed to escape contamination and to exert some influence on the city's mechanical routines, its impact often affected only the surface of those routines, not their sources. Unlike some of his contemporaries who believed that an external imitation of nature in urban architecture, dress, and manners was sufficient to naturalize the city, Emerson at his most perceptive recognized that such naturalization could occur only by redirecting the underlying forces that had created the external urban routine.

As a poet, hopeful that words had power, Emerson believed that part of redirecting the urban forces consisted in redefining those forces. It is not surprising, therefore, that he should describe seemingly mechanical processes in "organic" terms. Many literary precedents existed, of course, for applying organic metaphors to a nation as a whole, both in its racial aspects (the race growing or dying like an animal or plant) and in its social aspects (as the Elizabethans' "body politic"). Young Emerson was responding to these precedents as early as 1824 when he called the "literary growth" of the New England Puritans "the first bursting of a nation from the bud" and argued that Franklin and Jonathan Edwards were "such a fruit as might be expected from such a tree" (*JMN*, 2, 197).[26] Also available to describe civilized development was the time-honored (and timeworn) metaphor of planting, which at its most subtle combined the rational process of

26. In a lecture on "France or Urbanity" in 1854, Emerson told his audience that "the ancients believe the world was a huge animal," and he suggested that "Italy, Germany, India, America, are the stomachs of Behemoth" (Houghton manuscript 202.4). Nicoloff, *Emerson on Race and History*, esp. pp. 142–74, discusses Emerson's treatment of the "Saxon" race as an organism.

founding with an implication that the cooperation of natural forces was essential to the growth of that rational foundation. Following this convention, Emerson could look at the American continent and watch "Trade sow cities / Like shells along the shore" (*W*, 9, 18) or could contend that "the chain of Western railroads from Chicago to the Pacific has planted cities and civilization in less time than it costs to bring an orchard into bearing" (*W*, 7, 161). He was also familiar with the traditional means of personifying, or "humanizing," a city, especially by means of feminine nouns and pronouns ("she," "mother," "queen"), and he often applied this device to Boston.[27]

Despite such precedents, however, Emerson's generation of Romantics was the first to have to face the problem of applying natural metaphors to the growing industrial city. If, after contemplating the Parthenon, the Pyramids, and England's abbeys, Emerson could argue that "these temples grew

27. Ginestier, in *The Poet and the Machine*, p. 45, argues that "the city is maternal, the crowd which it contains feminine (*la foule*), and its hostility implies something contrary to nature." To refer to a city by a feminine pronoun is common even in the twentieth century, though increasingly "it" or some other neutral term is used to describe the modern industrial metropolis. As Lewis Mumford implies, the feminine pronoun may be a holdover from a preindustrial past, when the urban community was much more obviously an extension of the home or maternal womb—a projection symbolized by the very walls of the ancient and medieval cities. With the rise of post-Renaissance capitalism and later modern industry and their embodiment in gridiron or "open" cities, the maternal qualities of the city became less obvious. If the city remained "feminine," it became not so much a mother to be worshipped as a mistress to be exploited or wooed. Or, in its guises as a machine, it became neuter or even masculine in gender. When Henry Adams, in *The Education*, contrasts the modern Dynamo to the medieval Virgin, he is pointing among other things to a major metaphorical development of urban imagery.

as grows the grass" (*W*, 9, 7–8), his desire to make his writing speak to his own age also prompted him to speak of the aggressively modern city in organic terms. At his most organically affirmative, in fact, he argued that the industrial urban processes of his era were natural processes. In 1863, as he watched two American armies destroy the nation's cities, he was moved to remark that "there is no unemployed force in Nature. All decomposition is recomposition. War disorganizes, but it is to reorganize. Weeks, months pass—a new harvest; trade springs up, and there stand new cities, new homes, all rebuilt and sleepy with permanence" (*W*, 10, 248). In his 1844 essay "Nature," Emerson was even more explicit: "We talk of deviations from natural life, as if artificial life were not also natural. . . . If we consider how much we are nature's, we need not be superstitious about towns, as if that terrific or benefic force did not find us there also, and fashion cities. Nature, who made the mason, made the house" (*W*, 3, 182–83).

Two objections can be raised to Emerson's application of organic metaphors to the industrial city, and both are valid to a limited extent. The first objection is that a merely verbal manipulation of metaphor does not necessarily alter the actual substance of the metaphor's referent. To call civilized, mechanical, and industrial forces "organic" and "natural" need not make the actual functioning of such forces any less artificial. The second objection is that, in order to treat the modern city as organic, Emerson was forced to redefine the term "nature"—to treat nature not as the physical environment upon which man was imposing his urban rhythms and forms but as the universal or divine "Power" that created and sustained all physical objects and processes, whether urban or nonurban. Such a solution might have Transcendental sanction, but it risks being of only limited empirical value to human beings concerned with confronting their environment precisely and effectively, whether in life or in art.

Against these objections, two defenses seem to emerge —though rarely systematically—from the corpus of Emerson's writing. One defense involves his treatment of the relation of the "natural" man to the modern city. The other defense hinges on his use of organicism as a strategy or dramatic method rather than as a generic or teleological doctrine. Though each defense presents its peculiar problems and possibilities, both centrally involve Emerson's attempt to decide what he meant by "human nature."

With rare exceptions, Emerson applied organic metaphors to the emerging metropolises of science and industry only when talking about the human element in cities. It was the presence of men that made the city organic, and if their presence was not in itself sufficient to naturalize the city, it was certainly essential. Natural physical objects and processes usually entered the city creatively less by means of their own force (such as a cleansing rainstorm or warming sunshine) than by means of man's efforts. Man had assembled the Jardin des Plantes in Paris, had allowed grassy squares and trees to remain in the midst of Boston's buildings, and had channeled water through a man-made form in order to create a blithe New York fountain. Even man's own artifacts could be considered "natural" to the extent that they involved the expression of his essential nature. As Emerson argued in a relatively late essay, "Works and Days," "Our nineteenth century is the age of tools. They grew out of our structure. . . . All the tools and engines on earth are only extensions of [our] limbs and senses" (*W*, 7, 157). The railroad and telegraph could be organic unifiers not because they physically linked city and country or city and city but because they allowed *men* to come together. If the modern city were to be internally organic and organically related to its hinterland, the unification must occur through the agency of human nature—through man's correct use of his powers of seeing, saying, and physically acting.

When asserting his individualistic Transcendentalism most hyperbolically, Emerson argued that the creative vision of Man Thinking or Seeing did not distinguish between urban and nonurban objects, since all "experience" was merely a projection of the Over-Soul through the channel of the inspired seer. "The Intellect builds the universe and is the key to all it contains," he asserted in his essay "Natural History of Intellect." "It is not then cities or mountains, or animals, or globes that any longer commands us, but only man; not the fact, but so much of man as is in the fact" (*W*, *12*, 5). In an early lecture on English literature he asked his audience to "observe how every belief . . . clothes itself with societies, houses, cities, language, ceremonies, newspapers" (*EL*, *1*, 219). Even if the poet's power did not extend to an actual creation of the objects experienced, it often allowed the visual manipulation of those objects by a single act of spontaneous (that is, organic) perception. Thus, "by a few strokes," the poet "delineates, as on air, the sun, the mountain, the camp, the city, the hero, the maiden, not different from what we know them, but only lifted from the ground and afloat before the eye" (*W*, *1*, 51). At the poet's words, "All that we reckoned settled shakes and rattles; and literatures, cities, climates, religions, leave their foundations and dance before our eyes" (*W*, 2, 311).[28]

28. In 1836, while preparing his essay on *Nature*, Emerson wrote in his journal: "The man is the creator of his world. I choose to pursue certain thoughts to enter certain states of mind, & forthwith I seem to walk into woods by known ways & to hear wood birds & see pines &

More characteristically, however, Emerson urged his seer less to "create" visual experience or to manipulate unstable empirical data than to interpret or "experience" such data organically. The modern city might at least appear organically unified and organically related to its environment if the poet looked at it from the proper "angle of vision." Recent scholarship has stressed the assimilating or encompassing aspects of what might be called Emerson's panoramic or telescopic vision.[29] To the extent that Emerson believed that "the fact detached is ugly" (*J*, 5, 54) and that "nothing but is beautiful in the Whole" (*JMN*, 5, 26), he attempted to find a spot—physical if possible, imaginary when necessary—from which the seer, in an instantaneous and spontaneous act of perception, could experience the city as a visual whole and as part of its natural environment. There was thus a strong moral and aesthetic drive behind his interest in urban objects as proper subjects for "picturesque" art—that is, art that bound its contents into a unified visual image or "picture."

While traveling in Europe, Emerson applied to urban settings his own powers of panoramic vision. Like most of his contemporary artists, he continually attempted to gain a "bird's-eye view" of the cities he visited—to relate both the city's buildings to one another and the city as a whole to its natural setting. Looking down on Milan from the top of that city's cathedral, for example, he could exclaim, "Neighbored by this army of marble saints & martyrs, with scores of exquisitely sculptured pinnacles rising & flowering all around you, the noble city of Milan beneath, and all the Alps in the

---

birches. I choose to pursue certain other thoughts, & lo! I seem to visit the wharves & market" (*JMN*, 5, 172).

29. See esp. Paul, *Emerson's Angle of Vision*, pp. 73–74, and Hopkins, *Spires of Form*, pp. 82–83.

horizon,—it is one of the grandest views on earth" (*JMN, 4,* 190).[30] He applied the same strategy whenever possible to American cities. His most favorable remarks on New York, for example, came when he painted an imaginary picture of that city in the context of its bay, the sky overhead, and its continental hinterland. In his poem "Monadnoc" he allowed "the spruce clerk / From South Cove and City Wharf" to climb the mountain until the "city-tops" of Boston became "a glimmering haze" (*W*, 9, 71).

Though such panoramic views might not change the city in any physical sense, they might change the attitude of the observer enough to allow him to accept the urban environment as a legitimate or "natural" object of his fusing or "organic" vision. At its most negative, distant, or diffusing, such an "ensphering" vision might involve the denial of the city qua city. At its most creative, however—at what Emerson called middle-distance—the panoramic vision enabled the observer to affirm that individual "mechanical" objects and processes contributed to a pattern broader and even better than their individual natures might imply at closer range.[31]

30. Cooper frequently used the term "birds'-eye view" to indicate his goal of vision (e.g. *Excursions in Italy,* 1, 111, 145). His panoramic views of Paris and London are quite striking (*Gleanings in France,* pp. 90–91; *Residence in France,* 1, 158–59; *Gleanings in England,* p. 47). Hawthorne and Melville maneuvered for similar perspectives while in Europe. For Hawthorne's application of this technique to an American environment, see *American Notebooks,* pp. 35, 42.

31. Two striking passages on the problems involved in the panoramic view are Hawthorne, *Works,* 3, 199–200, and Cooper, *Excursions in Switzerland,* 1, 232–33. Paul, in *Emerson's Angle of Vision,* p. 76, chooses to call this perspective a "democratic vision"—"the wider look in which all things are alike and equalized." Paul oversimplifies, however, when he argues that Emerson assigned the eye's ensphering function basically to "the country" and its atomizing function basically

Assimilation of the modern city might also take place, if paradoxically, by another mode of "seeing"—that of the "microscopic" or "microcosmic" vision.[32] Though Emerson's own writings did not exhibit this method of seeing in practice as much as did the work of Melville, Thoreau, Hawthorne, or Whitman, he nevertheless recognized its theoretical importance. To the extent that the entire universe was an organism, animated by the spontaneous and yet purposeful impulse of a single divine principle, any object within that universe might be treated as a functional microcosm of the whole. "This magic lanthorn with fresh pictures, this microcosm," Emerson wrote in 1832, "this Bridal of the earth & sky, this God's wonder—we cannot take to pieces like a machine, but we may study its miracles apart, one at a time, & learn how to find the whole world & every one of its pebbles a tongue" (*JMN*, *4*, 60). If "the improvement that a man makes in one part of his knowledge affects every other part" (*JMN*, 3, 204), then the true poetic observer might profitably explore urban as well as nonurban objects—might "convert the daily and hourly event of New York, of Boston, into universal symbols" (*W*, *12*, 43). "If we had eyes to see it," Emerson wrote in his second "Nature" essay, "a bit of stone from the city wall would certify us of the necessity that man must exist, as readily as the city"

to "the city" (p. 73). In theory, at least, Emerson asserted that the poet's eye might operate rationally, analytically, and atomistically on the country as well as the city (remember Thoreau's systematic classification of plants and animals) and that the eye might treat synthetically the city as well as the country.

32. "Some men see microscopically: some see telescopically," Emerson wrote in 1829. "One magnifies & one micrifies. One exaggerates the familiar & homely into notice & honour; & one brings the great & the infinite home to our eye" (*JMN*, 3, 150). Both forms of vision, he believed, had their valid place in the human makeup.

(*W*, 3, 182).[33] Of course, such certification of the individual urban object's microcosmic relation to the total organism of the city and, beyond that, of the universe conflicted with Emerson's criticism of urban forms and functions as "artificial" and "superficial." Nevertheless, the theory's inconsistency was compensated for by the freedom it gave the practicing poet both to criticize urban life for its deviations from "organic" patterns and impulses and to insist that all aspects of the modern city were legitimately organic material for the poet's art.

The actual practicing or active poet, however, faced a crucial problem not encountered as centrally by the stationary aloof seer. This was the problem of time and its spatial equivalent, motion. Though the world might move and change beneath the gaze of the aloof seer, his encompassing vision could continue to provide a unitary, fusing experience at each moment of the temporal sequence. Emerson realized, however, that no actual finite poet could find such a stable perspective except in rare moments—perhaps only by projecting a better Self onto that vantage point. Most poets, even those of genius, were as much explorers for an undiscovered unity as describers of that unity. Their organically fusing experiences had to be gathered, so to speak, on the run. The poet could not hope to unify visually the movement of the modern

33. If Emerson urged treatment of some objects over others, his motive (aside from mere personal preference) was not based as much on a belief in a rural-urban dichotomy as on a preference for the fresh and vital over the static and conventional. Because previous artists had used urban settings to the point of making them mundane, he often advocated rural settings, but he also opposed the treatment of natural objects in too conventional a manner and would argue in contrast that art should deal with railroads and politics. His iconoclasm was often a strategic means that pointed toward a goal of balanced and comprehensive art and life.

city unless his eye was capable of following and even anticipating that movement—capable, that is, of making the poet both historian of and prophet to the urban civilization of his time. Emerson could write his wife that "I have just sucked all Concord & Boston too like a sponge to write Geo. Bradford a letter" (*L*, *4*, 463), and he was aware that such "organic" absorption of urban experience was at heart a temporal process.

Though the Poet Seeing might avoid to a certain extent the problem of time—finding in instantaneous and momentary encompassment a denial of the ultimate relevance of time—the Poet Speaking could never disregard the temporal problem. At his most perceptive, Emerson knew what T. S. Eliot has stated on behalf of the twentieth-century poet—that "Words move . . . Only in time."[34] In the attempt to describe a temporal experience organically, the poet was creating a new temporal experience in the form of verbal activity.[35] The organic portrayal of experience, therefore, involved the interaction of the poet and the environment—of two temporally expressed forces—both in the gathering of the material for the poem (or any man-made artifact) and in the new expression of this raw material in the poem itself. Thus, Emerson might attempt to "encompass" the city not by hoisting his vision aloft but by moving *around* the city or by guiding his roving eye *through* the city. Not only did he view Milan from the top of its cathedral, but he borrowed a coach, "made the circuit of the City and as travellers say 'killed it thoroughly' " (*JMN*, *4*, 190).

34. T. S. Eliot, "Burnt Norton," in *The Complete Poems and Plays, 1909–1950* (New York, 1958), p. 121. Emerson's Transcendental affirmation at its most searching was the belief that "Words, after speech, reach / Into the silence."

35. Note Emerson's comment that "language is a city to the building of which every human being has brought a stone" (*W*, *8*, 199).

Scholars may justly object that Emerson's own "thoroughness" of exploration seems rather skimpy when compared to Whitman's treatment of New York, Melville's description of Liverpool, or Hawthorne's presentation of Rome. It is equally obvious, however, that Emerson could appreciate such thoroughness in others, even when sensing its Transcendental limitations. After reading Carlyle's *Diamond Necklace* in 1837, he wrote his friend:

> I thought as I read this piece that your strange genius was the instant fruit of your London. It is the aroma of Babylon. Such as the great metropolis, such is this style: so vast, enormous, related to all the world, & so endless in details. I think you see as pictures every street, church, parliament-house, barrack, baker's shop, mutton-stall, forge, wharf, & ship, and whatever stands, creeps, rolls, or swims thereabouts, & make all your own. Hence your encyclopediacal allusion to all knowables, and the virtues and vices of your panoramic pages. Well, it is your own; and it is English; and every word stands for somewhat; and it cheers and fortifies me. (*Corr*, 161)

When Emerson visited London in 1847, Carlyle served as his guide or tutor in the art of exploring. "At noon or later we walked forth to Hyde Park, and the palaces, about two miles from here, to the National Gallery, and to the Strand, Carlyle melting all Westminster and London into his talk and laughter, as he goes" (*J*, 7, 345).[36] Some weeks later Emerson recorded in his journal his own less involved attempts to fol-

36. Interesting in comparison is Thoreau's description of his conversation with Whitman: "He told us that he loved to ride up and down Broadway all day on an omnibus, sitting beside the driver, listening to the roar of the carts, and sometimes gesticulating and declaiming Homer at the top of his voice" (*Correspondence*, p. 441).

low Carlyle's method: "I stayed in London till I had become acquainted with all the styles of face in the street, and till I had found the suburbs and then straggling houses on each end of the city. Then I took a cab, left my farewell cards, and came home" (*J*, 7, 489). Whatever the inadequacies of Emerson's conscious explorations, they represented his rather determined attempt to follow his advice to the American Scholar:

> If it were only for a vocabulary, the scholar would be covetous of action. Life is our dictionary. Years are well spent in country labors; in town; in the insight into trades and manufactures; in frank intercourse with many men and women; in science; in art; to the one end of mastering in all their facts a language by which to illustrate and embody our perceptions. (*W*, *1*, 97–98)

Emerson's interest in making the city organic led him almost inevitably to an interest in the human who had created the language of "facts"—the Hero or Man of Action. If the seer was the necessary human channel through which the Over-Soul "perceived" the modern city and the speaking poet the necessary channel through which the Over-Soul described the city, the Hero was the necessary channel through which the Over-Soul built and sustained the physical urban artifact. If the seer used the natural material of light and the sayer the natural qualities of sound, the Man of Action worked with the tangible materials of nature. "For man is the end of nature," Emerson argued in 1841;

> nothing so easily organizes itself in every part of the universe as he; no moss, no lichen is so easily born; and he takes along with him and puts out from himself the

> whole apparatus of society and condition *extempore*, as an army encamps in a desert, and where all was just now blowing sand, creates a white city in an hour, a government, a market, a place for feasting, for conversation, and for love. (*W*, 1, 317–18)

Knowledgeable men of action might build organically an urban civilization out of natural resources, he stated in 1850, because they "esteem wealth to be the assimilation of nature to themselves, the converting of the sap and juices of the planet to the incarnation and nutriment of their design" (*W*, 6, 93).

To describe the human force behind the erection and expansion of cities, Emerson sometimes used his persona of the Man of Action as a synecdoche for an actual group of human city-builders. "All the marked events of our day, all the cities, all the colonizations, may be traced back to their origin in a private brain," he argued in 1850 (*W*, 6, 251). A few years later, in his lecture "Success," he repeated: "There is no prosperity, trade, art, city, or great material wealth of any kind, but if you trace it home, you will find it rooted in a thought of some individual man" (*W*, 7, 296–97). Such a man had not merely projected impotent thought onto a hostile or indifferent natural environment; he had implemented his dreams through his energetic will. "What is the city in which we sit here," Emerson asked a Bostonian audience, "but an aggregate of incongruous materials which have obeyed the will of some man?" (*W*, 6, 43). He indicated in 1852 that the role of city-builder was intensely relevant to the American context: "I like that New England, like Greece, should owe its power to the genius of its people. There is no prosperity here, no trade, or art, or city, or great wealth of any kind, but, if you trace it home, you will find it rooted in the energy of some individual" (*J*, 8, 276). In several journal passages he even pointed to specific men for whom his builder provided a convenient abbreviation. "In each town you visit," he noted in 1851 while preparing his lecture "Fate,"

> there is some man who is in his brain and performance an explanation of all that meets the eye there. . . . If you see him, all will become plain. Mr. Erastus Bigelow, Mr. McElrath, Mr. Lawrence, Mr. Crocker, Mr. Vanderbilt, the old Ratch and Rodman, Jackson and Lowell, the Dwights at Springfield, Mr. Forbes, are each a walking city, and, wherever you put them, will build one. (*J*, 8, 222–23).[37]

Just as creatively active men might transform natural energy into organic urban processes (organic in the sense of being the products of the human organism and functioning toward an end intrinsic in or proper to the natural energy on which they were based), so these men might find ways to relate their industrial towns in a creatively organic manner to the natural hinterlands of the towns. The Seer might link town and country by finding a vantage point from which he could see both in a single act of perception. The Sayer might suggest unity by linking town and country verbally. When stringing together a series of nouns in a sentence, Emerson invariably included both urban and nonurban objects. He would have acknowledged such linking to be merely mechanical had he not believed in the unifying aims of the listing process itself.

The Man of Action, however, most characteristically linked city and country by a purposeful continuity of behavior

37. In using this journal passage in his essay "Fate," Emerson listed the towns to which he was referring (*W*, 6, 42–43).

—by moving between the city and country in such a way as to unify them. It is highly significant that, during his period of greatest Transcendental assertion, Emerson could write:

> Solitude is naught and society is naught. Alternate them and the good of each is seen. You can soon learn all that society can teach you for one while. . . . After some interval when these [natural] delights have been sucked dry, accept again the opportunities of society. The same scenes revisited shall wear a new face, shall yield a higher culture. Undulation, alternation is the condition of progress, of life. (*J*, 4, 473).

He very purposefully chose the railroad, symbol of the rising industrial force, as symbol also of the human movement that might unify city and hinterland: "the esthetic value of railroads," he remarked in his essay "Culture," "is to unite the advantages of town and country life, neither of which we can spare" (*W*, 6, 148).[38] We need travel only a short imaginative distance on Emerson's railroad to find ourselves on Whitman's open road or passage to India or on Hart Crane's bridge.

Emerson's desire to find varieties of human movement that might unify city and country under organic auspices was also a desire to discover the kinds of "natural" men most capable of such organic movement. As Emerson's journals, letters, essays, and lectures attest time and again, he was intensely

38. Thoreau treated the Fitchburg Railroad in similar fashion: "I usually go to the village along its causeway, and am, as it were, related to society by this link" (*Walden*, Chap. 5). Such undulation between society and solitude, Emerson said, was a necessary illustration of the creative "circle of nature" (*J*, 5, 54–55).

interested in the "Classes of Men" into which nature seemed to have divided mankind.[39] Though all men were radically equal in their sharing of the Over-Soul, they varied as widely in their individual "natural" powers as did the forms of the nonhuman environment.[40] Whether Emerson conceived nonhuman nature in terms of a chain of being or in terms of nineteenth-century evolutionary theories,[41] he used this natural hierarchy primarily as a metaphor for the human hierarchy—as a vertical mirror in which men might read not only their common qualities but their differences. One of the most important indexes determining whether or not an individual belonged near the top of the human scale as part of the "natural aristocracy" was his power to reconcile human creations such as the city with the forces and forms of his natural environment. The natural aristocrat's "excellence," Emerson argued, "is facility of adaptation and of transition, through

39. See Emerson's 1860 lecture on "Classes of Men" (Houghton manuscript 205.6) for a late statement of this recurring theme in his work. In this lecture he reminded his audience that "the two abiding and supreme classes who impress their stamp on the world, and carry on its business," were "the artist and hero"—classes, he admitted, which seemed "rarely united in one person."

40. Useful introductions to Emerson's conception of "natural aristocracy," in addition to Whicher, Paul, and Matthiessen, are Kenneth Kurtz, "The Sources and Development of Emerson's Representative Men" (Unpublished doctoral dissertation, Yale University, 1947); Perry Miller, "Emersonian Genius and the American Democracy," *New England Quarterly*, 26 (1953), 27–44; and John O. McCormick, "Emerson's Theory of Human Greatness," *New England Quarterly*, 26 (1953), 291–314.

41. See Joseph Warren Beach, *The Concept of Nature in Nineteenth-Century English Poetry* (New York, 1937), Chaps. 11 and 12, for indications of ways in which Emerson's conception of nature was influenced by these views.

many related points, to wide contrasts and extremes" (*W*, *6*, 137). In affirming the possibilities of reconciling movements, therefore, he was also affirming the possibilities implied in "human nature."

Emerson's attempt to find "natural" human movements that might reconcile city and country is most significant when discussed in the context of the literary traditions available to him—traditions that often used such movement less to unify city and country than to affirm their necessary separateness. Such movement had more characteristically resulted in destructive interaction than in creative fusion. In tragedy the moving individual might be killed; in comedy he might be "converted." In either case the polar environments between which he moved remained essentially unchanged. In much of the popular literature of the eighteenth and early nineteenth century, for example, the "natural man" might enter the metropolis either as a country bumpkin or as a noble savage, either to condemn the city or to learn from and be accepted by it, but rarely to "redeem" it with natural virtues from his previous environment. Conversely, when the urban hero of this period journeyed out into a pastoral landscape or a society of noble savages, it was generally with the purpose of *escaping* from the city, rarely for the purpose of applying truly creative urban values to the natural environment.[42] Traditional literature often gave the natural man power over the city only by making him a barbarian invader come to destroy urban life. Similarly, the urban dweller usually could exert an influence

42. An obvious example of constant environments is Shakespeare's *Midsummer Night's Dream*. When Tom Jones moves between the relatively unchanging environments of Somersetshire and London, only he is altered. The same is true of Pip and his worlds in *Great Expectations*. See also Hoxie Neal Fairchild, *The Noble Savage: A Study in Romantic Naturalism* (New York, 1928), esp. pp. 42–45, 262–63.

over a natural environment only at the cost of corrupting that environment.[43]

When such traditional interpretations of the moving hero and the dichotomous environments were applied to an American setting by American artists of Emerson's era, they acquired special poignancy, for a major objective of the American dream—of the City of the West—was the creative reconciliation of high civilization and untouched nature through the active agency of the divinely inspired or nobly motivated individual who fulfilled his own nature *through* this reconciliation. Failure to achieve such unification not only would suggest the need to modify severely the national expectations but would point to the limits of mankind's ability to achieve a lasting, because "naturally" rooted, progress. To the extent that civilized progress implied the destruction of the American savage, for example, it represented a new admission of the validity of the traditional conception of *non*reconciliation. On the basis of this conception Parkman lamented in *The Conspiracy of Pontiac* (1851) that "for a mausoleum, the city has risen above the forest hero."[44] The average American writer could affirm the ideal existence of the savage only by escaping from his urban environment to a natural setting so far separated in time or space from the city as to offer no dan-

43. Note Gibbon's treatment of the Goths' invasion of the Roman Empire or the upsetting impact of Coleridge's Ancient Mariner upon the wedding guests who have assembled at the start of that poem. Conversely, in Sidney's *Arcadia* the coming of urban man threatens to cause the downfall of a pastoral society. In a number of Scott's Scottish novels, the growing metropolis threatens a heretofore isolated hinterland community.

44. Quoted in Roy Harvey Pearce, *The Savages of America: A Study of the Indian and the Idea of Civilization* (Baltimore, 1953), p. 167. Pearce argues that "the noble Savage lived on in spirit precisely because he no longer lived on in the flesh" (p. 194).

ger of actual confrontation or interaction. In a similar manner, the American mind did not know whether to treat the figure of the white pioneer as a carrier of civilization into the American wilderness under a banner of manifest destiny, as a mediator who functioned "to soften the contrast between the dark forest and the city," or as the embodier of a Romantic desire to escape from civilization.[45]

Like their fellow countrymen, American writers also seemed caught at times between their desire to find a hero who might reconcile environments and their use of more common literary approaches to the hero's function. The rustic entering the city, as made into a stock character by developing American dramatists, was not functionally different from his prototypes in English and Continental drama.[46] The protagonist of Charles Brockton Brown's *Edgar Huntley* moved between New York and the American wilderness—in a pattern resembling a midsummer nightmare—without doing more than affirming the horrible disparity between the civilized and the wild. Though Cooper often stressed that his best urban heroes and best natural heroes (Judge Temple and Natty Bumppo in *The Pioneers,* Ludlow and Tiller in *The Water Witch*) were brothers under the skin, he found no totally satisfactory way in which to allow their interactions to reconcile their respective environments.[47] A number of the provincials of Hawthorne and Melville—for example, the protagon-

45. Arthur K. Moore, *The Frontier Mind: A Cultural Analysis of the Kentucky Frontiersman* (Lexington, 1957), p. 174 and passim; Smith, *Virgin Land,* Chaps. 5 and 6.

46. Glenn H. Blayney, "City Life in American Drama, 1825–1860," in A. Dayle Wallace and Woodburn O. Ross, eds., *Studies in Honor of John Wilcox* (Detroit, 1958), pp. 111–14, 122–23.

47. See the excellent comments on Cooper in Donald Davie, *The Heyday of Sir Walter Scott* (London, 1961), esp. Chap. 10.

ists of "David Swan," "My Kinsman, Major Molineux," and *Redburn*—entered the city with high hopes but without displaying strong reconciling powers. Conversely, the reforming urbanites of *The Blithedale Romance* journeyed to the country with hopes of unification, only to discover that, "as regarded society at large, we stood in a position of new hostility, rather than new brotherhood," and that "the yeoman and the scholar . . . are two distinct individuals, and can never be melted or welded into one substance."[48] In light both of historical actuality and of the traditional literary pattern of this actuality, Emerson's lament in 1844 becomes representative of a major fear in nineteenth-century American thought. "I wish to have rural strength and religion for my children," he said, "and I wish city facility and polish. I find with chagrin that I cannot have both" (*J*, 6, 506).

The continuing attempt to find a way to "have both," in spite of the almost impossible difficulties involved, is one of the striking characteristics of the American literature of Emerson's era.[49] Admitting the dichotomous aspects of urban culture and nature, many major American writers nevertheless attempted to treat such a dichotomy not as final but as provisional. Their heroes' roles as men in motion became important agents of a process that hopefully would lead to reconciliation of all aspects of the American environment. Cooper shuttled such protagonists as Cornelius Littlepage and

48. Hawthorne, *Works*, 5, 343, 394.

49. The extremes that Richard Chase, in *The American Novel and Its Tradition* (Garden City, 1957), believes English novelists have attempted to reconcile (see Chap. 1) are often "social" extremes. The extremes that one major variety of American Romanticism seeks to reconcile are more metaphysical in nature, and reconciliation must often take place by what Chase calls "limited and special means"—means suggested by Feidelson in *Symbolism and American Literature*.

Miles Wallingford back and forth between city, countryside, and wilderness in order that they might come to creative terms with both the virtues and limitations of all these environments. Melville's Pierre, though ultimately doomed by an imagination seeking solutions beyond human power, was at least initially blessed by an ideal combination of rural experience and "annual visits to the city; where *naturally* mingling [my italics] in a large and polished society, Pierre had insensibly formed himself in the airier graces of life, without enfeebling the vigor derived from a martial race, and fostered in the country's clarion air."[50] Hawthorne could suggest that "the wild life of the streets has perhaps as unforgettable a charm, to those who have once thoroughly imbibed in it, as the life of the forest or the prairie," and the protagonists of each of his major novels embodied in their movements some version of the pattern of attempted reconciliation.[51] Even Thoreau, for all his intense dislike of many aspects of urban life, was willing at times to praise them with faint damning —to recognize that, in his role as Transcendental affirmer, he must make at least a nominal gesture toward reconciliation with modern urban life. Praising the Londoner Milton, he reminded himself of his resolution to "be native to the universe." Though he loved Concord best, he said, "I am glad when I discover, in oceans and wildernesses far away, the materials out of which a million Concords can be made,—indeed unless I discover them, I am lost myself,—that there too I am at home. . . . Though the city is no more attractive to me than ever, yet

50. Melville, *Works*, 7, 5.

51. Hawthorne, *Works*, 7, 344. See Coverdale's remarks in *The Blithedale Romance*, on his return to Boston from the Farm (*Works*, 6, 486). In *W*, 6, 114–15, Emerson comes to a similar conclusion with regard to this variety of "Arcadian fanaticism."

I see less difference between a city and some dismallest swamp than formerly."[52]

Emerson too—as this study has stressed—looked on the denial of the city as useful dialectical strategy, but weak philosophy. Escape from the city, for his man of action, was not an ultimately satisfactory solution to the pressing problems confronting modern man. It had true value only as part of a cyclical dramatic motion whose other half was return to the city. Although Emerson was intrigued by European literature's escapist Romanticism, in both its negatively Transcendental and primitivistic varieties, he was more basically committed to the affirmative, reforming element in European Romanticism, as manifested especially in the writing of Goethe and Carlyle. He borrowed both from the French Revolution's Noble Savage, who symbolized the reforming impulse in natural man, and from the Romantic's archetypal prophet who emerged from his studies in the metropolis to preach to all the world. The result was an organic partnership between an American Adam who resembled in many ways a cisatlantic Carlyle and a dynamic Cosmopolitan from the City of the West who had many of the lineaments of a Goethe. If any individual could unify the natural and urban environments of America, Emerson believed it would be this moving, circling, exploring, encompassing Western Cosmopolitan.

In one form, the Cosmopolitan began his reconciling movement in a natural environment and proceeded toward and into the urban world. As a "man of nature," he did not protest against urban ways by staying remote from the city or by advancing destructively on it. Rather, he entered the city to *re*form its patterns, to reinforce it "with new blood from the woods and mountains. Wild men, John Baptists,

52. Thoreau, *Journals*, 2, 47.

Hermit Peters, John Knoxes, utter the savage sentiment of Nature in the heart of commercial capitals" (*W*, 7, 95). Emerson argued on a number of occasions that "the city is always recruited from the country" (*W*, 7, 140). "The city would have died out, rotted and exploded, long ago," he stated in 1841, "but that it was reinforced from the fields. It is only country which came to town day before yesterday that is city and court to-day" (*W*, 3, 129).

As Emerson used the phrase, however, "new blood from the woods and mountains" had not only a biological but—as should be expected—a metaphorical meaning. It was this meaning of "natural" that allowed him, in one of his self-projections, to identify the wild reformer with "my own class —. . . the few worshippers of the Muse—wild & sacred" (*L*, 3, 20). Regardless of his varying conceptions of his own role, he often stressed the virtues of the natural man who dared approach the city creatively. At the very least, the concept of natural man could offer protective armor for the active man of imagination who desired to confront an urban environment: "The poet, the orator, bred in the woods, whose senses have been nourished by their fair and appeasing changes, year after year, without design and without heed—shall not lose their lesson altogether, in the roar of cities or the broil of politics" (*W*, 1, 31). At best, the natural man might use his original experiences not only to protect himself from the city, but to refashion the city according to natural principles.

Carlyle, Emerson believed, was such a natural man. In the Scotsman's Highland experiences lay the seeds which were flowering into the creative literary conquest of London. Reviewing Carlyle's *Past and Present* in the *Dial*, Emerson emphasized the strength of a man whom elsewhere he would call a "Gulliver among the Lilliputians" (*J*, 6, 395):

> Carlyle is the first domestication of the modern system, with its infinity of details, into style. We have been civilizing very fast, building London and Paris, and now planting New England and India, New Holland and Oregon,—and it has not appeared in literature; there has been no analogous expansion and recomposition in books. Carlyle's style is the first emergence of all this wealth and labor with which the world has gone with child so long. London and Europe, tunnelled, graded, corn-lawed, with trade-nobility, and East and West Indies for dependencies; and America, with the Rocky Hills in the horizon, have never before been conquered in literature. This is the first invasion and conquest. (*W*, *12*, 390)

"This man upholds & propels civilization," Emerson had written of Carlyle several years before. "He knows & loves the heavenly stars, and sees fields below with trees & animals. He sees towered cities; royal houses; & poor man's chambers, & reports the good he sees, God through him telling this generation also that he has beholden his work & sees that it is good. He discharges his duty as one of the World's Scholars" (*JMN*, 5, 358–59). Emerson hoped that the "first invasion" that this English Scholar had made into "the modern system" would be carried even further by the American Scholar, whose natural roots in the continent of "the Rocky Hills" would lend strength to his reconciling confrontation of modern urban civilization.

The drama of organic reconciliation might begin in the city as well as in nature, however. Emerson once portrayed this humane reconciliation by an imaginary "meeting of gentlemen" representing both America's natural and urban environments. To the rural representatives at this imaginary meeting, he stated: "What we want when you come to see us is country culture. We have town culture enough and to spare. Show us your own, inimitable and charming to us, O Countryman!" (*J*, 6, 197). One of the most striking aspects of this and similar passages in his essays is Emerson's identification with the *urban* "gentlemen." The "we" was not merely the so-called editorial first person plural. It indicated one of the primary roles Emerson played in his desire to be a reconciler. More basic to his writings than the natural man who came to the city was the urban man who appreciated "nature" both in himself and in his environment and therefore attempted to productively naturalize the city. Emerson's lectures and essays were not usually addressed to "wild men" and farmers any more than Wordsworth's poetry was directed toward idiot boys or solitary reapers. He intended instead to articulate the challenge of "Nature" to urban audiences, a challenge not to destroy but to remake the city according to the most authoritative organic specifications—specifically, according to the organic natures of the city dwellers themselves. When he praised the farmer and farm life, he was generally developing a strategic contrast to urban patterns within a dialectical framework rather than advocating farming as an ideal life for the best "class" of urban men.

The farming persona (and he is just that—a dramatically conceived figure) who appears in Emerson's essay "Farming" (*W*, 7, 137–54) does not seem to be as much a human being as an admirable object of a natural landscape: "He is permanent, clings to his land as the rocks do" (p. 139). The farmer's greatest asset was his "*naturel* . . . his constitutional excellence," but this "excellence" was basically "that uncorrupted behavior which we admire in animals" (pp. 153–

54). The farmer's life was thus a "natural," organic life, in contrast to the "artificial" lives of many urban dwellers (p. 154), but it was not the existence most suited to the expression of the highest energies of the American scholars, poets, or heroes. Strategically, it was useful to point to the farmer as "a slow person, timed to Nature, and not to city watches" (p. 138), but Emerson also believed that the farmer's natural time-sense represented less a conscious choice than an inability to cope with the pace of urban routine. The farmer was a "slow, narrow man" (p. 139); he was not the reconciler Emerson so fervently desired. His farm was not the locus for organic unification of city and nature, but "an asylum" where men might hide "if they do not succeed in society" (p. 138).

Like other natural resources, however, Emerson's idealized farmer played a vital role in the process of reconciliation. Though not himself the reconciler, he symbolized the natural source of such reconciliation. "The men in cities," Emerson said, "who are the centres of energy, the driving-wheels of trade, politics or practical arts, and the women of beauty and genius, are the children or grandchildren of farmers, and are spending the energies which their fathers' hardy, silent life accumulated in frosty furrows, in poverty, necessity and darkness" (pp. 140–41).[53] Nevertheless, the farmer and his

53. Emerson often noted the way in which the "flower" of the rural population was more interested in succeeding in an urban than in a rural environment (e.g. *W*, 1, 368; *W*, 6, 108–09; *J*, 8, 174). Though he disliked some of the materialistic motives that brought such young people to the city, he recognized that they could not "fulfill" their potentials as human beings by remaining on the farm. "I do not wish to overstate this doctrine of labor, or insist that every man should be a farmer, any more than that every man should be a lexicographer," he said in his 1841 lecture on "Man the Reformer." "The doctrine of the Farm is merely this, that every man ought to stand in primary relations with the work of the world" (*W*, 1, 240–41). When Emerson was

landscape represented at their best only one aspect of "human nature." Reconciliation of city and country on organic terms could come only through the agency of those individuals who represented within themselves *both* the urban and natural poles of human possibility. The Western Cosmopolitan, not the Noble Savage, had the best opportunity—and the greatest desire—to unify his rural and urban worlds, for both were his "organic" domain.[54]

The imaginative Cosmopolitan initiated the movement toward reconciliation by leaving periodically (at least in imagination) the "artificial life of cities" in order to explore "the laws of the creation" in "the fresh and fragrant fields" (*EL*, 1, 11). In order to be effective, the movement from city to country needed to be motivated first by a sincere (that is, "natural") desire to learn nature's lessons, not by a desire to impose a mechanical or rationalistic form onto nature: "A dilettantism in nature is barren and unworthy. The fop of fields is no better than his brother of Broadway" (*W*, 3, 177). Any such halfhearted action toward reconciliation—one not motivated by genuine love of reconciliation—"was tentative, a piece of the city carried out into the fields, and was the city still, and no new fact, and could not inspire enthusiasm" (*W*, 3, 101–02). In order to find organically useful material

not using the farmer as a strategic contrast to the urban man's misuse of his powers, the latter tended to have the advantage in any comparison of the two (see, for example, *JMN*, 5, 301, 461).

54. As early as 1823, while delighting in "the fine woodlands" of Connecticut during a walking tour of that state, Emerson had observed that "the good people who live in them do not esteem them. It is the people born in town who are intoxicated with being in the country" (*JMN*, 2, 225). The "city boy," he argued many years later, generally possessed a "finer perception" than "the owner of the wood-lot" (*W*, 7, 298).

for his urban environment, the Cosmopolitan needed temporarily to "lose himself" in nature—to find by loving immersion in the "incredible beauty" of the landscape a lesson that might subsequently be applied to remedy "the ugliness of towns and palaces" (*W*, 3, 171–73). In his narrative poem "The Adirondacs," Emerson admonished a group of Boston's leaders who went camping in the woods:

> Look to yourselves, ye polished gentlemen!
> No city airs or art pass current here.
> Your rank is all reversed; let men of cloth
> Bow to the stalwart churls in overalls:
> *They* are the doctors of the wilderness,
> And we the low-prized laymen. (*W*, 9, 185).

Near the conclusion of this rather long poem, however, he stressed the ultimate purpose that brought such men to the wilderness—a purpose beyond mere spiritual refreshment:

> We flee away from cities, but we bring
> The best of cities with us, these learned classifiers
> Men knowing what they seek, armed eyes of experts.
> We praise the guide, we praise the forest life:
> But will we sacrifice our dear-bought lore
> Of books and arts and trained experiment,
> Or count the Sioux a match of Agassiz?
> O no, not we! (*W*, 9, 193)

Such "learned classification" was not merely rational or mechanistic when performed in the spirit of loving communion with nature. The "urban mind" need not deny its appropriate functions in order to find in a rural environment organic food that might enrich the city.

Because Emerson believed that genuine learning of the

lessons of nature did not lead to stasis in the Cosmopolitan but to renewed dialectical movement toward reconciliation, he questioned the human sufficiency of merely one-way movement from city to country. Though he admired the Transcendentalists for the courage, dedication, and idealism that prompted them to "withdraw themselves from the common labors and competitions of the market and the caucus," he questioned whether withdrawal was the most adequate way of working for the high ideals they professed. The Transcendentalists were "striking work, and crying out for something worthy to do!" Their conception of "worthy" action, however, seemed not only too inhuman at times but even falsely "divine." When Emerson noted that "to their lofty dreams the writings of Iliads or Hamlets, or the building of cities or empires seems drudgery," he was showing not only the positive but the sinister side of their idealism—an idealism sometimes more destructive or sterile than productive and reconciling. From their "solitary and critical way of living," he believed, "no solid fruit has yet appeared to justify their separation" (*W*, *I*, 340–41).

Emerson's point was not really that the Transcendentalists' escape from the city was unworthy or even that it lacked practical consequences. (The urban observer of their withdrawal might find "fruitful" application to his paved environment, and had the motives of the Transcendentalists been merely practical, rational, and manipulative, they would have been, in Emerson's eyes, little better than fops of the fields.) Rather, he wished to emphasize that withdrawal was only half of the organic drama. This cycle could bear fruit only when the Cosmopolitan, either personally or by means of his art, brought the lessons of nature back to the city, brought back a desire for reconciliation not on the city's artificial terms but on the terms of nature. "The poet, in utter solitude remembering his spontaneous thoughts and recording them, is found to have recorded that which men in crowded cities find true for them also" (*W*, *1*, 103). In 1841 Emerson wrote in his journal: "In the lonely woods I remember London, and think I should like to be initiated in the exclusive circles." Such a movement toward reconciliation "has this condition that it be of the greatest kind, such conquest as grand genius makes, and so the individual demonstrates his natural aristocracy, best of the best" (*J*, 6, 95).

Almost all of Emerson's "representative men" (both those in and outside his book on the subject) exemplified in action his belief in the desirability and possibility of reconciliation. No individual was a "complete Man." Even the greatest of actual men revealed a "lopsided" character due to overdevelopment of one or more faculties at the expense of other equally vital ones. However, the large majority of Emerson's men of stature proved their worth by showing in various degrees an ability to join the urban and natural worlds. The "Great Men" of his lectures on "Biography" in 1835—Michelangelo, Luther, Milton, Fox, and Burke—all represented a creative confronting of the city by the reforming power of their "natural" force.[55] The subjects of *Representative Men*—individuals as diverse as Swedenborg, Montaigne, Shakespeare, and Napoleon—also shared this fusing power. Love of the city and the power to reconcile that city with the organic universe were not mutually exclusive when found in the makeup of the "representative" Cosmopolitan. Emerson treated Plato, for example, as an intensely—almost provincially—urbane Idealist "monstrously fond of Athens" (*W*, *4*, 71). Love of urban life, however, was the very basis of Plato's

55. E.g. *EL*, *1*, 113, 151.

desire "to reconcile his poetry with the appearance of the world, and build a bridge from the streets of cities to the Atlantis" (*W*, *4*, 61). Montaigne was "sufficiently related to the world to do justice to Paris or London, and, at the same time, a vigorous and original thinker, whom cities can not overawe, but who uses them" (*W*, *4*, 162). Goethe—"the cow from which all [the] milk" of nineteenth-century thought had been "drawn" (*J*, *8*, 214)—was a particularly good example on which Emerson could conclude his book. As a supreme instance of the modern reconciler, Goethe indicated that even the modern industrial city might be made the organic and productive home of those men of stature who were sufficiently alive to their own naturally based powers. On one hand, Emerson stressed, Goethe was comfortably at the center of his urban society:

> I suppose the worldly tone of his tales grew out of the calculations of self-culture. It was the infirmity of an admirable scholar, who loved the world out of gratitude; who knew where libraries, galleries, architecture, laboratories, savans and leisure were to be had, and who did not quite trust the compensations of poverty and nakedness. Socrates loved Athens; Montaigne, Paris; and Madame de Stael said she was only vulnerable on that side (namely, of Paris). It has its favorable aspect. . . . This man was entirely home and happy in his century and the world. (*W*, *4*, 288)

Goethe was great, however, because he did not take his beloved urban environment for granted. Instead, at his best moments, he challenged his urban civilization to become aware of its highest organic possibilities. "Coming into an over-civilized time and country," Emerson noted, "when original talent was oppressed under the load of books and *mechanical* auxiliaries [my italics] and the distracting variety of claims," Goethe had "taught men how to dispose of this mountainous miscellany and make it subservient" (*W*, 4, 289).

> He has clothed our modern existence with poetry. Amid littleness and detail, he detected the Genius of life, the old cunning Proteus, nestling close beside us, and showed that the dulness and prose we ascribe to the age was only another of his masks . . . that he had put off a gay uniform for a fatigue dress, and was not a whit less vivacious or rich in Liverpool or the Hague than once in Rome and Antioch. He sought him in public squares and main streets, in boulevard and hotels; and, in the solidest kingdom of routine and the senses, he showed the lurking daemonic power. (*W*, 4, 273–74)

Looking at the example of Goethe, Emerson could assert with varying degrees of certainty that the modern urban world arising rapidly in America need not, for all its machines, be inorganic. Organicism was, after all, a metaphorical rather than a literal concept.[56] It implied basically being true to one's own inner nature—by which Emerson meant

56. Like Melville, Hawthorne, and other contemporaries, Emerson was certainly capable of drawing upon negative connotations of organic metaphors—of referring to "the city's poisoning spleen" (*W*, 9, 49), of comparing two dollar-loving urban societies to "a society of bores in an oak tree" and "a great society of cheese mites" (*J*, 8, 175), and of arguing that "cities churches colleges all go for the quadruped interest" (*L*, 5, 17). He was not arguing, however, as Zola and Hardy would later argue, that the traits of lower organisms were the strongest features of man's nature. Rather he was pointing to men's willful perversion of their higher powers. The animality of the most able men, he argued, was the result of their misuse of the powers of free choice; it was Emerson's version of sin. "The material is nothing," he stated in 1839,

generally one's highest nature. The modern city could become organic by directing "the old cunning Proteus" of natural power into channels most conducive to the moral and intellectual growth of its inhabitants. The organic city could not ask man to imitate the routines of animals, savages, or even farmers, however suited such routines might be to their "natural" possessors. The truly urban man's nature demanded something more challenging than merely working in the rural soil. Without denying his roots in rural nature, the Cosmopolitan remained true to his own organic potential by looking toward a modern urban world that, at its best, could give him in abundance the men, artifacts, and ideas his evolving and dramatically oriented spirit needed and desired. Organic form was not enough. It was merely a means to higher human ends:

> Great cities, enormous populations, are disgusting, like the population of cheese, like hills of ants, or swarms

---

> bitumen, wood, or stone; the proportion is all. Proportion makes permanence, beauty, grandeur. So it is with this daily life; here lie the same materials for all men, the common day, the common men, the common woes, necessities, and, deep under all, the uplifting sentiment of the Good. Out of these selfsame elements the sot builts his sty and the hero his prevailing character,—Pantheon, shall I say. (*J*, 5, 356)

Cf. Thoreau's remark to H. G. O. Blake: "It is not enough to be industrious; so are the ants. What are you industrious about?" (*Correspondence*, p. 493). Emerson would probably have agreed with Christopher Tunnard, who warns of the dangers of a merely biological approach to the modern city—an approach that seeks solutions to urban problems "outside the economic pattern in the insect world of cells, efficiency and minimum standards. The solution which denies the city," argues Tunnard, "is not born of the artist's vision of Utopia; it springs from ignorance, anti-intellectual prejudice, or contempt for human beings" (*The City of Man*, pp. 46–47).

of fleas,—the more the worse. But if they contain Merlins and Corneliuses, Friar Bacons and Crichtons, if road-makers, mathematicians, astronomers, chemists; good kings like Alfred; poets like Chaucer; inventors, farmers, and sailors, who know the elements, and can make them work; memories, imaginations, combinings, perseverances, arts, music, and not maggots;—then the more the merrier. Open the gates, let the miracle of generation go on. (*J*, 7, 514–15)

6. "The Freedom of the City"

> *Would you have been born like a gipsy in a hedge, and preferred your freedom on a heath, and the range of a planet which had no shed or boscage to cover you from sun and wind, to this towered and citied world?* (W, 1, 311)

> *"Did you give Athens the best laws?" "No," replied Solon, "but the best it would receive."* (*J*, 10, 243)

> *Let every man shovel out his own snow, and the whole city will be passable.* (*J*, 5, 437)

In the title essay of *Society and Solitude* Emerson described "a humorist" who "left the city" in order to "conceal himself" in the natural landscape (*W*, 7, 3–4). The humor of this attempt lay in its being an impossible action. Emerson recognized that the modern world of urban society made it increasingly difficult for any individual, like Huck Finn, to "light out for the territories." When Huck arrived, he was likely to find a newly risen city there ahead of him. In 1867, as Emerson observed the expansion of the Western railroad system, he saw that "now a market at each station makes a small New York near to every farm" (*J*, 10, 184). Throughout his life, in fact, he had recognized that the existence of cities was as inevitable as the existence of mankind itself. "Let the river roll which way it will," he said in 1850, "cities will rise on its banks" (*J*, 8, 90). If Stephen Whicher is correct in arguing that Emerson's writings after his first series of *Essays* show an increasingly stoic resignation in the face of limiting, complex, and even painful "experience,"[1] then such a posture included necessarily an acquiescence to the world of the city.

Emerson is done an injustice, however, if his increasingly explicit concern with "society" is treated merely as a sign of the defeat of his most radical dreams of individual human greatness. In turning to "urban experience," Emerson also saw himself as taking on an even greater challenge to personal development than that offered by nonhuman nature. As he watched the physical frontier disappear and industrial cities arise in the era before the Civil War, he found evidence that human beings were more than a match for their continental hinterlands. "Civilization mounts and climbs," he asserted in an essay on "Works and Days." "Malthus, when he stated that the mouths went on multiplying geometrically and the food only arithmetically, forgot to say that the human mind was also a factor in political economy, and that the augmenting wants of society would be met by an augmenting power of invention" (*W*, 7, 162). In a lecture on "Resources" in 1863, Emerson celebrated the growing "triumph of man over nature" and argued optimistically that "armed with his machinery man can dive, can fly, can see atoms like a gnat; he can peer into Uranus with his telescope, or knock down cities with his fists of gunpowder" (*U*, 23).

At the very time Emerson delivered this lecture, however, native armies were knocking down cities of his own nation. The Civil War was a dramatic reminder to him and his contemporaries of a question more crucial than whether man could master his natural environment. The really crucial question, Emerson had always realized—whether he thought about it in the Christian terms of his ministerial days, in the

1. Whicher, *Freedom and Fate*, esp. pp. 72–93, 126–40.

Romantic terms of his most radically Transcendental days, or in the more humanistic terms of his later years—was whether man could master himself. Emerson's increasing interest in natural science was at heart an interest in the scientists themselves.[2] Even as poet, he was less concerned with natural symbols than with the human symbol-makers—or rather, with man as "natural" symbol. Pope's assertion in the eighteenth century that "the proper study of mankind is Man" had been intended to put an end to unsettling inquiry about the nature of the universe. When Emerson put a similar question in the nineteenth century, he made it the starting point of his poetic inquiry. In his writings men increasingly became known not by their reflections in external nonhuman nature, but by their reflections in a social environment. It would be foolish to deny Emerson's lifelong love of woods and mountains, stars and sea. For insights into the "old cunning Proteus" of life, however, he turned increasingly from the landscape to the *man*scape of the modern city. "What is a man," he asked in his essay "Art," "but a finer and compacter landscape than the horizon figures,—nature's eclecticism?" (*W*, 2, 352). For Emerson, the term "city" referred only secondarily to the physical artifact of streets and buildings; primarily, it was a metonym for the interaction of its human community. In urban ways and woes lay not only convenient but essential material for any Romantically oriented poet who wished to come to terms with the problem of modern man.

Although Emerson said many realistic things about mod-

2. The articles on Emerson's interest in natural science are too numerous to list. The best ones point to his use of the natural fact as a metaphor. See Harry H. Clark, "Emerson and Science," *Philological Quarterly*, 10 (1931), 225–60.

ern urban society, the basic impulse that led him to deal with the city was not so much a doctrine of literary "realism" as an interest in the possibilities of Romantic exploration. It was comparable, though not identical, to the exploring impulse that brought the novels of Melville and Hawthorne increasingly toward the center of urban life—an impulse that gave a significant pattern to the succession of urban locales from Salem to Rome in Hawthorne's major novels and that structured Melville's symbolic progression from the lands of *Typee* and *Omoo* to the enigmatic and nightmarish urban worlds of Pierre's New York, Bartleby the Scrivener's Wall Street, Israel Potter's London, and the Confidence Man's moving city, the *Fidèle*.[3] Emerson's impulse was a less vigorous form of the one that prompted Whitman to walk through the streets of New York looking for "the new romance of reality that is ten-fold deeper than anything born of the litterateurs."[4] Like other Romantics, Emerson was less interested in the external facts or urban routine than in the "inner" meaning of those facts. Nearer in spirit to the romancer than to the

3. Note, for example, Melville's treatment of London in *Israel Potter:* "Among the things of the capital, Israel for more than forty years was yet to disappear as one entering at dusk into a thick wood. Nor did ever the German forest, nor Tasso's enchanted one, contain in its depths more things of horror than eventually were revealed in the secret clefts, gulfs, caves and dens of London" (*Works, 11,* 203). The city, Melville argued in *Pierre,* was the home of the "darker, though truer aspect of things" (*Works,* 9, 94). Hawthorne preferred "the darker and dingier streets" of cities because he there had "a sense of being in the midst of life, and of having got hold of something real" (*English Notebooks,* p. 13).

4. Charles I. Glicksberg, ed., *Walt Whitman and the Civil War* (Philadelphia, 1933), p. 24. Whitman spoke of his "Illusions of youth! Dreams of a child of the Bowery!" (p. 54) in a manner similar to the way in which Wordsworth had spoken of his "intimations of immortality."

novelist of manners, he gave less thought to the way men behaved in the modern city than to the source of "life" that empowered such behavior. In 1843 he expressed his interest in a letter to Margaret Fuller: "The life lived, the thing done is a paltry & drivelling affair, as far as I know it . . . Yet I love life —never little,—and now, I think, more & more, entertained & puzzled though I be by this lubricity of it, & inaccessibleness of its pith & heart. The variety of our vital game delights me" (*L,* 3, 178).[5] As poet, therefore, Emerson was most happy with the city when it offered him, in its "facts," intriguing evidence of the power behind the facts. After one trip to Boston, he wished he had the power of "mesmerism," so that he might increase his own ability to ferret out the meaning of the "vital game." "Each man has facts that I want," he complained,

> and, though I talk with him, I cannot get at them for want of the clue. He does not know what to do with the facts; I know. . . . Here is all Boston,—all railroads, all manufacturers, and trade, in the head of this well-informed merchant at my side: what would not I give for a peep at his rows and rows of facts! . . . It is for this

5. American Romantics were intensely interested in what the modern city had to offer in the way of "human life." As Whitman said in *Leaves of Grass,* "This is the city . . . and I am one of the citizens; / Whatever interests the rest interests me." Hawthorne often referred to his "passion for thronged streets and the intensest bustle of human life" (*English Notebooks,* p. 591). In Liverpool, Redburn is "filled . . . with wonder and delight" at the large docks, which are "full of life and commotion" (*Works,* 5, 206). Even Thoreau, while in New York in 1843, remarked that "every thing there disappoints me but the crowd. . . . The crowd is something new and to be attended to" (*Correspondence,* p. 107).

> news, these facts, that I go to Boston, and visit A and B and C. Boston were ten times Boston if I could learn what I go thither for. (*J*, 7, 258–59)

In his essay on "The Poet," Emerson explained what he wished to do with such urban material. "The chief value of the new fact," he said, "is to enhance the great and constant fact of Life" (*W*, 3, 19). Often, even against his predispositions, he was forced to affirm that the modern city gave much evidence of this indwelling vitality. While visiting New York in 1843 he transcended his Concordian tastes sufficiently to observe:

> In this last year of extreme depression, as it is called, nine hundred houses have been built in N.Y. which would make a pretty town elsewhere. And when I hear the words "hard times," & "no business," I look from the speaker to the passing thousands who tramp so energetically the thoroughfare, to rolling carriages, to loaded drays, to criers & ringers & beckoners (for all are so thoroughly alive that a finger or a wink suffices) and then to these long & lengthening streets—and ferries leading to suburban cities for Brooklyn already counts 40,000; and these irresistible affirmations do quite outroar & drown the feeble querulousness of the protesters, and I greatly prefer this to all the American cities. (*L*, 3, 152–53)

Sometimes, in fact, as Emerson watched the vital movement of the most admirable sections of urban society, he was led to feel that his personal dislikes of the city showed less about the city's inadequacies than about his own. "I meet in the street people full of life," he said in 1849 after one of his innumerable trips to Boston. "I am, of course, at ebb tide; they at flood; they seem to have come from the South, or from the West, or from Europe. I see them pass with envy at this gift which includes all gifts" (*J*, *8*, 13).

Emerson's criticisms of urban civilization, however, derived less from a sense of his own inadequacies than from his Romantic expectations. His frequent disillusionment with urban life came not from a feeling that the city was unimportant to man, but from his demanding expectations that the city achieve a vastly fuller "life" than it had yet done. In 1830 Emerson found a symbol for the Romantic dream and its frustration in Dr. Edward D. Clarke's description "of the entrance of Moscow—All splendour & promise till you enter the gate, & then you look before & behind but only cottages & shops" (*JMN*, 3, 198). When Emerson used this passage in a lecture in 1836, he made some revealing changes: "One is reminded of Dr. Clarke's well known description of the entrance of Moscow, which at a distance showed a splendid collection of domes and minarets and filled the traveller with a tumult [of] pleasing expectations, but when once he had passed the gates and entered the city he found nothing but narrow streets and plain tenements" (*EL*, *1*, 374).[6] In sub-

6. Hawthorne and Melville also commented on the failure of the real city to live up to its Romantic promises. A distant view of London at sunset gave Hawthorne a "glorious and sombre picture, dusky, awful, but irresistibly attractive, like a young man's dream of the great world, foretelling at that distance a grandeur never to be fully realized" (*Works*, 7, 263). Melville's Redburn wishes while in England to fill "my Yankee soul with romantic thoughts"—a wish that makes his disappointment all the greater. Eugene Arden, in a suggestive article on "The Evil City in American Fiction," *New York History*, 35 (1954), 259–79, argues that "the New York novel has always been able to draw on either half of the cultural dichotomy—which recognized New York as both the city of light and the city of darkness" (p. 278).

stituting "narrow streets and plain tenements" for "cottages & shops," he was reminding his audience of the very real urban world around them and of the gap between what that world was and what it might be. Whether he crusaded fervently for ideal American Scholars or whether he bound his pursuit empirically to Representative Men, Emerson was searching for varieties of human "life" that might point to a fulfillment of his dream of an ideal community.

As Emerson insisted throughout his career, the sine qua non of truly human life was the priceless possession of freedom. The "great gift of God" was "the endowment of the human race with liberty" (*Y*, 164). His concern for human freedom therefore became a central key to his evaluation of modern civilization. Since he believed that "the true test of civilization is, not the census, nor the size of cities, nor the crops . . . but the kind of man the country turns out" (*W*, 7, 31), his judgment of the city's worth continually revolved around two questions: first, how much and what kinds of freedom did the city give its human members? second, how did the individual members use their freedom?

Emerson's attitude toward "the freedom of cities" fluctuated between the poles of his complex temperament. In 1861, for example, he argued, "People receive as compliment the freedom of cities. 'T is a sham gift, like so many other doings. The personage, 't is likely, who receives it, is some poet, or some politician. What freedom will it give him? . . . I cannot see that the freedom of such a town as ours can be given to any adult who does not possess it already" (*J*, 9, 329). Though a ceremonial freedom might be specious, a truly functional freedom might prove highly valuable. While in England in 1848, Emerson saved his lecture earnings instead of sending them home to pay some accumulating debts because he did not "wish to prejudice my freedom in London . . . for that would be to forfeit the main object of my visit here" (*L*, 4, 14). In an essay in *The Conduct of Life* he argued that "wealth requires, besides the crust of bread and the roof,—the freedom of the city, the freedom of the earth, travelling, machinery, the benefits of science, music and fine arts, the best culture and the best company. He is the rich man who can avail himself of all men's faculties" (*W*, 6, 89).

In its positive connotations, "freedom of the city" actually had two different meanings. On one hand, it referred to an individual's freedom *from* the city—an independence predicated upon the individual's moral virtue. As Emerson stated in his eulogy of Thoreau, borrowing a remark from Aristotle: "One who surpasses his fellow citizens in virtue is no longer a part of the city. Their law is not for him, since he is a law to himself" (*W*, 10, 477). Speaking of Plato's personal virtue, Emerson could urge, "Let such be free of the city and above the law" (*W*, 4, 89).[7] He referred to the same quality in 1840 when he argued "that one man is a counterpoise to a city,—that a man is stronger than a city, that his solitude is more prevalent and beneficent than the concert of crowds" (*J*, 5, 474). Similarly, in 1850 he could assert: "Not to be bruised by the bruisers, not to despond in cities, is a mark of merit" (*J*, 8, 91). In the essay on "Culture" in *The Conduct of Life*, Emerson applied this freedom to the individual's actual role as a social participant: "We can ill spare the commanding

7. Emerson argued in 1838,

Not insulation of place, but independence of spirit is essential, and it is only as the garden, the cottage, the forest, and the rock, are a sort of mechanical aid to this that they are of value. Think alone, and all places are friendly and sacred. The poets who have lived in cities have been hermits still. Inspiration makes solitude anywhere. (*W*, 7, 174)

social benefits of cities; they must be used, yet cautiously and haughtily,—and will yield their best values to him who best can do without them" (*W*, 6, 155).

Mere freedom from the city was not sufficient for Emerson, however. It implied the individual's ability to keep the urban routine from harming him, but it gave no assurance that the individual could use his virtue creatively to help others achieve a similar freedom. Therefore, Emerson also used the term to refer to the power of action. In this sense he could argue that eloquent genius "has the freedom of the city" (*W*, 10, 53) and could praise "the men who fear no city, but by whom cities stand" (*W*, 7, 322). Carlyle had told him that London "had well served" such possessors of active freedom in England (*W*, 5, 18), and Emerson observed such power in Goethe and Carlyle himself.[8] Most of Emerson's lectures and essays, in fact, seem addressed primarily to the men of active power rather than to those of merely defensive virtue. He sometimes attempted to console the men of "unaided virtue" (to use Melville's term), for example, in such essays as "Compensation," "Farming," "Domestic Life," or "Old Age." His most enthusiastic imaginative efforts, however, challenged men of active power to use their power in such a manner as to achieve the best *kinds* of possible human freedom. Power

8. Hawthorne interestingly expressed one way in which the city might give a usable freedom to the exploring artist. The "prime purpose and achievement" of his "aimless wanderings" in London, he said, "were to lose my way, and so to find it the more surely. . . . Having once fully yielded to its influence, I was in a manner free of the city, and could approach or keep away from it as I pleased" (*Works*, 7, 256–57). Charles Williams, in *The Image of the City and Other Essays*, ed. Anne Ridler (London, 1958), expresses a challenging view of the relationship of freedom and cities: "The main difference between the idea of the City and the idea of the Nation is that the first can involve the thought of choice. . . . We can deliberately found the City" (pp. 92–93).

itself was neutral and could therefore be used to destroy certain kinds of worthwhile freedoms or to enlarge others. Many of Emerson's essays, therefore, contain jeremiads against the dangers of misused power. In his journal for 1834 he pleaded, "Do not trust man, great God! with more power until he has learned to use his little power better" (*JMN*, 4, 335). As poet and prophet, he constantly blended consolation and challenge in his attempts to discuss the interrelationship of the two basic freedoms available to man in an urban world.

To the extent that virtue's freedom from the city was merely defensive—protecting man's spirit from the external world—and represented therefore a state of "being" rather than "doing" or "becoming," the modern city had little to offer it, and, conversely, it had little to offer the modern city. On the other hand, those men with active power—the natural aristocrats, as Emerson often called them—could gain a great deal from and contribute a great deal to their urban environment. The freedom of these men of action was always only a relative or (in terms of Transcendental possibility) "second-best" freedom, operating only in relation to the specific limits and necessities of finite experience and able inevitably to achieve only limited ends.

Emerson sometimes referred to the city as "the kingdom of Talent" (*J*, 6, 210) rather than of genius. The term "Talent," however, was as widely ranging in connotations as the possibilities of finite experience. Emerson often criticized the misuses of talent, but he recognized that in its upper limits it bordered on genius—in fact, was often a tool used creatively by genius.[9] Though the city was not inherently the home of

9. In a letter of 1841, Emerson remarked that "next to the Culture of Man the demonstration of a talent is the most attractive thing" (*L*, 2, 394–95). In *Representative Men* he spoke of "original talent" (*W*,

genius, it was characteristically the home of many individual geniuses. Working within the finite limits of urban civilization, these natural aristocrats accepted some of its limits as necessary tools in order to transform other of its limits into expressions of their personal power. Three such tools were those recognized by Emerson as basic attributes of the City of the West and, consequently, of the modern city—large space, rapid motion, and human heterogeneity.

Though urban space had an external or objective meaning, Emerson was more basically concerned with its relative or psychological meaning when applied to the problem of individual human freedom. When he talked about proper "urban scale," he was in fact talking about "human scale." The physical size of the modern city had no real significance until that size was compared to the psychological size of the individuals who confronted the city. Emerson enjoyed citing Leo Bizantinus' remarks to an audience of Athenians who were laughing at his wife's and his small size: "yet as little as we are, when we fall out, the city of Byzantium is not big enough to hold us" (*JMN*, 3, 170).[10] "Proper" urban scale was relative to what each individual conceived to be his own proper capacities. Emerson did not protest against gigantic cities as much as against little-minded men. "The absence of ideas" in the human community, he argued, "reduces all to the same poorness" (*J*, 8, 364). When he argued that "cities degrade us by magnifying trifles" (*W*, 6, 153) or that New York was

---

4, 289), and in a lecture of 1838 he reminded his audience that "the man of genius should occupy the whole space between God or pure mind and the multitude of uneducated men" (*W*, 1, 182). Centrally relevant to Emerson's conception of "talent" is his discussion in his essay "Fate" (*W*, 6, 150) of the relationship of finite limits and finite powers.

10. Cf. *JMN*, 5, 171, and *J*, 8, 408–09.

"only a colossal 'Mr. Potter's Shop'" (*L,* 4, 189–90), he was in fact protesting against men's refusal to use their urban environment in the proper way—to enlarge their capacities. Similarly, he could complain that "the personal communications are greatly narrowed" (*L,* 3, 156) and that "all the young people are near-sighted in the towns" (*J,* 5, 225). Criticism not of the urban artifact but of the urban artificer was implied in his observation in 1847 that "we live in Lilliput" (*J,* 7, 254).

The large-minded man, Emerson believed, need not fear the large city, since "after a little experience he makes the discovery that there are no large cities" (*W,* 6, 222). In the large scale of the modern city, the natural aristocrat might find both a physical and a symbolic tool for freely expressing and enlarging his own powers.[11] "He who aspires to be the English poet," Emerson argued in *English Traits,* "must be as large as London, not in the same kind as London, but in his own kind" (*W,* 5, 257). What he said of the house and the public building could also apply to the total city when used by man at his best:

> It is very fit that man should build good houses. Such an irritable, susceptible, invalid, beauty-loving creature as he is, should not dwell in a pen. His understanding, his eye, his hand are fitly employed on Persian Terraces, Egyptian Temples, and European Palaces. . . . I look upon

11. Consequently, American writers could protest that existing cities were too dense or too small. "One inconvenience I sometimes experienced in so small a house," Thoreau remarked playfully of his hut at Walden, was "the difficulty of getting to a sufficient distance from my guests when we begin to utter the big thoughts in big words. . . . Individuals, like nations, must have suitable broad and natural boundaries, even a considerable neutral ground, between them" (*Walden,* Chap. 6).

> the stately architecture of Persia and Egypt as a real part of the human heaven as much as a poem or a charity. Justice can be administered on a heath, and God can be worshipped in a barn. It is, nevertheless, fit that Justice should be administered in a stately hall open to the sun and air and to nations; and that God should be honored in temples whose proportion and decoration harmonize rather with the works of nature than with the sheds we build for the domestic animals. (*J*, 5, 27–28)

As Emerson noted in a lecture in 1853 on the "Anglo-American," "It is the American discovery, that, it is as easy to occupy large space, & do much work as, to occupy a small space, & do little."[12] America's leaders, he believed, possessed the power to occupy large urban space, but he recognized that the crucial problem was whether such leaders would use this space in a manner beneficial to those Americans whose personal powers were not as great.

The same moral and psychological considerations governed Emerson's evaluation of the "freeing" or "limiting" tendencies of urban motion. Many city dwellers were "immoveably bounded" by superficial or uncreatively cyclical movement because they lacked "liquidity of hope or genius" (*L*, 4, 376). Their motion was not liberating because it was "aimless" (*W*, 6, 208). It lacked creative purpose because it placed more value on the motion itself than on the inner human source of this motion. Emerson could thus assert in one mood that "avarice, ambition, almost all talents, are restless and vagrant; they go up to the cities; but Religion is a good rooter" (*J*, 6, 265). Such an attitude toward movement in the city, he said, made its holders into mere "city dolls."

12. Houghton manuscript 202.2.

The most creative urban movement, however, resulted from the actions of men who desired to free themselves from unnecessary limitations; "power is what they want, not candy," Emerson stated (*W*, 6, 93). For men with expansive aims, the rate of movement was less important than the direction of movement:

> If some persons are credible, a man cannot honestly get a livelihood by trade in the city. His integrity would be disqualification. He might, however, they agree, if he had sufficient time to build up a credit for honesty; but no poor man proceeding on borrowed capital can afford to wait so long. What does this show? Why, that the true way now of beginning is to play the hero in commerce, as it has been done in war, in church, in schools, in state, not begin with borrowed capital, but . . . begin with his hands, and earn one cent; then two; then a dollar; then stock a basket; then a barrow; then a booth; then a shop; & then a warehouse; & not on this dangerous balloon of a credit, make his first structure. (*JMN*, 5, 412)[13]

To those urban leaders who combined strong wills with high purposes, the modern means of motion offered innumerable possibilities for the liberation of human powers. Because of the electric telegraph, Emerson noted in 1864, "men now communicate from England to Bombay, from Boston to San Francisco, from Boston to Paris, and to Egypt, in little more time than it would take two guests . . . to join each other from

13. In 1824 Emerson observed that "Dr. Johnson was so poor when he first came to London, that he was obliged to live for weeks on four pence half penny pr day—and to walk with Savage the streets all night, for want of lodging" (*JMN*, 2, 378).

the two sides of the drawing-room" (*U*, 59). Similarly, the railroad need not dehumanize its users, provided they used it for humanizing purposes. As Emerson observed in 1843, "The Americans take to the little contrivance as if it were the cradle in which they were born" (*J*, 6, 336). Becoming used to such contrivances of modern industrial civilization was prerequisite to using these tools creatively.

More crucial than space or motion, however, to the problem of man's freedom in the modern city was the factor of urban complexity. Emerson realized that many men found the heterogeneity of modern urban life more bewildering than liberating. Again, however, his judgment was based as much on psychological as on physical considerations. Perhaps the major danger of the city's heterogeneity was not that such variety was inherently too limiting, but that it might be too freeing—might encourage finite man to attempt to take advantage of too many opportunities and so tempt him to dissipate his energies. "We are wasted with our versatility," sighed Emerson in 1850; "with the eagerness to grasp on every possible side, we all run to nothing. . . . I stay away from Boston, only because I cannot begin there to see those whom I should wish, the men and the things" (*J*, 8, 155).

Standing before the superabundance of the city's heterogeneous opportunities, Emerson saw great possibilities for each individual to find that "calling" most suited to him. His harshest complaints were directed not against the city's complexity but against the individual's refusal to use that complexity in the name of freedom for himself and others. Emerson constantly attacked the conformity he witnessed in the city—a conformity all the more ludicrous or pathetic because of the city's immense potential. "As you approach cities," he complained in an early sermon, "and as people are crowded together, they naturally come to regard each other's opinion much more. . . . Men cease to regard great principles, they turn from looking at truth itself, they turn from seeking simple duty, to consider *what is agreeable to other people*" (Y, 47–48). Men were "ground down to the same tame and timid mediocrity" in the cities, he argued a few years later, not because of lack of opportunity for individual expression but "from the fear of offending and the desire of display" (*EL*, 1, 20–21). A similar charge in one of his most used sermons, "Trust Yourself," anticipated his famous essay on "Self-Reliance": "I am afraid of this great tendency to uniformity of action and conversation among men. . . . The ends of action are the same, but the means of manner are infinitely various" (Y, 106). Emerson realized it was diversity, not conformity, that structured and impelled the drama of human life he loved so much.[14]

Urban conformity was the product of psychological needs, not external necessity. For the natural aristocrat, the heterogeneity of the modern city might offer at the least an environment of laissez-faire. The common man might feel pathetically lonely in the city and might express this loneliness in an attempt to conform to some "safe" standard of mediocrity, but the natural aristocrat could find the freedom to be alone without being lonely—to go his individual way and not be bothered by others. As Carlyle wrote Emerson in 1836, a year after moving to London, "I cannot say that this huge blind monster of a City is without some sort of charm

14. In a lecture on "Society" in 1837, Emerson argued that "the Division of labor" was a "wonderfully mutual convenience" for all able members of the society (*EL*, 2, 100). For other of his attacks on conformity, see *W*, 2, 23–24, and his remark in an 1837 lecture on "The Present Age" that "decorum is a sign of the inaction of the higher faculties" (*EL*, 2, 162).

for me. It leaves one alone, to go his own road unmolested. Deep in your soul you take up your protest against it, defy it, and even despise it; but need not divide yourself from it for that" (*Corr*, 145). Six months later he again wrote his American friend: "In the very hugeness of the monstrous City, contradiction cancelling contradiction, one finds a sort of composure for oneself that is not to be met with elsewhere perhaps in the world" (*Corr*, 153). In 1853 he was still pressing the same view, arguing that in summer "London is not a bad place at all. . . . Out of La Trappe, which does not suit a Protestant man, there is perhaps no place where one can be so perfectly alone" (*Corr*, 494). Emerson observed a similar phenomenon in Paris while traveling there in 1833: "Young men are very fond of Paris, partly, no doubt, because of the perfect freedom—freedom from observation as well as interference" (*JMN*, 4, 201).[15]

To the natural aristocrat with creative purpose, however, the city was not merely a neutral or indifferent environment. It offered him positive resources in its unusually high concentration of dramatic opportunities and other natural aristocrats. "The greater number of men you collect together," Emerson argued in 1829, "the greater is the chance of finding great talents and virtues" (Y, 46).[16] He recognized that in the leading men of Shakespeare's London lay much valuable

15. In *U*, 28, and *J*, 10, 43, Emerson discussed the "freedom" that one might find in a "city hotel." Note Hawthorne's remarks about the "freedom" that Rome seemed to offer the artist (*Works*, 6, 158–59; 10, 76–77).

16. In one lecture Emerson observed that "the large cities are phalansteries; and the theorists draw all their arguments from facts already taking place in our experience" (*Works*, 10, 357–58). In his 1864 lecture on "Social Aims" he argued that "for certain social needs there are great advantages in a central capital, which represents the power and genius of the nation" (*U*, 36). See his comment in 1842 on

material for the great bard himself. "It was impossible that such an observer as Shakspear [sic] could walk in the same city from year to year with his renowned group without gathering some fruit from their accomplishment and learning" (*EL*, *1*, 316). Emerson found such human resources in the cities of the past and the present, of Europe and America. "What a town was Florence," he exclaimed in 1864, "with Dante, Ghiberti, Giotto, Brunellischi, Da Vinci, Michael Angelo, Raffaelli, Cellini, Guicciardini, Machiavelli, Savonarola, Alfieri, Galileo!" (*J*, *10*, 5). He made similar lists of Boston's distinguished citizens.[17] In 1842 he wrote a friend in Berlin that "you are very rich in men to have in one city so large a proportion of the most conspicuous persons in Europe" (*L*, *3*, 77).[18] Though such men and their productions were available to a degree outside the city, the city's power of concentration made these resources much more conveniently available to the creative individual. "London, New York, Boston," Emerson said, "are phalanxes ready-made, where you shall find concerts, books, balls, medical lectures, prayers, or Punch and Judy, according to your fancy, on any night or day" (*J*, *6*, 314).

One of Emerson's most forceful statements of the liberating and dramatic opportunities offered by the heterogeneous city occurred in his essay on "Culture," which was first given as a lecture in Pittsburgh, a city of the West, in 1851:

> A man should live in or near a large town, because, let his own genius be what it may, it will repel quite as

the Fourierists' proposal to make Constantinople the Transcendental metropolis of the world (*L*, *3*, 21).

17. See, for example, *J*, *6*, 290; *9*, 303, 568; *10*, 235.

18. Carlyle had reminded Emerson that London, for all its faults, "turned out good men" (*W*, *5*, 18).

> much of agreeable and valuable talent as it draws, and, in a city, the total attraction of all the citizens is sure to conquer, first or last, every repulsion, and drag the most improbable hermit within its walls some day in the year. . . .
>
> Cities give us collision. . . . We must remember the high social possibilities of a million of men. The best bribe which London offers to-day to the imagination is that in such a vast variety of people and conditions one can believe there is room for persons of romantic character to exist, and that the poet, the mystic and hero may hope to confront their counterparts. (*W*, 6, 148–50)

Emerson never denied, of course, that such "high social possibilities" had their limitations. Throughout his life his doctrine of compensation continued to assert that "it is impossible & absurd to get anything without its price."[19] No finite power could be acquired without also accepting some finite limit, and he criticized the city most harshly when he believed that its citizens, through either necessity or choice, were paying too much "freedom" or "life" for their urban opportunities. He continued to affirm, however, that the wise and purposeful man of genuine ability could choose urban resources that were creative tools as well as disciplining limits and thus gave more liberating power than they took. Carlyle had suggested such enlarging compensations to Emerson in a letter

19. The statement comes from Emerson's 1837 lecture on "Trades and Professions" *EL*, 2, 127). In the first chapter of *Walden*, Thoreau defined "the cost of a thing" as "the amount of what I will call life which is required to be exchanged for it, immediately or in the long run." Most of his contemporary Romantics would have agreed with him. See Henry F. Pommer, "The Content and Basis of Emerson's Belief in Compensation," *PMLA*, 77 (1962), 248–53.

of 1835: "I have dwelt and swum now for about a year in this World-Mahlstrom of London; with much pain, which however has given me many thoughts, more than a counterbalance for that" (*Corr*, 131).

The very heterogeneity of the city, in fact, made possible the natural aristocrat's expansion of his finite and limited powers, for it extended immensely the number and variety of finite limits from which he could choose. Though Emerson's Transcendental dream was to find infinite power in all things, he recognized that for even the most able men "Life is a selection, no more. . . . The Library is gradually made inestimable," he argued in 1846, "by taking out from the superabounding mass of books all but the best. . . . Things collect very fast of themselves; the difference between house and house is the wise omissions" (*J*, 7, 203–04). By making a "Mahlstrom" of opportunities available, the city increased the individual's opportunities to make "wise omissions"—a process that involved both choosing the individual "calling" best suited to himself and creating finite objects of value that others might use in turn as tools of liberation.

Choosing between heterogeneous objects, in fact, appealed to the whole experimental and dramatic side of Emerson—the side that allowed him as poet, prophet, and historian to draw upon and test many varieties of traditional urban metaphor. "All life is an experiment," he asserted in 1842. "The more experiments you make, the better" (*J*, 6, 302). To make mistakes while experimenting was unfortunately inevitable, but mistakes were preferable to no experimentation at all, for man's finite freedom could be asserted only through the experimenting process itself—a process at the heart of the dialectical drama within which Emerson structured his thought. The result of every finite experiment was, after all, primarily the occasion for a further experiment. In the city, where millions of experimental results were juxtaposed each day, the city's leaders might find lessons that would allow them to make more adequate experiments and achieve more lasting, because more creative, results. "In our cities," Emerson argued in his essay on "Beauty," "an ugly building is soon removed and is never repeated, but any beautiful building is copied and improved upon, so that all masons and carpenters work to repeat and preserve the agreeable forms, whilst the ugly ones die out" (*W*, 6, 295–96).

By increasing his personal freedom of choice and expression through creative experiment—through an affirmation of the continuing experimental and dramatic process itself—the natural aristocrat was freeing not only himself but the other citizens in the urban community. "Every man who removes into this city with any purchasable talent or skill in him," Emerson argued in his essay on "Wealth," "gives to every man's labor in the city a new worth" (*W*, 6, 104–05). One individual would affect the rest of the city in that way only if he were a microcosmic part of an organic human community. Emerson wished to treat mankind as a whole as the social equivalent of the World Spirit, and he showed an increasing willingness to affirm that men's cities were central symbols of the total organic community. "I admire that poetry which no man wrote," he said in 1856, "no poet less than the genius of humanity itself, and which is to be read . . . in the effect of pictures, or sculptures, or drama, or cities, or sciences, on me" (*J*, 9, 37). In using his own life freely and creatively, the individual contributed organically to the life of the community. The value of individual works, Emerson noted in "Wealth," was thus "much enhanced by the numbers of men who can share their enjoyment. In the Greek cities it was reckoned profane that any person should pretend a property in a work of art, which belonged to all who could behold it" (*W*, 6, 98–99). Whatever the limitations of individual experiments in freedom—with all the dramatic tensions such experiments spawned—they produced a total urban artifact that pointed to the creative principle of the universe. When "the performance of steam and iron locomotive on any iron road," Emerson said in 1861, was "continued or repeated for many miles . . . and directed on Boston or New York," it acquired "an incredible grandeur. All the details are performed by very narrow, ordinary people, but the total effect seems quite out of reach of any one man, and a godlike gift" (*J*, 9, 301).

Emerson's advocation of a laissez-faire policy in municipal and national government, therefore, was based not only on a desire for individual freedom but also on a desire for an organic community. Mere laws could not by themselves force individuals to interact creatively. Such communal interaction was at heart primarily the result of individuals who used their freedom creatively and therefore responsibly. "Let every man shovel out his own snow," urged Emerson, "and the whole city will be passable" (*J*, 5, 437).[20] The community could not grow, he believed, without the freely given contributions of individuals, and its laws therefore needed to protect and encourage their freedom. But Emerson also recognized

20. Note Emerson's attitude toward laissez-faire government in Y, 77. In his essay on "The Method of Nature" he asked: "If I see nothing to admire in the unit, shall I admire a million units? Men stand in awe of the city, but do not honor any individual citizens" (*W*, 1, 193). Relevant if routine studies are Alexander Kern, "Emerson and Economics," *New England Quarterly*, 13 (1940), 678–96, esp. 691–93, and John C. Gerber, "Emerson and the Political Economics," *New England Quarterly*, 22 (1949), esp. 338–46. In *Freedom and Fate*, Whicher offers brief but perceptive remarks on Emerson's view of "organic" community (see esp. pp. 130–31).

that, without the opportunities provided by the community, the individual could never realize his fullest earthly potential. By helping the community grow, he provided a basis for his own further growth. At its best, the relationship between the citizen and the city was that of a creative spiral of mutual growth, based on the love of each for the other.

On May 15, 1861, Emerson delivered in the city of his birth a lecture entitled "Boston." For the purposes of this study, the date is symbolically appropriate. Coming exactly one month after President Lincoln had declared that a state of insurrection existed in the United States, the lecture can be treated as a coda to one era in American history. Filled with fragments of many previous lectures, written on several sizes and shades of paper, containing in manuscript many rearranged pages and deleted remarks, the lecture also shows an Emerson who was approaching the conclusion of his period of greatest public activity—a writer increasingly less concerned with new visions than with revisions. To the extent that the lecture has any structure at all, however, it dramatizes Emerson's continuing concern with the potentially creative relationship of the free individual and the unified community. In terms almost Hegelian in their ultimate dramatic implication, he argues that "Boston never wanted a good principle of rebellion in it, from the planting until now" (*W*, 12, 203). For this reason the city's annals "are great historical lines, inextricably national; part of the history of political liberty" (p. 188). Boston, as Emerson presents it, is in essence a Western city. The lecture asserts optimistically that within this increasingly modern urban community the American can still fulfill his capacities as Hero, Poet, and Scholar. "Boston" treats such individual fulfillment as, in finite terms, both a product and a cause of the human unity of the city—a unity based on an organic alliance with nature, with history, and with God.[21]

The opening remarks of "Boston" link the city to natural forces by discussing the impact of "climate and air" on its way of life.[22] Nature itself, in fact, has created a heterogeneous environment in which human freedom can find its most various means of expression. "Who lives one year in Boston ranges through all the climates of the globe," says Emerson. "And if the character of the people has a larger range and greater versatility, causing them to exhibit equal dexterity in what are elsewhere reckoned incompatible works, perhaps they may thank their climate of extremes" (p. 185). Pointing to the heterogeneous individuality that creates the vital life of human Boston, he applies to his own city Vasari's remarks on Florence: "the desire for glory and honor is powerfully generated by the air of that place, in the men of every profession; whereby all who possess talent are impelled to struggle that they may not remain in the same grade with those whom they perceive to be only men like themselves . . . but all labor by every means to be foremost" (pp. 185–86).

21. Though I have taken most quotations from the printed form of this lecture in *W*, *12*, 182–211, my remarks are also based on an examination of the manuscript of the lecture in the Houghton Library (202.6), which contains several pages not used in the printed version. The themes and structure of this lecture are closely related to those of Emerson's "Historical Discourse" in Concord in 1835—though more emphasis is placed, in the later lecture, on the organic qualities of the community and on the role of the artist in this community—and to those of his poem "Boston" (*W*, *9*, 212–16), some of which is printed with the lecture.

22. See Hopkins, *Spires of Form*, p. 144. Emerson draws a metaphorical connection between the influences of "air" and "spiritual influence."

Having found for Boston an organic spot in nature, Emerson next searches for the city's organic relation to human history. "Of great cities you cannot compute the influence," he argues. "Each great city gathers . . . values and delights for mankind, and comes to be the brag of its age and population" (p. 187). He progresses briefly through the major urban symbols of the historical City of Man.

> The Greeks . . . praised Athens, the "Violet City." It was said of Rome in its proudest days, looking at the vast radiation of the privilege of Roman citizenship through the then-known world,—"the extent of the city and of the world is the same" . . . London now for a thousand years has been in an affirmative or energizing mood; *has not stopped growing.*[23] Linnaeus, like a naturalist, esteeming the globe a big egg, called London the *punctum saliens* in the yolk of the world. (pp. 187–88)

Next in historical line, as far as Emerson's lecture is concerned, is one of America's own cities of the West, Boston. "This town of Boston has a history. . . . I do not speak with any fondness, but the language of coldest history, when I say that Boston commands attention as the town which was appointed in the destiny of nations to lead the civilization of North America" (p. 188).

Boston's role as a lode star of American civilization resulted from the crucial experiment undertaken by the city from its beginning—an experiment in the creative use of freedom. Boston's leaders engaged patiently in the task of "building their empire by due degrees" (p. 199). Their efforts

23. My italics. Emerson's comment on the continuing growth of London is especially interesting in light of his remarks in *English Traits* and reinforces my analysis of the earlier work.

on behalf of creativity and freedom allowed the city to liberate itself from natural and economic necessity in an upward movement toward fulfillment of both the individual and his community. Boston progressed because it did not desire freedom merely for the sake of freedom. Rather, it "accepted the divine ordination that man is for use; that intelligent being exists to the utmost use; and that his ruin is to live for pleasure and for show" (p. 205). Using their freedom in the name of creative power, Boston's people produced "planters of towns, fellers of the forest, builders of mills and forges, builders of roads, and farmers to till and harvest corn for the world." Working creatively with natural and economic resources, they slowly prepared themselves for the creation of "epic poems and dramas" (p. 204).

Boston's first creative experiment involved the mastering of external nature. Emerson symbolizes this experiment by describing the founders' attempt to find a suitable location for the town. Though the location finally chosen was organically appropriate ("How easy it is, after the city is built, to see where it ought to stand"), Emerson portrays the original settlers as men "not at all accustomed to the rough task of discoverers" (p. 191). He is thus able to trace within the history of Boston itself the increasing power of the exploring spirit of man. By means of this increasing power, external nature slowly comes under man's dominion. The original wilderness seemed filled with danger ("they exaggerated their troubles. Bears and wolves were many; but early, they believed there were lions"), but man's power is eventually able to humanize this environment—not only externally but by mastering the fears of his own mind—and "Nature has . . . been of peaceable behavior ever since" (p. 192). As Boston's people learned how to use the power of external nature for creative purposes, they also learned to liberate their minds from internal limits. Founding their new city in an era when "the superstition which hung over the new ocean had not yet been scattered" (p. 192), they increasingly asserted the creative aspects of their religious idealism. Emerson was impressed by "how rich and expansive a culture—not so much a culture as a higher life—they owed to the promptings of this sentiment" (p. 194).

As might be expected from the Romantic way in which Emerson used religious metaphors, his references to "religious sentiment" seem at base a reference to man's creative imagination—"always enlarging, firing man, prompting the pursuit of the vast, the beautiful, the unattainable" (p. 197). The victory of the idealistic mind in Boston's historical development was ultimately a victory for art and the artist. Boston's creative spirit was moving toward a fulfillment that "unites itself by natural affinity to the highest minds of the world; nourishes itself on Plato and Dante, Michael Angelo and Milton; on whatever is pure and sublime in art" (p. 197). Emerson lists a series of Boston-born writers who exhibited this exploring spirit in their writings and argues that since 1820 "the Renaissance" has come to Boston art.[24]

Since Boston "infused all the Union with its blood" (p. 207), however, the Boston Renaissance was also an American Renaissance. Treated in its widest possible national context, Boston foreshadowed a true City of the West. In a spirit similar to Whitman's, Emerson chants a hymn to the creative spirit and its national environment—a "new country" that can "speak to the imagination and offer swing and play to the confined powers":

24. The term "Renaissance" appears in the manuscript but not in the printed text.

> What should hinder that this America, so long kept in reserve from the intellectual races until they should grow to it, glimpses being afforded which spoke to the imagination, yet the first shore hid until science and art should be ripe to propose it as a fixed aim, and a man should be found who would sail steadily west sixty-eight days from the port of Palos to find it,—what should hinder that this New Atlantis should have its happy ports, its mountains of security, its gardens fit for human abode, where all elements were right for the health, power, and virtue of man. (pp. 199–200)[25]

"Emancipation," Emerson asserts, *is* "the American idea" (p. 200). The American's freedom inevitably has "its sinister side" in its liability to misuse, but if applied creatively, his freedom "leads to heavenly places" (p. 200).

These "heavenly places" are an aging Emerson's version of a figurative New Jerusalem. "There is a Columbia of thought and art and character," he argues, "which is the last and endless sequel of Columbus's adventures" (p. 201). America's "consciousness of power and sustained assertion of it" (p. 205) offers the continuing possibility of creating a proper national home for his Man of the West or New Cosmopolitan—a New Atlantis or New Columbia that will both support and be supported by the free assertions of America's eternally youthful spirit. "Youth and health like a stirring town, above a torpid place where nothing is doing. In Boston they were sure to see something going forward before the year was out. For this was the moving principle itself, the *primum*

25. In the manuscript Emerson has crossed out "this dream of philosophers, poets, & adventurers, the Fortunate Isles" and substituted "New Atlantis," crossed out "holy land" in favor of "mountains of security," and substituted "gardens" for "paradises."

mobile, a living mind agitating the mass" (p. 206). Emerson knows that Boston, like America, like the world, is far from perfect. He points to the "many black lines of cruel injustice" in both its past and present, and he admits that "all manner of vices can be found in this, as in every great city" (p. 208). But Emerson does not choose to dwell on Boston's sins. The purpose of his essay, like most of his essays, is not to damn man for his imperfections, but to point to what man can ideally become by means of creative experimentation within the context of the human drama. He argues that "a community, as a man, is entitled to be judged by his best," and he asserts that Boston's best is its very affirmation of the creative process. "The genius of Boston is seen in her real independence, productive power and northern acuteness of mind —which is in nature hostile to oppression. It is a good city as cities go" (p. 208).

In his conclusion Emerson significantly chooses an organic metaphor to describe the human community of Boston:

> And thus our little city thrives and enlarges, striking deep roots, and sending out boughs and buds, and propagating itself like a banyan over the continent. Greater cities there are that sprung from it, full of its blood and name and traditions. It is very willing to be outnumbered and outgrown, so long as they carry forward its life of civil and religious freedom, of education, of social order, and of loyalty to law. (p. 209)

Neither Boston nor its individual citizen is mechanical or static. The order of one and the freedom of the other support their mutual powers of growth. Boston is organic because it is human—because its history embodies the growth of man's powers. Boston's support of "civil and religious freedom" is not support of social anarchy. Out of the individual's freedom, Emerson asserts optimistically, will spring a genuine love of the community that supports his freedom. Out of the individual's love will spring the only lasting basis for a creative community in the essential West that is America.

Emerson asserts such love in the concluding paragraph of his lecture by applying a personal pronoun to Boston:

> Here stands to-day, as of yore, our little city of the rocks; here let it stand forever, on the man-bearing granite of the North! Let her stand fast by herself! She has grown great. She is filled with strangers, but she can only prosper by adhering to her faith. Let every child that is born of her and every child of her adoption see to it to keep the name of Boston as clean as the sun; and in distant ages her motto shall be the prayer of millions on all the hills that gird the town, "As with our Fathers, so God be with us!" (p. 211)

The city's creativity, its ability to "mother" noble men, is based on the same impulse of love that allows the poet to create a lasting work of art. Though a Western city, "filled with strangers," Boston is also a "city of the rocks." The city's independent spirit—the ability to "stand fast by herself" in the face of the gigantic, rapid, and heterogeneous forces of the modern world—is not ultimately defensive. Rather it is a means to a unifying end—a unity with nature ("the hills that gird the town"), with the best aspects of history's City of Man ("our Fathers"), and with the challenging transcendental vision of a figurative City of God.

Emerson's concluding attitude toward Boston is thus more optimistic than that expressed by many later American writers toward the increasingly urban civilization of modern America. His cautious optimism, however, is still relevant. It was based on his belief that, at the heart of the dialectical dramas in which the city participated and which it focused through concentration, the city contained its own modes of self-criticism and, hence, potential growth. The increasing scale, the increasingly rapid movement, and the increasing heterogeneity of the modern city symbolized many dehumanizing dangers, but these dangers seemed to Emerson the inescapable underside of their creative potential. Even behind his darkest use of urban material lay an experimenting idealism. In his very attempt to explore dramatically the meaning of the city and the humane uses of that meaning, Emerson, like many American writers, asserted his "freedom of the city" and its traditional metaphorical uses.

Bibliographic Note

1. Emerson and "The Age of Cities"

To the extent that I can list my indebtedness, four studies of Emerson have most strongly influenced my treatment of his thought, literary theories, and practice: Ralph L. Rusk, *The Life of Ralph Waldo Emerson* (New York, 1949); Stephen E. Whicher, *Freedom and Fate: An Inner Life of Ralph Waldo Emerson* (Philadelphia, 1953); F. O. Matthiessen, *American Renaissance: Art and Expression in the Age of Emerson and Whitman* (New York, 1941); and Charles Feidelson, *Symbolism and American Literature* (Chicago, 1953). I have also profited by discussions of Emerson's artistic craft and theories in Sherman Paul, *Emerson's Angle of Vision: Man and Nature in American Experience* (Cambridge, Mass., 1952), and Jonathan Bishop, *Emerson on the Soul* (Cambridge, Mass., 1964). Of the many studies of Emerson's attempts to be relevant to the affairs and problems of his own era, I have found the following the most useful: Daniel Aaron, *Men of Good Hope: A Story of American Progressives* (New York, 1951), Chap. 1; Perry Miller, "Emersonian Genius and the American Democracy," *New England Quarterly*, 26 (1953), 27–44; and Henry Nash Smith, "Emerson's Problem of Vocation—A Note on 'The American Scholar,'" *New England Quarterly*, 12 (1939), 52–67. Frederick I. Carpenter, in *American Literature and the Dream* (New York, 1955), argues—probably too simply—that Emerson's essays "had as their main theme the application of the scholarship, or wisdom of man, to the problems of the present." Though not specifically on Emerson, Perry Miller's *The Raven and the Whale: The War of Words and Wits in the Era of Poe and*

Melville (New York, 1956) offers stimulating hints as to the problems facing American writers who wished to make their work effective in an urbanizing world. David R. Weimer's *The City as Metaphor* (New York, 1966), published shortly before my own study went to press, applies similar analytical techniques to the treatment of urban material by American writers from Whitman to Auden.

My attempt to develop an "urban" context for Emerson, though literary in aim, owes less to specifically literary studies than to works with a social, historical, or philosophical orientation. Of the few major studies of American attitudes toward urban civilization, the best is Anselm L. Strauss, *Images of the American City* (New York, 1961). Morton and Lucia White, *The Intellectual Versus the City from Thomas Jefferson to Frank Lloyd Wright* (Cambridge, Mass., 1962), is somewhat rigid and one-sided in its scheme and assumptions. Blanche Houseman Gelfant, *The American City Novel* (Norman, Okla., 1954), lacks adequately sophisticated tools of literary analysis. A useful, if necessarily simplified, outline of urban attitudes can be drawn from Christopher Tunnard and Henry Hope Reed, *American Skyline: The Growth and Form of Our Cities and Towns* (New York, 1953). More provocative and wide-ranging is Tunnard's *The City of Man* (New York, 1953). John W. Reps' *The Making of Urban America: A History of City Planning in the United States* (Princeton, 1965) is as valuable for its urban maps as for its text. The pictures, structure, and working assumptions of John A. Kouwenhoven's *The Columbia Historical Portrait of New York* (Garden City, 1953) offer stimulating hints as to the development of American urban imagery; more case studies of this nature are needed. A valuable approach to the problem, especially in its attempt to formulate psychological and visual categories for the analysis of urban imagery, is Kevin Lynch, *The Image of the City* (Cambridge, Mass., 1960). And it was inevitable that I should confront the brilliantly imaginative and justly controversial studies by Lewis Mumford, *The Culture of Cities* (New York, 1938) and *The City in History: Its Origins, Its Transformations, and Its Prospects* (New York, 1961).

2. City of the West

Any contemporary study of the image of the West must come to terms with Henry Nash Smith, *Virgin Land: The American West as Symbol and Myth* (Cambridge, Mass., 1950); one might, however, find an equally pioneering study of the "Western" spirit in Constance Rourke, *American Humor: A Study of the National Character* (New York, 1931). The most outstanding recent study of Western imagery is Edwin Fussell, *Frontier: American Literature and the American West* (Princeton, 1965), notable especially for its close literary analysis of the works of major nineteenth-century American writers. Consistently stimulating—especially as a study of the new "Westerner" and his intellectual dilemmas—is R. W. B. Lewis, *The American Adam: Innocence, Tragedy and Tradition in the Nineteenth Century* (Chicago, 1955). Humane and something of a cross between Smith, Fussell, and Lewis is Wilson O. Clough, *The Necessary Earth: Nature and Solitude in American Literature* (Austin, Tex., 1964). Though it contains interesting suggestions as to the basis of a westward-looking American imagination, Howard Mumford Jones' *O Strange New World. American Culture: the Formative Years* (New York, 1964) strikes me as rather old-fashioned. Two aspects of the image of the West receive stimulating treatment in Roy Harvey Pearce, *The Savages of America: A Study of the Indian and the Idea of Civilization* (Baltimore, 1953), and Arthur K. Moore, *The Frontier Mind: A Cultural Analysis of the Kentucky Frontiersman* (Lexington, 1957). Also valuable as a discussion of the impact of Western imagery on American literary aims is Benjamin T. Spencer, *The Quest for Nationality: An American Literary Campaign* (Syracuse, 1957).

The historical basis for an image of a City of the West is suggested by Richard C. Wade, *The Urban Frontier: The Rise of Western Cities, 1790–1830* (Cambridge, Mass., 1959), but the perceptive reader can find many similar patterns emerging from Carl Bridenbaugh's two fact-heavy studies of colonial American cities, *Cities in the Wilderness: Urban Life in America, 1625–1742* (New York, 1938) and *Cities in Revolt: Urban Life in America, 1743–1776* (New York, 1955). See also Theodore Hornberger, "Three Self-Conscious Wests," *Southwest Review,* 26 (1941), 424–48. Two routine, but relevant, articles on Emerson are Ernest Marchand, "Emerson and the Frontier," *American Literature,* 3 (1931), 149–74—obviously influenced by the Turner thesis, but interesting in its portrayal of Emerson's fascination with "the drama of an unfolding society"—and John Q. Anderson, "Emerson and 'Manifest Destiny,'" *Boston Public Library Quarterly,* 7 (1955), 23–33.

3. The City of God

One of the most important recent studies to stress adequately the dramatic relevance of religious rhetoric to the development of America's conception of itself is Charles L. Sanford, *The Quest for Paradise: Europe and the American Moral*

Imagination (Urbana, Ill., 1961). No study of the intellectual and American foundations of this Christian and Romantic melodrama can avoid Perry Miller's monumental two-volume study of *The New England Mind* (Cambridge, Mass., 1953–1954). Both Feidelson's *Symbolism and American Literature* and Lewis' *The American Adam* have examined, though in different ways, the impact of the dichotomizing imagination on the literature of Emerson's era. Highly usable in establishing such literary continuities between Puritanism and the American Renaissance is Miller's *Errand into the Wilderness* (Cambridge, Mass., 1956), esp. his chapters "From Edwards to Emerson" and "The End of the World." See also the excellent article by Alan Heimert, "Puritanism, the Wilderness, and the Frontier," *New England Quarterly*, 26 (1953), 361–82, and a more limited study by Eugene Arden, "The Evil City in American Fiction," *New York History*, 35 (1954), 259–79. Somewhat derivative from Miller is Loren Baritz' chapter on Emerson in his recent study, *City on a Hill: A History of Ideas and Myths in America* (New York, 1964); the metaphor of the title is applied rather vaguely. Relevant and perceptive studies of Emerson are Newton Arvin, "The House of Pain: Emerson and the Tragic Sense," *Hudson Review*, 12 (1959), 37–53, and Clark Griffith, " 'Emersonianism' and 'Poeism': Some Versions of the Romantic Sensibility," *Modern Language Quarterly*, 22 (1961), 125–34.

A full-length study is needed on the theme of pilgrimage in American literature. A guide to some of the problems such a study would face is Bernard Blackstone's exploration of English Romantics, *The Lost Travellers: A Romantic Theme with Variations* (London, 1962). Special aspects of this theme can be found in Nathalia Wright, *Melville's Use of the Bible* (Durham, N.C., 1949); James Baird, *Ishmael: A Study of the*

Symbolic Mode in Primitivism (Baltimore, 1956), Chap. 14; Charles Williams, *The Image of the City and Other Essays,* ed. Anne Ridler (London, 1958), esp. Ridler's introduction and Williams' chapter on "The Image of the City in English Verse"; Dorothy Sayers, *Papers on Dante* (London, 1954), esp. her chapter on Dis; Roland M. Frye, *God, Man, and Satan* (Princeton, 1960); George H. Williams, *Wilderness and Paradise in Biblical Thought* (New York, 1962); Samuel C. Chew, *The Pilgrimage of Life* (New Haven, 1962); Cyclone Covey, *The American Pilgrimage* (New York, 1961); and David E. Smith, *John Bunyan in America* (Bloomington, 1966).

4. The City of Man

My understanding of Emerson's attitudes toward history is due mainly to Whicher, *Freedom and Fate,* esp. Chaps. 7 and 8; Philip L. Nicoloff, *Emerson on Race and History* (New York, 1961); Mildred Silver, "Emerson and the Idea of Progress," *American Literature, 12* (1940), 1–19; and A. Robert Caponigri, "Brownson and Emerson: Nature and History," *New England Quarterly, 18* (1945), 368–77. None of these studies, however, takes adequate account of Emerson's interest in history as a literary possibility as well as a moral lesson. Reinhold Niebuhr's *The Self and the Dramas of History* (New York, 1955) contains many interesting suggestions that might be applied usefully to Emerson's own aesthetic and moral sense of history. A helpful background for Emerson's explorations of Europe emerges from two recent studies, Cushing Strout, *The American Image of the Old World* (New York, 1963), and Nathalia Wright, *American Novelists in Italy* (Philadelphia, 1965). Useful, though by no means comprehensive, introductions to the impact of classical themes and literature on American literature are Richard M. Gummere, *The American Colonial Mind and the Classical Tradition* (Cambridge, Mass., 1963), and Jones, *O Strange New World*, esp. Chaps. 7–9.

5. The Organic City

Almost all recent major studies of Emerson's literary achievement have stressed the "organic" theories of life, thought, and art that he held in common with many American and European Romantics. In addition to Matthiesson, Feidelson, Whicher, Paul, and Bishop, see Charles R. Metzger, *Emerson and Greenough: Pioneers of a Transcendental Esthetic* (Berkeley, 1954); Vivian C. Hopkins, *Spires of Form: A Study of Emerson's Aesthetic Theory* (Cambridge, Mass., 1951); and Richard P. Adams, "Emerson and the Organic Metaphor," *PMLA*, 69 (1954), 117–30. A context for Emerson's organic theories is provided by such standard studies as Frank Kermode, *Romantic Image* (London, 1957); M. H. Abrams, *The Mirror and the Lamp: Romantic Theory and the Critical Tradition* (New York, 1953); René Wellek, "The Concept of Romanticism in Literary History," in *Concepts of Criticism* (New Haven, 1963), pp. 128–97; and Morse Peckham, "Toward a Theory of Romanticism," *PMLA*, 66 (1951), 5–23. Leo Marx relates such theories to a more traditional "pastoral" ideal and drama in *The Machine in the Garden: Technology and the Pastoral Ideal in America* (New York, 1964). Few literary studies have been attempted on the machine and the modern industrial city as "Romantic" or "organic" forces; one of the best is Paul Ginestier, *The Poet and the Machine*, trans. Martin B. Friedman (Chapel Hill, N.C., 1961).

6. "The Freedom of the City"

Emerson's concern with freedom is an important theme of Rusk's and Whicher's biographies. The question of urban possibilities and perils for the modern individual is evoked brilliantly in Mumford's *The Culture of Cities* and *The City in History*. My thoughts on this matter have also been stimulated by Paul and Percival Goodman, *Communitas: Means of Livelihood and Ways of Life* (New York, revised edition, 1960), and Jane Jacobs, *The Death and Life of Great American Cities* (New York, 1961).

Index

Index

Index

Index

Index